Employee Share Schemes

Equity Reward for Private Companies

1st Edition

Thomas Dalby

© 2018 – Claritax Books Ltd

All rights reserved. No part of this publication may be reproduced or distributed in any form or by any means, or stored in a database or retrieval system, without the prior written permission of the publishers.

Official material is reproduced under the terms of the Open Government Licence (see www.nationalarchives.gov.uk/doc/open-government-licence).

Disclaimer

This publication is sold with the understanding that neither the publishers nor the authors, with regard to this publication, are engaged in providing legal or professional services.

The material contained in this publication does not constitute tax advice and readers are advised that they should always obtain such professional advice before acting, or refraining from acting, on any information contained in this book. Readers are also advised that UK tax law is subject to frequent and unpredictable change.

Every effort has been taken to compile the contents of this book accurately and carefully. However, neither the publisher nor the author can accept any responsibility or liability to any person, whether a purchaser of this book or not, in respect of anything done or omitted to be done by any such person in reliance, partly or wholly, on any part or on the whole of the contents of this book.

Claritax Books is a trading name of Claritax Books Ltd.

>Claritax Books Ltd
>6 Grosvenor Park Road
>Chester
>CH1 1QQ

>Company number 07658388
>VAT number 114 9371 20

Law date

The text is based on the tax law as at 1 July 2018.

First edition July 2018

Employee Share Schemes

Equity Reward for Private Companies

1st Edition

Thomas Dalby

Published by:

Claritax Books Ltd
6 Grosvenor Park Road
Chester, CH1 1QQ

www.claritaxbooks.com

ISBN: 978-1-912386-03-1

Other titles from Claritax Books

Other titles from Claritax Books include:

- A-Z of Plant & Machinery
- Advising British Expats
- Capital Allowances
- Construction Industry Scheme
- Discovery Assessments
- Employee Benefits & Expenses
- Employment Status
- Enterprise Investment Scheme
- Entrepreneurs' Relief
- Financial Planning with Trusts
- Furnished Holiday Lettings
- Main Residence Relief
- Pension Tax Guide
- Research & Development
- Residence: The Definition in Practice
- Stamp Duty Land Tax
- Tax Chamber Hearings
- Tax Losses
- VAT Registration

See www.claritaxbooks.com for details of further titles due for publication in the coming months.

About the author

Thomas Dalby LLB, CTA is head of share schemes at Gabelle, the specialist tax advisory firm, covering most aspects of employee reward.

Thomas trained at the Bar before being seduced by the glamour and excitement of tax, joining Deloitte in 1996 and moving into the firm's employee reward practice in 2000. He has advised on and implemented all of the statutory share schemes, assisting clients with the design of awards, their grant, reporting obligations through to the exercise of share awards and their implications in the context of a transaction.

Thomas can be contacted at thomas.dalby@gabelletax.com.

Preface

To put it mildly, the law on the taxation of employees' shares is complex: the legislation is densely written, employs a range of unfamiliar concepts and has an extensive jargon all of its own.

The purpose of this book is to try to de-mystify the law in this area and to act as a clear and accessible guide to equity reward. The focus of this volume is on private companies, as employee share schemes can be a powerful tool for smaller businesses wanting to recruit and retain the best people, and it is the author's view that equity reward is under-used by many companies, who could otherwise benefit.

This book would not have been possible without the patience and kindly resolution of Ray Chidell, the support of Paula Tallon and the rest of the team at Gabelle, and the forbearance of my wife, Catharine.

Nottinghamshire

June 2018

Abbreviations

AIM	Alternative Investment Market
AMV	Actual market value
BIM	Business Income Manual
CFD	Contract for difference
CG	Capital Gains Manual
CGT	Capital gains tax
Ch	Chapter
Ch D	Chancery Division
CSOP	Company share option plans
CTA	Corporation Tax Act
DOTAS	Disclosure of tax avoidance schemes
EBT	Employee benefit trust
EBIT	Earnings before interest and tax
EBITDA	EBIT with depreciation and amortisation added back
EFRBS	Employer-financed retirement benefits scheme
EIM	Employment Income Manual
EMI	Enterprise management incentive
EOT	Employee ownership trust
ER	Entrepreneurs' relief
ERSM	Employment Related Securities Manual
ESC	Extra statutory concession
ESS	Employee share scheme
ETASSUM	Employee Tax Advantaged Share Scheme User Manual
EWHC	England and Wales High Court
FA	Finance Act
FTT	First-tier Tribunal
FURBS	Funded unapproved retirement benefits scheme
GAAP	Generally accepted accounting principles
GAAR	General anti-abuse rule
HMRC	Her Majesty's Revenue & Customs
IHT	Inheritance tax
IHTA 1984	Inheritance Tax Act 1984
IP	Intellectual property
ITA 2007	Income Tax Act 2007
ITEPA 2003	Income Tax (Earnings and Pensions) Act 2003
ITTOIA 2005	Income Tax (Trading and Other Income) Act 2005
JSOP	Joint share ownership plan
NAV	Net asset value
NIC	National Insurance contributions
NIM	National Insurance Manual

PAT	Profit after tax
PAYE	Pay as you earn
P/E ratio	Price/earnings ratio
PERDa	(Private companies) price/earnings ratio database
Pt.	Part
RCA	Readily convertible asset
RV	Restricted value
S.	Section
SAV	(HMRC) Shares and Assets Valuation
SAYE	Save as you earn
Sch.	Schedule
SI	Statutory instrument
SIP	Share incentive plan
SSCBA 1992	Social Security Contributions and Benefits Act 1992
TAAR	Targeted anti-avoidance rule
TC	Tax cases
TCGA 1992	Taxation of Chargeable Gains Act 1992
TIOPA 2010	Taxation (International and Other Provisions) Act 2010
TMA 1970	Taxes Management Act 1970
UKSC	UK Supreme Court
UMV	Unrestricted market value

Table of contents

Other titles from Claritax Books iv
About the author v
Preface vii
Abbreviations viii

PART 1: BACKGROUND AND FIRST PRINCIPLES
1. **The legislative background**
   1.1   Finance Act 2003 3
   1.2   Underlying principles 4
   1.3   Scope of the legislation 5
   1.4   Retrospective effect 11
   1.5   Founders' shares 11
   1.6   Slaying myths about elections 11

2. **Valuation**
   2.1   Background 13
   2.2   Information standards 15
   2.3   Valuation approaches 17
   2.4   Minority shareholdings 21
   2.5   Share rights v personal rights 22
   2.6   Key valuation terms used in ITEPA 2003 25

PART 2: TAXATION OF EMPLOYEE SECURITIES
3. **Acquisition of securities**
   3.1   Introduction to share awards 29
   3.2   Acquiring securities – looking at the deal 30
   3.3   Restricted securities 31
   3.4   Chapter 3C – securities acquired for less than
           market value 43
   3.5   Share options 47

4. **Post-acquisition changes**
   4.1   The legislative objective 52
   4.2   Chapters 3A and 3B – non-commercial changes in
           Value 52
   4.3   Convertible securities 57

xi

	4.4	Chapter 4 – post acquisition benefits 62
	4.5	Chapter 4A – shares in spin-out companies 63

5. Disposal of shares
	5.1	Expectations as to treatment 68
	5.2	Restricted securities 68
	5.3	Convertible securities 74
	5.4	Chapter 3C – securities acquired at less than market value 79
	5.5	Chapter 3D – disposal of securities for more than market value 80
	5.6	CGT on disposing of securities 85
	5.7	Entrepreneurs' relief 88

PART 3: COMPANY CONSIDERATIONS
6. Corporation tax
	6.1	CTA 2009, Part 12 – introduction 93
	6.2	Basic qualification conditions 93
	6.3	Relief on acquisition of shares (Chapter 2) 96
	6.4	Relief for share options (Chapter 3) 96
	6.5	Restricted securities (Chapter 4) 98
	6.6	Convertible securities (Chapter 5) 99
	6.7	Mobile employees 99
	6.8	Other corporation tax reliefs 100
	6.9	Relief for the costs of establishing a share scheme 100

7. Operation of PAYE and NIC
	7.1	Basic principles 102
	7.2	PAYE on acquisition of securities 102
	7.3	PAYE on post-acquisition charges 102
	7.4	Readily convertible assets 104
	7.5	Section 222 106
	7.6	Transferring NIC liabilities 108

8. Reporting and accounting
	8.1	The reporting regime 110
	8.2	Accounting for employee share awards 114

PART 4: IMPLEMENTING SHARE SCHEMES
9. Designing an employee share scheme
- 9.1 The basic elements of a share scheme 119
- 9.2 Immediate ownership v options 120
- 9.3 "Vesting" and performance conditions 123
- 9.4 Treatment of leavers 124
- 9.5 Exit strategy 129
- 9.6 Dilution 130
- 9.7 Communication 133

10. What shares to use in the plan
- 10.1 The basics 134
- 10.2 Employee classes 135
- 10.3 Growth shares 136
- 10.4 Company law considerations 140

11. Employee share schemes and employee trusts
- 11.1 Employee trusts and share schemes in general 145
- 11.2 Establishing an employee trust 147
- 11.3 Funding an employee trust 149
- 11.4 Acquiring shares from employees or other Shareholders 150
- 11.5 Using EBT assets to satisfy share awards – CGT 151
- 11.6 Using EBT assets to satisfy share awards – disguised remuneration 154
- 11.7 Using EBT assets to satisfy share awards – CT relief 158
- 11.8 Transactions 158

PART 5: STATUTORY SHARE SCHEMES
12. Introduction to the statutory schemes
- 12.1 An overview 163
- 12.2 Enterprise management incentives 164
- 12.3 Company share option plans 166
- 12.4 SAYE 169
- 12.5 Share incentive plans 171
- 12.6 The statutory schemes in an OMB context 176
- 12.7 Comparison between statutory and non-statutory remuneration – example 178

13. Enterprise management incentives (EMI)
- 13.1 Eligibility for qualifying EMI options – company 181
- 13.2 Eligibility – shares 192
- 13.3 Eligibility – employees 193
- 13.4 Establishing the scheme 197
- 13.5 Employee tax treatment 203
- 13.6 Company tax position 213
- 13.7 Company transactions 213
- 13.8 Amending options 221
- 13.9 Leavers 222
- 13.10 Reporting 223

14. Company share option plans (CSOP)
- 14.1 Eligibility for a Schedule 4 CSOP 225
- 14.2 Establishing the scheme 227
- 14.3 Employee tax treatment 231
- 14.4 Company tax treatment 232
- 14.5 Transactions 233
- 14.6 Leavers 235
- 14.7 Amending options 237
- 14.8 Reporting 238

15. Share incentive plans (SIP)
- 15.1 Eligibility for a Schedule 2 SIP 239
- 15.2 Establishing the scheme 241
- 15.3 SIP awards 242
- 15.4 Employee tax treatment 248
- 15.5 Company tax position 252
- 15.6 Employee share trust taxation 255
- 15.7 Disqualifying events 255
- 15.8 Company transactions 256
- 15.9 Reporting 257

Table of legislation 259
Index of cases 267
General index 269

Part 1: Background and first principles

1. The legislative background

1.1 Finance Act 2003

The taxation of employees' shares has largely developed during the post-war period, marching in approximate pace with the increasing sophistication of the capital markets, and the current legislative regime can be traced back to FA 2003, Sch. 22.

Before the changes implemented by FA 2003, Parliament and the profession had been through a long process of consultation on the second of the re-write projects that was enacted as the *Income Tax (Earnings and Pensions) Act* 2003, and which came into force on 6 April 2003.

ITEPA 2003 made few changes to the way that employees' shares were taxed, but was largely considered to have successfully pulled together the disparate threads that had developed over the previous 20 years and presented them in a manner that had a semblance of coherence.

FA 2003 represented a complete revision of the rules on employees' shares, codifying them in a new Part 7 of the Act and broadened the scope of the rules to apply to most forms of securities, taking a wrecking hammer to the freshly re-written ITEPA 2003 in the process.

The Budget was given on 9 April 2003, the changes meriting only a line in the Chancellor's statement. There was no pre-warning that changes would be made and no consultation on the draft legislation, the government justifying its approach on the basis that the revised legislative regime was intended to counter avoidance. It is rumoured that the government went so far as to assign the drafting of the various chapters of the new ITEPA 2003, Pt. 7 to separate law firms, none of whom were given sight of the others' contributions, leading to the sense of inconsistency between the various provisions of Part 7.

The Budget changes revised the existing tax charges on options, convertible shares and restricted securities and introduced a raft of

Part 1: Background and first principles

new anti-avoidance provisions aimed at preventing the manipulation of the value of employees' shares.

Parliamentary scrutiny of the new legislation was limited, with the government brushing aside most attempts to review or revise the rules with the argument that this was anti-avoidance legislation and was not, therefore, open to scrutiny.

The lateness of the Budget and the staggered introduction of the new regime meant that three separate regimes could apply to employee shares acquired in 2003, with different treatments potentially applying to shares acquired before the Budget day, between the Budget day and 16 April 2003, or after 16 April.

Two other schedules to the *Finance Act* had a lasting impact on employee share schemes: Sch. 23 (now enacted as CTA 2009, Pt. 12), which legislated for corporation tax deductions for awards of employee shares, and Sch. 24 (now enacted as CTA 2009, Pt. 20), which limits deductions for contributions to employee benefit trusts and similar structures.

1.2 Underlying principles

The main principle underlying the FA 2003 regime is that value "gifted" to an employee will always be treated as taxable employment income, while organic growth in the value of securities will benefit from capital treatment.

Taking the most basic situation, if an employee is gifted shares, the initial value of the shares will be treated as a payment of taxable employment income on the date of receipt, but any uplift in value will be taxed when the shares are disposed of under the capital gains tax regime. If the employer undertakes a transaction that inflates the value of the employee's shares then that transaction will also be treated as having given rise to taxable employment income, unless it can be shown to have been a commercial transaction; if the employee is allowed to sell the shares for more than their market value, then the difference between the value of the proceeds and the market value of the shares will be treated as taxable employment income too.

The implementation of this principle in the legislation is explored in greater detail below; although it will be up to the reader to determine to what extent the legislation actually delivers on its promise.

1.3 Scope of the legislation

1.3.1 *"Employee"*

ITEPA 2003, s. 4 uses a standard definition of "employee", defining the term by reference to someone who works under a contract of employment or apprenticeship. The s. 4 definition also includes Crown employees.

ITEPA 2003, s. 5 broadens the scope of the legislation so that references to "employees" in the legislation apply equally to office holders unless the legislation explicitly excludes office holders.

For the purposes of the tax regime set out in ITEPA 2003, Pt. 7, no distinction is drawn between employees and directors or other office holders; shares acquired by directors, including non-executive directors, are always potentially within the scope of the employment-related securities regime.

1.3.2 *"Securities"*

ITEPA 2003, s. 420 sets out a comprehensive list of things that count as "securities", which extends to virtually any instrument that a company can issue and draws no distinction between a UK and overseas company.

The list in s. 420 includes:

- shares;
- rights under contracts of insurance;
- debentures and similar company debt instruments;
- warrants and other instruments granting an entitlement to subscribe for shares;
- depository receipts and similar documents acknowledging that the holder has an interest in securities held by another person;
- units in a collective investment scheme;
- futures and options, other than "securities options";

- contracts for difference ("CFDs") and contracts similar to CFDs; and
- assets within the scope of ITA 2007, Pt. 10A.

The legislation defines a "securities option" as a right to acquire securities, to which separate rules apply, other than an option granted to avoid tax or NIC (HMRC term this sort of option an "avoidance option"). The impact of this anti-avoidance rule is to bring this type of option within the scope of other anti-avoidance legislation in ITEPA 2003, Pt. 7.

ITEPA 2003, s. 420 explicitly excludes a number of instruments from its definition of "securities". These can be broadly split into three groups:

- cash-like instruments (cheques, bankers' drafts, etc.), which fall to be taxed under the general earnings charge in ITEPA 2003, s. 62;
- documents conferring or evidencing an interest in real property (leases, etc.), which also fall within the general earnings charge; and
- certain insurance products, which either fall to be taxed under the pension income rules in ITEPA 2003, Pt. 9 (annuity contracts, etc.) or do not confer a realisable benefit on the employee (for example, contracts of insurance that have no surrender value).

1.3.3 "Employment-related securities"

The starting point of the legislation is that securities acquired "by reason of an employment" will be subject to the regime of charges in ITEPA 2003, Pt. 7.

The employment in question can be that of the person acquiring the shares or that of some other person. At its basic level, this provision prevents an employer from awarding shares to an employee's spouse and then arguing that the shares are not employment-related securities, because the employee didn't actually acquire them. It also has the wider implication that shares acquired by a company, trust or partnership could fall within the scope of the legislation if a link can be drawn between the acquisition and a particular employee.

Example 1: employment-related securities (1)

Pauline is a director of Custard plc, which is quoted on AIM. Shares in Custard plc are gifted to Stephen, Pauline's husband, by the company, as a thank-you for Pauline's long service.

As Stephen received the shares by reason of Pauline's employment with Custard plc, the shares will be treated as employment-related securities and Pauline will be taxed as if she herself had received the shares.

The legislation is not limited to securities issued by a person's employer; securities issued by an unconnected company can also be treated as employment-related securities.

Example 2: employment-related securities (2)

Charles is employed by Cream Ltd, an advertising agency. Under its contract with Custard plc, part of its fee is paid in Custard plc shares, a number of which are gifted by Cream Ltd to Charles as a bonus for his good performance with the company.

As Charles has received the Custard plc shares as payment for his work with Cream Ltd, they will be treated as employment-related securities.

The rules on employment-related securities stop applying on the earliest of the following dates:

- the date on which the securities are transferred to somebody who is not an "associated person";
- the death of the employee; and
- where the individual in question is no longer employed, the seventh anniversary of the later of the date on which the securities were acquired and the date the person ceased employment.

For the purposes of the employment-related securities regime, an associated person is defined as the employee, or if someone else acquired the securities, the person who acquired them and their "relevant linked persons". (The use of nested definitions in ITEPA 2003, Pt. 7 does little to improve its intelligibility!).

Any person who is a member of the same household as, or connected with, the employee/original share recipient will be treated as a relevant linked person. The legislation carves out a number of exceptions: a company is not treated as relevant linked person if it is:

- the employer;
- the person from whom the employment-related securities were acquired;
- the person who made the right to acquire the employment-related securities available; or
- the person who issued the employment-related securities.

The seven-year rule means that, in most cases, securities held by an ex-employee will fall outside the scope of the employment-related securities regime seven years after the employment ceased. In the unlikely event that an ex-employee receives securities after his or her employment has come to an end, then he or she will have to wait a further seven years before the new securities fall outside the employment-related securities rules.

Example 3: the seven-year rule

Costas is awarded shares in his employer company in November 2015. In January 2016 he is made redundant, but is allowed to keep the shares, because he is treated as a "good leaver" under the company's share scheme.

After Costas leaves, a project that Costas had been working on comes into fruition, becoming very profitable. The board, as a goodwill gesture, makes a further award of shares to Costas in August 2016.

In May 2023, the company arranges for an employee share trust to buy the shares from Costas for more than their market value. As this date falls more than seven years after Costas left the company, the shares that he acquired in November 2015 will not be treated as employment-related securities and no tax charges will arise under ITEPA 2003 on those shares. But the shares acquired in August 2016 are still treated as employment-related securities and Costas will be treated as having received taxable employment income in respect of those shares, as they were repurchased for more than their market value (see **5.5** below).

1.3.4 "By reason of employment"

Section 421B contains the critical rules to determine whether securities fall within the scope of ITEPA 2003, Pt. 7. The starting point is common-sense: if securities are acquired by reason of a person's employment, then they will be within the scope of Part 7 by reference to that person.

However, the legislation is broadened by a deeming provision in s. 421B(3):

> "3) A right or opportunity to acquire securities or an interest in securities made available by a person's employer, or by a person connected with a person's employer, is to be regarded for the purposes of subsection (1) as available by reason of an employment of that person unless—
>
> (a) the person by whom the right or opportunity is made available is an individual, and
>
> (b) the right or opportunity is made available in the normal course of the domestic, family or personal relationships of that person."

In plain language: if an individual acquires shares issued by a company connected with his or her employer, then those shares will almost always be treated as employment-related securities.

The only exception to this is where someone is acquiring shares from another individual with whom there is a demonstrable family tie, or who is a member of the same household or if there is some other very close tie.

Needless to say, given the scope for the abuse of this exception, HMRC (and purchasers of businesses too) are known to apply a very sceptical approach to this rule; practitioners should be warned to expect a strong degree of cynicism if employers develop convenient deep friendships with their employees!

Care is also needed because this "safe haven" provision does not protect family members who work in the business and it is transparently clear that they are receiving the shares by way of remuneration.

Example 1: family and domestic relationships

Pauline leaves Custard plc and sets up her own company. Pauline employs her son and two unrelated people on her board of directors. Pauline arranges for all three to be awarded 2,000 shares each in the company.

Although the award of shares to Pauline's son would seem to fall within the exemption in s. 421B(3), the fact that he is receiving the same number of shares at the same time as the other directors strongly suggests that he is acquiring them by reason of his employment, not by reason of his relationship with Pauline.

In their guidance, HMRC have stated that they regard shares in a close company that are issued to friends or family of the controlling shareholder as potentially falling within the exemption in s. 421B(3); the exemption is not just limited to shares or securities that are transferred from one person to another.

A point to be aware of is that securities transferred by one family member to another may not be employment-related securities in the hands of the recipient, but the person gifting the shares potentially remains within the scope of the rules on employment-related securities with respect to those securities.

The legislation makes it clear that the employment in question can be an existing employment, a former employment or a prospective employment.

Example 2: prospective employment

Reena and Raveen intend to invest in Cream Ltd. Reena has agreed with the existing shareholders of Cream Ltd that she will take a seat on the board of directors. Raveen does not intend to become involved with the running of the company and is not offered a position by Cream Ltd. A year later, Raveen is co-opted onto the board by other investors as their representative.

In Reena's case, the position is very clear; she intends to join the board and to become a director, and her shares will be treated as employment-related securities because they are being acquired in respect of a prospective employment.

Raveen's case is different. She had no intention of serving on the board of Cream Ltd and, at the time that she acquired the shares, it cannot be said that she was acquiring shares in a prospective employer company. Her shares will not, therefore, fall within the scope of Part 7.

1.4 Retrospective effect

Although a small number of the specific charges under Part 7 can only apply to shares acquired after the FA 2003 legislation came into force, the essential definition of "employment-related securities" is not time limited: an individual may have acquired securities long before 2003, but his securities will still be within the scope of Part 7 if the circumstances in which he acquired them fit within those defined in s. 421B.

1.5 Founders' shares

Before FA 2003, the founders of a business were often able to argue that their shareholdings fell outside the rules on employment-related securities, as they had acquired their shareholdings by virtue of their activity as an investor into the business, rather than by virtue of their role as a director of the company.

After FA 2003 a "founders' shares argument" is no longer sustainable; most people founding companies intend to sit on the board of the company and are often entered into the books of the company as directors on its incorporation. The effect of this is that they have a prospective employment with the company at the time that the shares are issued to them: their shares are unarguably within the definition of employment-related securities in s. 421B of ITEPA 2003, and the regime in ITEPA 2003, Pt. 7 will apply to those shares.

For this reason, it is essential to consider the impact of ITEPA 2003, Pt. 7 whenever a transaction is being undertaken in company shares.

1.6 Slaying myths about elections

A final point to make in this chapter is that it is not possible to make an election to escape ITEPA 2003, Pt. 7. Although we will encounter a number of election regimes in the course of this book, none of these should be seen as a "silver bullet"; in each case the elections only serve to modify the ITEPA 2003, Pt. 7 regime; they do not disapply it as a totality.

2. Valuation

2.1 Background

The bedrock of the rules governing the taxation of employment-related securities and the operation of employee share schemes is the value of shares acquired by employees and transactions that could affect that value. It is essential for anyone advising clients on employee share schemes to understand the principles of business valuation and their application to employment-related securities.

Although valuation can seem to be a complex scientific and mathematical process, it is ultimately underpinned by subjective judgements made by the individual valuer: even the most complicated valuation models, which assess the opportunity cost of owning shares, are based on assumptions made by the valuer; a valuation is only as good as the experience and judgement of the individual valuer.

The purpose of this chapter is to give an overview of typical approaches to valuation for tax purposes and to their application in the context of employment-related securities, rather than serve as a "how to" guide to share valuation or to discussion of the methodologies used in commercial valuations.

Before *Finance Act* 2003, all employee share valuations were calculated by reference to the "money's worth value" of the shares in question. This is derived from the decision in *Weight v Salmon* and the wording of the charging provisions in the legislation, currently enacted as ITEPA 2003, s. 62:

> **"62 Earnings**
>
>   (1) This section explains what is meant by "earnings" in the employment income Parts.
>   (2) In those Parts "earnings", in relation to an employment, means—
>   (a) any salary, wages or fee,
>   (b) any gratuity or other profit or incidental benefit of any kind obtained by the employee if it is money or money's worth, or

  (c) anything else that constitutes an emolument of the employment.

(3) For the purposes of subsection (2) "money's worth" means something that is—

  (a) of direct monetary value to the employee, or

  (b) capable of being converted into money or something of direct monetary value to the employee.

(4) ...."

After FA 2003, ITEPA 2003, s. 421 stipulates that the value of employment-related securities for the purposes of all of the charges arising under ITEPA 2003, Part 7 will be determined in accordance with the rules in TCGA 1992, Part VIII. In relation to unquoted shares, these are set out in TCGA 1992, s 273:

"273 Unquoted shares and securities

(1) The provisions of subsection (3) below shall have effect in any case where, in relation to an asset to which this section applies, there falls to be determined by virtue of section 272(1) the price which the asset might reasonably be expected to fetch on a sale in the open market.

(2) The assets to which this section applies are shares and securities which are not listed on a recognised stock exchange at the time as at which their market value for the purposes of tax on chargeable gains falls to be determined.

(3) For the purposes of a determination falling within subsection (1) above, it shall be assumed that, in the open market which is postulated for the purposes of that determination, there is available to any prospective purchaser of the asset in question all the information which a prudent prospective purchaser of the asset might reasonably require if he were proposing to purchase it from a willing vendor by private treaty and at arm's length."

In addition to the legislation, there is an extensive corpus of case law governing the interpretation of s. 273.

Valuation

In practical terms, the money's worth value of unquoted shares is estimated based on the price realisable on a potential sale of the shares; the money's worth valuation approach and the TCGA 1992 rules differ in the information that can be taken into account in valuing the securities. This is explained at **2.2** below.

Case: *Weight v Salmon* (1935) 19 TC 174

2.2 Information standards

The key difference between the money's worth valuation and the TCGA 1992 valuation standards is the assumptions that must be made about the parties to a hypothetical transaction in the securities that are being valued.

ITEPA 2003, s. 62(3) makes the identity of one of the transacting parties clear, i.e. the employee. The TCGA 1992 approach, on the other hand, does not allow the valuer to make any assumptions at all about the identity of the transacting parties.

In practical terms, this has a significant impact on the information that can be taken into account in valuing the securities:

- a money's worth valuation must take into account the knowledge and information available to that individual employee;
- a TCGA 1992 valuation can only take into account the information that would be made available to a person who is otherwise unconnected with the company by reason of his or her shareholding.

Example: information standards

Cate is a director of La Gata Building Services Limited. She is invited to acquire 500 shares in the capital of the company, out of an issued share capital of 100,000 shares, at a price of £1.00 per share.

Cate acquired her shares in August. In November of the same year, La Gata Building Services Limited is acquired by Catkin Construction Limited for consideration of £10 per share. Cate was involved in negotiating the acquisition on behalf of the board of directors, who communicated the transaction to the minority shareholders once due diligence was complete, and the terms of the offer had been finalised a fortnight before the transaction completed.

In valuing the shares issued to Cate for TCGA 1992 purposes, a valuer would only take into account the information that would be available to a person holding half of 1% of the share capital of the company and the information that a person attempting to buy a shareholding of that size would be able to have access to – for a shareholding of this size, it is unlikely that this would be anything more substantial than the information in the public domain. Assuming that no details of the deal had leaked or been briefed by either of the parties, it is unlikely that details of the deal would be available to the public and the transaction would not be taken into account in valuing Cate's shares for TCGA 1992 purposes.

Valuing the shares on the money's worth basis changes this; this is because Cate is fully aware of the transaction and her knowledge of the transaction means that she would be unlikely to transact at a price that did not substantially reflect the impending transaction value.

In this admittedly extreme example, the money's worth value would be significantly different to the TCGA 1992 value.

In most cases, the amount of information available to an employee is not likely to be significantly greater than the information that would be available to a third party, which will mean that often there will not be a significant difference between the TCGA 1992 value and the money's worth value.

In the example given above, the shareholding was very small, meaning that for TCGA 1992 purposes, the parties would only have access to publicly available information. As the size of a shareholding to be valued increases, the amount of information that would be treated as available to the parties increases: someone mulling the acquisition of a controlling interest in a company would rightly ask for management information and would in all likelihood be granted access to it.

2.3 Valuation approaches

2.3.1 Choosing an approach

HMRC, in their approach to valuation, tend to favour one of four valuation methodologies, valuing by reference to:

- the company's net asset position;
- the dividend yield on the shares;
- a multiple of earnings; or
- if there is an industry accepted methodology, using that approach.

The objective of these methodologies is to establish at what price a willing purchaser and a willing seller would transact.

2.3.2 Net asset value

For a non-trading entity, like a property holding company or investment company, the value in the company and its shares will be the company's asset base, in which case the company's net asset value ("NAV") will give a best estimate of the company's value.

In assessing the NAV, a purchaser will wish to ensure that the assets and liabilities of the company, as shown in the accounts, fairly represent their market value. For the purposes of a tax valuation, the information admissible in the valuation process may be significantly limited, if the shareholding in question is small; this can mean that the hypothetical purchaser of shares may not have enough information to make more than a cursory analysis of the company's balance sheet position.

It is not generally appropriate to value a trading company on the basis of its NAV, as it is usually the trade that a potential purchaser would be interested in acquiring; in a real-world context, buyers often decline to purchase the cash and other assets of a trading company. If a trading company does have a significant asset base that is directly linked to its trade (for example, trading premises) it may be necessary to make adjustments to a valuation undertaken using a different methodology to reflect the value of those assets.

2.3.3 Dividend yield

Valuing shares by reference to dividend yield is an approach that is rarely taken in a private company context. While dividend yield can be a good way to assess the value and performance of a publicly listed company, there are factors that are specific to private companies that mean that this approach is rarely adopted for fiscal valuation purposes:

- the owners of the business are often performing managerial functions and are choosing to take their remuneration in the form of dividends instead of drawing a market rate salary, to enjoy a tax and NIC saving;
- the owners of the business may be wealthy individuals who do not need the additional dividend income and are waiting on an eventual capital gain;
- if the company is backed by institutional investors, the company's debt commitments may mean that it is not able to pay dividends;
- if the company is a start-up, or involved in biotech or software development, it is unlikely to have distributable reserves or profits;
- if the company in question is a subsidiary of another company, the dividend history may be more reflective of the parent company's cash requirements than the performance of the subsidiary; or
- the shares in question might be of a new class without any dividend history.

2.3.4 Multiple of earnings

For a trading company the preferred methodology is to calculate the company's value by reference to a multiple of the company's earnings. Ideally a company will be valued by reference to a multiple derived from the price/earnings ratios ("P/E ratios") of comparable listed companies. The P/E ratios are calculated by dividing the company's market capitalisation (i.e. the number of shares in issue multiplied by the price per share) by its profit after tax.

Because it is difficult to compare one company directly with another, valuers will typically put together a group of comparator companies to derive a multiple based on their combined P/E ratios, in the hope that this might smooth out pricing effects that are not connected with the companies' performance (for example, market hype over a company's product pipe-line that may not be ultimately justified).

There are a number of problems with this approach for smaller private companies:

- most listed companies will be many times larger than the company in question, allowing them economies of scale and position in the market that a smaller company would not enjoy;
- public companies are rarely constrained to one geographical region, meaning that they are shielded from local economic conditions;
- most public companies are significantly more highly diversified than private companies, often with a degree of vertical integration into their supply chain, in a way that is not feasible for private companies.

For these reasons, a private company may decide that a better approach would be to look at earnings multiples derived from transactions in similar sized companies, and a number of organisations publish data on private company transactions and deal multiples.

Example: multiples

Cate is now on the board of Catkin Construction Limited and is mulling a proposal to offer shares to the employees of the company.

The company has 250,000 shares in issue and its key financial data for the year is as follows:

EBIT	1,800,000
EBITDA	2,000,000
PAT	1,280,000

Part 1: Background and first principles

(EBIT is the company's earnings before interest and tax, EBITDA is the EBIT with depreciation and amortisation added back in, and PAT is profit after tax.)

In considering the company's value, she reviews the P/E ratios of the listed companies in her sector that she feels are closest to Catkin Construction Limited in terms of trade and financial position:

	Market cap £bn	P/E ratio
Gargantua plc	2.086	12.25
Pantagruel plc	1.407	21.06
Gog plc	0.973	89.91
Magog plc	1.115	17.01
Brobdingnag plc	0.784	8.86
Median		17.01
Median excluding Gog plc		14.63

The P/E ratio for Gog plc is clearly an outlier and Cate excludes Gog plc from her calculations. But even if Gog plc is excluded from the calculation, the 14.63x multiple suggests that Catkin Construction plc would be worth around £19m, which seems too high to Cate, given her knowledge of the industry and recent transactions.

Cate looks instead to the Private Company Price Earnings Ratio Database ('PERDa'), which can be found at PERDa.net, and sees that they are reporting average EBIT multiples of 7x, based on companies with an average EBIT of £2.5m and average total valuations of £17.5m. Because of the difference in scale between Catkin Construction Limited and the companies recorded in PERDa, Cate discounts the multiple by 40% to give a multiple of 4.2, giving an implied valuation of £7.5m for the company.

2.3.5 Industry-specific methodologies

Some industries have specific methodologies for valuing companies, which are commonly used in transactions. HMRC will accept valuations based on these methods if they are well established within the industry and there is publicly available information supporting them.

Examples of industry-specific methods include:

- asset management companies, which are valued by reference to a percentage of their assets under management;
- risk-bearing insurers, which are valued by reference to their balance sheet values; and
- financial advisers, which are valued by reference to a multiple of their recurring turnover.

2.4 Minority shareholdings

The size of the shareholding that is being valued has an impact above and beyond the amount and quality of information that can be used in the valuation process. The value of a shareholding is unlikely to be a simple pro-rata split of the whole company value, unless the shareholders are selling *en bloc* to someone buying the whole capital of the company.

In company law terms, the size of a shareholding impacts on the decision-making power that it gives its holder:

- a person holding 75% or more of a company's share capital will have almost total control over the company, able to pass special resolutions on his or her own (allowing him or her to amend the articles of association, for example) and able to initiate a company sale;
- a holding of more than 50% but less than 75% allows the shareholder to pass ordinary resolutions (governing matters like dividend payments), but the shareholder must find others willing to cooperate in passing a special resolution;
- someone holding more than 25% but less than 50% can block special resolutions, but will not be able to pass ordinary or special resolutions without the assistance of other shareholders; and
- holdings of less than 25% cannot obstruct special resolutions, becoming progressively less influential – a shareholding of less than 10% is unlikely to give its holder any material influence over the affairs of the company.

Valuers often apply a discount to reflect the differential rights that different sized shareholdings confer on their holders, to reflect the fact that a small shareholding is worth very much less than a simple pro-rata split of the company's value.

Example: minority discounts

Catkin Construction Limited was proposing to make share awards to two key employees from shares held in an employee share trust of 5,000 and 75,000 shares; 2% and 30% of the share capital respectively.

Based on the £7.5m company valuation that Cate had derived for the company, Cate determines that the following discounts should be applied to the pro-rata valuation of £30.00 per share:

- for the holding of 5,000 shares, Cate determines that a discount of 75% should be applied, because the shareholding is so small and uninfluential, meaning that the value attributable to the holding is £37,500 (i.e. 5,000 x £30.00 @ 25% or £7.50 per share);
- the holding of 75,000 shares would allow the employee to block special resolutions, but would not allow the employee to force the sale of the company or even to declare dividends on his or her shareholding and, for that reason, Cate determines that a discount of 35% should be applied, meaning that the value of the holding for tax purposes will be £1,462,500 (i.e. 75,000 x £30.00 @ 65% or £19.50 per share).

2.5 Share rights v personal rights

As set out above, the TCGA 1992 valuation standard is based on a hypothetical transaction in the shares in question; the standard does not allow us to make any assumptions about the characteristics of either hypothetical party to that hypothetical transaction. This means that it is important to distinguish between rights that an individual has solely by virtue of owning the particular securities in question and rights that the shareholder enjoys in his or her capacity as a signatory to a shareholders' agreement or other contractual agreement (often referred to as share rights and personal rights, respectively).

For the purposes of the valuation standard, the key question is whether a third party purchaser, who is not party to any other agreement, would acquire the rights in question simply by owning the securities that are being valued.

Example: nature of rights

Cate owns 25,000 ordinary shares in the capital of Catkin Construction Limited, which represents 10% of the company's issued share capital. The articles of association of the company only provide for a single class of shares and do not set out how the capital of the company should be divided between the shareholders on a sale of the company, liquidation or return of capital.

The default position is that shares rank equally if the articles do not draw a differentiation between their rights.

Cate is also a signatory of a shareholders' agreement with the majority shareholder of Catkin Construction Limited. The terms of the agreement are that, on a sale of the company, Cate is entitled to receive 20% of the proceeds of sale, despite holding only 10% of the share capital.

A third party purchaser, who was not party to the shareholders' agreement, would not acquire the right to receiving the additional share of the proceeds simply by purchasing and holding the shares. The rights set out in the shareholders' agreement would not be taken into account for the purposes of the TCGA 1992 valuation standard.

This was the fact pattern in the Supreme Court decision in *Grays Timber v HMRC*, which was the first case to examine fully the employment-related securities regime. The case concerned the division of the proceeds of the sale of the company to a third party:

- the managing director of the company had a 6% shareholding, which would have entitled him to receive £0.4m of proceeds on the sale;
- however, under the terms of a shareholders' agreement, the managing director instead received proceeds of £1.4m;

- these special rights were not incorporated into the company's articles of association;
- HMRC argued that the rights conferred by the shareholders' agreement could not be taken into account in considering the market value of the managing directors' shareholding for the purposes of TCGA 1992, s. 273;
- HMRC argued that the value of the shares at the point of sale was £0.4m, meaning that the managing director had received £1m more for his shares than their market value.

Therefore, under the provisions in ITEPA 2003, Part 7, chapter 3D (see **5.5** below), the difference between the shares' market value and the proceeds that the managing director received was taxable employment income and subject to PAYE and NIC, not CGT.

The taxpayer's counsel had argued that there was a deep inconsistency between the chapters of ITEPA 2003, Part 7 in their treatment of the definition of market value: in Chapter 2 (Restricted Securities) the legislation seems to imply that rights that are personal to an employee should be taken into account for the purposes of the valuation standard (see **5.2** below); if personal rights can count toward the valuation of shares in one chapter of the legislation, why shouldn't they count in the other chapters?

The Supreme Court found against the taxpayer. A personal right that is extrinsic to the rights attached to the shares cannot be taken into account in most cases (ITEPA 2003, Part 7, Chapter 2 being an outlier). In his leading judgment, Lord Walker observed that:

> "It is regrettable that ITEPA 2003, which came into force on 6 April 2003 and was intended to rewrite income tax law (as affecting employment and pensions) in plain English, was almost at once overtaken by massive amendments which are in anything but plain English."

On the inconsistency of the legislation, he added:

> "I express the hope that Parliament may find time to review the complex and obscure provisions of Part 7 of ITEPA 2003."

Sadly, Parliament has yet to take up the challenge.

Case: *Grays Timber Products Limited v HMRC* [2010] UKSC 4

2.6 Key valuation terms used in ITEPA 2003

2.6.1 Restricted value or "RV"

This term is generally used to mean the "money's worth" value chargeable under ITEPA 2003, s. 62 (see **2.1** above).

2.6.2 AMV

Although the term is never spelt out in the legislation, it is widely taken to mean "actual market value" and is used in Part 7 to denote the TCGA 1992 value of securities, taking into account any restrictions that are placed on them.

2.6.3 UMV

The unrestricted market value of a security is the TCGA 1992 value of shares, disregarding any restrictions that have been placed on them.

Part 2: Taxation of employee securities

3. Acquisition of securities

3.1 Introduction to share awards

In essence, when an employee receives securities, any difference between the value that he or she receives in the shares and the price paid to acquire them will be treated as taxable employment income and will be subject to tax under one of the provisions of ITEPA 2003.

How the tax would be collected is discussed in **Chapter 7** below and the position of the employer company is set out in **Chapter 6**.

In the absence of the special regime of charges in ITEPA 2003, Pt. 7, an award of shares to an employee would constitute "money's worth" in the hands of the employee, which would fall to be taxed as general earnings under ITEPA 2003, Pt. 3, Chapter 1. (The ITEPA 2003 provisions, now found at s. 62(3), are an enactment of the 1935 House of Lords decision in *Weight v Salmon*.)

This means that the employee would normally be treated as having received taxable employment income on the date that he or she received the shares that had been awarded. The value subject to tax would be based on the money's worth received by the employee, as set out above in **Chapter 2**, this valuation standard is different to that developed for the purposes of TCGA 1992, Part VIII, as the information that can be taken into account for such a valuation is less restrictive than the usual CGT valuation standard, which is used throughout ITEPA 2003, Pt. 7.

These rules exist in parallel with ITEPA 2003, Pt. 7, which introduces modifications to the tax regime; often a single transaction can be apparently within the scope of a number of different taxing provisions, although in reality the rules have to be read together as forming a unified system and often the "common law" tax charge under ITEPA 2003, Pt. 3, Chapter 1 will only be visible if there is a material difference in the "money's worth" and TCGA 1992, Part VIII valuations.

Case: *Weight v Salmon* (1935) 19 TC 174

3.2 Acquiring securities – looking at the deal

In order to work out how an award of securities should be taxed there are two essential elements that need to be considered:

- The status of the securities themselves – are the securities convertible into other securities? Are there any restrictions on the rights of the securities?
- The terms of the offer of securities to the employee – does the employee have to pay anything to acquire the securities? Will the employee have to pay something for the securities now or in the future? Does the employee receive the securities now, or in the future? Do the terms of the offer to the employee impose additional restrictions on his or her rights to enjoy the securities?

These questions go back to the principle set out in **Chapter 1**:

- at what point does the employee receive value?
- how do we measure that value?
- and to what extent can the employee be said to have given consideration for the value that he or she has received?

If the securities' rights or the terms of the offer place a restriction on the employee's rights over the securities, then the employee can be seen to have received only a proportion of the value of the securities; the provisions of the restricted securities regime will need to be considered to establish how much value is treated as taxable employment income and when it will come into charge (discussed in detail at **3.3** below).

Where an employee receives securities, which are convertible into securities of another description, then that employee cannot be said to have received the whole benefit of the securities until they have undergone their conversion into the other type of securities. For this reason, the rules on convertible securities in ITEPA 2003, Pt. 7, Chapter 3 have the effect of disregarding the securities' conversion rights when they are acquired, deferring the bulk of the tax charge until the point that the employee receives value, when the conversion event takes place. These rules are discussed in detail in the next chapter.

If the deal is such that the employee has a right to acquire securities at a point in the future, then the rules on securities options in ITEPA 2003, Pt. 7, Chapter 5 will apply (see **3.5** below).

Finally, if an employee has agreed to pay something for the shares at a date in the future, or if the shares are not fully paid up when they are issued to the employee, the "normal" rules in Part 3, Chapter 1 would treat the promise to pay in the future as good consideration that would reduce or eliminate the tax charge on acquisition. The additional rules in Part 7, Chapter 3, discussed in full at **3.4** below, set out how to deal with this sort of transaction and the modifications that are needed to the basic regime.

3.3 Restricted securities

3.3.1 Before FA 2003

Before FA 2003 there had been two disjointed tax regimes in place that dealt with the situation where shares granted to employees were subject to a risk of forfeiture (the "conditional shares" regime) or subject to restrictions on their rights.

Although both regimes remain technically in force, they only apply to shares that were acquired by reason of employment before 16 April 2003 and, in consequence, are increasingly rarely encountered in practice.

These rules deferred tax charges, in whole or in part, from the date that the shares were acquired by the employee to the date the shares were disposed of or the employee otherwise came to a full enjoyment of the share rights.

In the case of the rules on conditional shares, the regime applied where an employee could be forced to dispose of his or her shares and brought the whole value of the shares into charge as taxable employment income at the point that the shares were sold or they ceased to be conditional. This could leave employees, who believed that their profits on selling their shares were capital and subject to tax at a maximum rate as low as 10%, suffering PAYE and NIC charges at far higher rates.

The rules were, on the whole, poorly understood by advisers and were seen to have unfair and perverse results for employees.

3.3.2 Finance Act 2003: restricted securities

In order to remedy some of the unfairness that was perceived to exist in the old rules, as well as to combat tax avoidance using securities, new rules were introduced in FA 2003. The new rules applied to all shares acquired on or after 16 April 2003 and came fully into force on 1 September 2003.

The rules on restricted securities are set out in ITEPA 2003, Pt. 7, Chapter 2 and their rationale is to defer tax charges until the point that an employee enjoys the value from his or her shares or other securities.

The principle underlying the rules is that where an employee acquires shares that are subject to a restriction that reduces their market value, then the value brought into tax when the shares acquired will be reduced to reflect the restrictions; when the restrictions are lifted or the shares are sold, then there will be a further tax charge to reflect the value "freed up" by the lifting of the restrictions.

There is an inherent problem in the drafting of the legislation, because it fails to take into account the impact of the change from a "money's worth" valuation of employees' shares to the TCGA 1992, Part VIII value: if a restriction is inherent in the shares' rights, it will be fully taken into account in valuing the shares, as a third party purchaser of those shares would be subject to the restriction; if a restriction is not an inherent share right, it will not be reflected in the valuation at all, because the hypothetical third party purchaser envisaged by the legislation and case law would not be treated as being bound by any restrictions that did not attach to the shares directly. This point is explored in more detail in **Chapter 2** above.

The profession and HMRC have tacitly come to a compromise, entertaining the polite fiction that the market value of shares can be affected in the ways envisaged by the legislation, and the courts have given a degree of support to this premise. Whether the courts would continue to entertain this view if the point were to be directly litigated is questionable, but the author suspects that it is not in the interests of taxpayers or HMRC to pursue the point to a court capable of decisively ruling on it and that the polite fiction will continue for so long as the legislation remains in force.

3.3.3 What are restricted securities?

ITEPA 2003, s. 423 defines a restricted security by looking at some of the key features of the rights conferred by the ownership of those securities.

Where the market value of the securities is treated as being reduced because of any arrangement or condition that falls within three broad categories, then they will be treated as restricted securities:

- restrictions on the right of employees to retain the shares, where the employee might be compelled to dispose of the securities without receiving the securities' market value in return;
- direct or indirect restrictions on the right of the employees to exercise all of the rights attaching to the shares, for example, the right to freely transfer the shares (an example of an indirect restriction would be where the employee suffered some penalty for exercising his or her rights); and
- restrictions on the rights of employees to retain the proceeds of selling their securities.

Example: restricted securities

Hitesh is awarded 1,000 B shares in his employer company, Tea Limited. The articles of association of Tea Limited state that anyone who holds B shares who leaves employment with the company must sell the shares for the lesser of their market value and the shares' nominal value.

Hitesh has acquired shares that have a forfeiture condition attaching to them, these are restricted securities for the purposes of ITEPA 2003, Pt. 7, Chapter 2.

The decision of the First-tier Tribunal in *Sjumarken* demonstrates that there is no need for a restriction to be something express and legally enforceable; it is enough to demonstrate that there is a *de facto* restriction on the rights of securities for them to constitute restricted securities for the purposes of the legislation.

In the *Sjumarken* case the taxpayer had received shares under the terms of a scheme that was organised by his employer company; the rules of the plan said that Mr Sjumarken could not sell his shares until a fixed period had expired, but that if he left the company this provision fell away. Mr Sjumarken left his employer and attempted to sell his shares, but was rebuffed by the plan administrators, who made Mr Sjumarken retain his shares until the fixed period had expired. The tribunal decided that the shares were restricted securities, even though the limit on Mr Sjumarken selling them was a matter of the practice of the scheme administrators, and not a feature of the rules.

ITEPA 2003, s. 424 exempts securities from the restricted securities rules in two situations, provided that there is not a tax avoidance motive underlying the structuring of the award of securities. The exemption applies where:

- the securities are not fully paid up and can be forfeited if any unpaid amounts are called and the call is not subsequently paid; or
- the securities are subject to forfeiture where the employee is dismissed for gross misconduct.

Because listed company shares can be freely traded by anyone on a market, shares in listed companies will only constitute restricted securities if there is a side agreement between the employees and the company forming a part of the terms under which the shares are awarded to the employees (although awards of interests in shares, rather than shares themselves – for example, under a joint ownership plan – may have intrinsic features that mean that the interest in shares constitutes a restricted security for these purposes).

For private companies, the position is less straightforward, and there may be features of a company's articles of association that mean that the shares will constitute restricted securities *per se*, without reference to an ancillary agreement.

Case: *Sjumarken v HMRC* [2015] UKFTT 375 (TC)

3.3.4 Private companies: interaction with the Companies Act 2006 model articles

As a matter of practice, HMRC treat limitations on an employee's right to sell his or her shares as a restriction for the purposes of Chapter 2.

A common example of such a restriction would be a right for the directors of a company to refuse to permit shares to be freely transferred; this typically takes the form of a provision in a company's articles of association regulating the transfer of shares and is very commonly encountered; as a matter of corporate governance most private companies are unwilling to allow their shares to be freely transferable. The commercial rationale for such provisions is that they prevent disgruntled shareholders from transferring shares to business competitors or to other persons unconnected with the company.

The Table A articles of association set out in the pre-2006 Companies Acts regulations only gave the directors the right to refuse to register the transfer of shares if the shares were not fully paid; this meant that the default position for companies was that their shares were not "restricted securities", unless they had adopted articles of association that over-rode the transfer provisions in Table A.

The model articles set out in the post-2006 legislation have reversed the position: the default articles of association for private companies now give the directors an unfettered discretion to refuse to register the transfer of shares, which means that shares in a private company incorporated under the 2006 Act will always constitute restricted securities unless the company's shareholders have taken the positive step of adopting articles that over-ride the transfer provisions.

Even where a company has adopted custom articles, the transfer provisions in those articles are likely to restrict the freedom of shareholders to transfer their shares freely.

Another provision which is often included in private company articles of association is a requirement for bankrupt shareholders to offer their shares for sale, often at par value, to the other shareholders. This provision is often encountered in family companies and is intended to prevent the value of a company from being dissipated by bankrupt family members. For the purposes of the legislation, this will also constitute a restriction and bring the shares within ITEPA 2003, Pt. 7, Chapter 2.

3.3.5 Forfeitable securities

In terms of the legislation, securities are said to be subject to forfeiture where a shareholder can be compelled to dispose of them without receiving consideration that is at least equal to the securities' market value. The obligation on a bankrupt member to offer shares for sale for nominal consideration, discussed at **3.3.4** above, constitutes a forfeiture condition for these purposes.

In broad terms, ITEPA 2003, s. 425 provides that where a forfeiture condition has a life of less than five years, the tax point is moved from the date on which the employee receives the shares to the date that the forfeiture condition lifts or, if sooner, the date on which the shares are sold.

Example

Tea Limited makes a further award of shares to Hitesh, which are subject to a condition that if he does not meet his sales targets over the following two years he will have to transfer the shares to the company's employee share trust for no consideration. If he meets the sales targets, the condition will lapse and Hitesh will be free to keep the shares.

Because the award of shares come with a forfeiture condition that lasts less than five years, Hitesh will not be treated as having received taxable employment income when the shares are awarded to him; the tax point is shifted to the date on which the forfeiture condition is lifted.

The rules on forfeitable securities are a part of the restricted securities regime, which means that the tax charge will be governed by ITEPA 2003, s. 426: when a forfeiture condition lifts there may be additional restrictions that need to be considered by the employee and by the company in calculating the amount subject to tax and whether there are any further tax charges that could arise in respect of the employee's shares.

3.3.6 Operation of the tax charge on acquisition

As set out above, when restricted securities are acquired by an employee, a tax charge may arise under one of the chapters of Part 7, principally Chapter 3C (*Acquisition of shares at less than market value*), Chapter 5 (*Securities options*) and Chapter 3 (*Convertible securities*).

For the purposes of the tax charges in Part 7, Chapter 2 has the effect of substituting the securities' restricted value (referred to as "AMV" in the legislation) for the value that would normally be derived from Part VIII TCGA 1992 (referred to as "UMV").

However, there is still a residual charge to tax under ITEPA 2003, Pt. 2, Chapter 1, which will be evaluated using a "money's worth" valuation, which may produce a different value.

Example: restricted securities

Tea Limited makes an award of shares to Martin, which are restricted securities. The company calculates that using a Part VIII TCGA 1992 valuation, the shares have an unrestricted value of £10 each, which implies that their AMV will be £9 per share (based on the assumption that the restrictions on the shares would depress their market value by 10%).

The company also considered the money's worth value of Martin's shares, which it calculated to be £9.50 per share.

Assuming that Martin does not elect to disapply the restricted securities rules, he will pay tax calculated by reference to the higher figure of £9.50 per share.

Although the restricted securities rules can reduce the value treated as taxable employment income when an employee acquires securities, there can be a significant opportunity cost: the proportion of the value of the securities which escapes tax when securities are acquired will be brought into charge when the securities are sold or the restrictions are lifted.

3.3.7 Operation of the tax charge on future events

While a detailed explanation of the operation of the tax charge properly belongs in the next chapter, it is useful to have an overview of the legislation, as it bears on decisions that the employees and employers need to take when restricted securities are acquired.

Where restricted or forfeitable securities are subject to one of the events listed in ITEPA 2003, s. 427, a tax charge will arise on the employee. The events are:

- the lifting or variation of restrictions; and
- the disposal of the restricted securities for consideration (there is an exemption that applies where the securities are disposed of to an "associated person").

The legislation sets out (at s. 428) a formula for calculating the tax charge. The formula is daunting at first sight, but the principle is relatively straightforward and the apparent complexity in the drafting reflects a degree of over-engineering by the draftsman, who clearly envisaged that a set of securities would possibly subject to a series of tax charges over its lifetime. In practice, it is extremely rare for an employee to incur more than one tax charge under these provisions. This is because most charges will be triggered when securities are sold and many employers prefer to take advantage of the regime of elections to opt out of the complications that the restricted securities rules bring with them (see **3.3.8** below).

As quoted in the legislation, the formula is given as:

UMV x (IUP-PCP-OP)-CE

The formula is intended to be used each time that there is a chargeable event in relation to the securities:

- **UMV** is the unrestricted value of the securities after the event has taken place;
- the expressions in brackets are intended to capture the proportion of the securities' value "released" by the chargeable event:
  - **IUP** is a calculation of the proportion of the value of the securities that was neither paid for by the employee nor subject to tax when they were acquired,
  - **PCP** is the proportion of the securities' value that has been taxed on earlier chargeable events; and
  - **OP** is the remaining proportion of the securities' value that is attributable to the restrictions after the chargeable event has taken place; and
- **CE** is the cost, if any, that the employee incurs to secure the release or lifting of the restrictions.

Acquisition of securities

These terms and their operation are explored in more detail, at **5.2** below, but their operation can be illustrated with a simple example (sadly, "simple" is a relative term in the context of the rules on restricted securities!):

Example 1: restricted securities – operating the charge (1)

In the example given above, Martin does not elect to disapply the restricted securities rules, and paid tax calculated on £9.50 per Tea Limited share when he acquired them.

Two years later, Tea Limited is taken over by Chai Corp. The shareholders, including Martin, receive £100 per share.

In this case:

- UMV will be £100 – the value of the consideration that Martin receives for the shares;
- IUP will be 0.05 – i.e. the £0.50 difference between the value on which Martin has paid tax and the UMV of the shares when he acquired them, divided by the UMV;
- PCP will be nil, as there have not been any earlier chargeable events;
- OP is also nil, as there is no difference between the restricted and unrestricted values of the consideration that Martin has received; and
- CE is nil, as Martin has not made a financial contribution to the sale process.

On this basis, the value treated as taxable employment income when Martin sells his shares will be £5.00 and the remainder of Martin's proceeds will be taxed under the CGT rules.

The way that the formula works means that if an employee pays for his or her shares and that initial payment is at least equal to or exceeds UMV, then no future charges to tax can arise under either the restricted or forfeitable securities regimes.

Example 2: restricted securities – operating the charge (2)

At the same time as he received his award of shares, Martin bought shares in Tea Limited and paid £10.00 per share; as before, he does not elect to disapply the restricted securities rules.

There is no tax to pay when Martin acquires his shares and on the sale to Chai Corp Martin will not be treated as having received any taxable employment income:

- As before, UMV will be £100;
- IUP will be nil, because Martin had paid for the full, unrestricted value of the shares when he acquired them; and
- PCP, OP and CE will be nil (and irrelevant in any case – if IUP is nil there can be no prior tax charge).

In some cases, the "money's worth" value of a share may equal or exceed UMV. In those cases, the employee will have been charged to tax under ITEPA 2003, Pt. 2, Chapter 1 on a value that is at least equal to UMV, which will mean that IUP will also be nil in these cases when considering the charge to tax under the restricted securities rules.

3.3.8 Effect of elections

The legislation provides for a regime of elections, allowing employers and employees to modify the tax treatment of securities under ITEPA 2003, Pt. 7, Chapter 2.

The four types of election are as follows:

- s. 425 – disapplies the forfeitable securities rules when securities are acquired;
- s. 430 – disapplies the effect of the remaining restrictions on shares after a chargeable event has taken place;
- s. 431(1) – disapplies the whole of the restricted securities regime when securities are acquired; and
- s. 431(2) – disapplies the effect of some restrictions when securities are acquired.

There is a comparatively short timescale for making these elections:

- elections under sections 425, 431(1) and 431(2) must be made within 14 days of the date on which the securities are acquired; and

- elections under s. 430 have to be made within 14 days of a chargeable event.

The elections must be made jointly by both the employee and employer company. There is no obligation to file them with HMRC, but they must be available for inspection.

In practice, elections under s. 425 are rarely, if ever, used. If an employee and employer wish to make the acquisition date the tax point for the acquisition of forfeitable securities then the likelihood is that they will wish to disapply the whole of the restricted securities regime, in which case an election under s. 431(1) would be more appropriate.

The circumstances in which elections under s. 431(2) might be used are limited; the only commercially sensible reason for disapplying some, but not all, of the restrictions attaching to securities might be where forfeitable securities have other restrictions applying to them and the parties are keen to take advantage of the forfeitable securities rules without wishing to worry about the tax effect of the other restrictions on the shares.

Elections under s. 430 are also comparatively rare, as the first chargeable event relating to an employee's securities is likely to be their sale. The main situation where a s. 430 election would be of use would be where forfeitable securities have been given to an employee and the forfeiture condition has lifted, but there are still outstanding restrictions on the shares.

The most frequently encountered election is the election to opt out of the restricted securities regime completely, set out in ITEPA 2003, s. 431(1).

Example: elections

Tea Limited makes a further award of shares to Martin, which are conditional on his meeting a performance target – if he does not meet the performance target by the third anniversary of grant, he will be obliged to sell the shares back to the company at par.

This is a forfeiture condition and it falls within the scope of ITEPA 2003, s. 425 because it has a lifespan of less than five years.

The shares are of the same class as those comprised in Martin's other share awards and carry the same restrictions.

If Martin and the company do nothing, then Martin will not be taxed when he receives the shares; instead, Martin will be treated as having received taxable employment income equal to the shares' restricted value when the forfeiture condition lifts and then there would be a further tax charge under the restricted securities rules when Martin sold the shares.

If Martin and the company make a s. 425 election, then Martin would be taxed on the shares' restricted value when he receives them, and would then suffer a charge under the restricted securities rules when he sells; Martin would not be refunded the tax that he suffered if he does not meet the performance conditions and is forced to sell the shares back at par – at best he would have realised a CGT loss.

Martin and the company could make a s. 431(2) election to ignore all of the restrictions on the shares other than the forfeiture condition – this would mean that Martin would not have an up-front tax charge: if the performance conditions are satisfied, Martin will pay tax on the UMV of the shares at that point and will not be subject to further tax charges under the restricted securities regime when he sells the shares; if the performance condition is not met, then the shares will be forfeit and Martin will not have suffered a "dry" tax charge. The same result would arise if Martin did nothing when the shares were awarded to him, but he and the company made a s. 430 election when the performance condition was achieved.

Finally, if Martin and the company made a s. 431(1) election when he acquired the shares, then neither the restricted securities rules nor the forfeitable shares rules would apply: Martin would pay income tax on the whole unrestricted value of the shares when he acquired them and would have no further exposure to the rules on restricted securities; however, he would run the risk that he paid tax in respect of shares that he subsequently loses.

Where an employee acquires shares through one of the tax-advantaged share schemes set out in statute (which are discussed in more detail at **Chapter 12** below) they may be deemed to have made s. 431(1) elections when their awards crystallise under ITEPA 2003, s. 431A – these rules are dealt with in more detail below.

If securities have been acquired as part of a tax avoidance scheme, then ITEPA 2003, s. 431B deems that a s. 431(1) election will have been made.

With the exception of the forfeitable securities rules, most employers see the restricted securities regime as an unnecessary complication that could hinder future transactions; it is very rare for a well-advised employer to wish to risk the potential future compliance obligations that arise from the restricted securities regime, and employers will usually make employee share awards dependent on the employee entering into a s. 431(1) election.

Elections are usually high up on the list of documents requested by purchasers of companies in due diligence processes; if elections have not been made or there are questions about their validity, the effect on due diligence processes can be entirely disproportionate to the tax at risk.

Although many employers are willing to take advantage of the forfeitable securities regime, most employers see the restricted securities regime as a risk and trap for the badly advised.

3.4 Chapter 3C – securities acquired for less than market value

3.4.1 The mischief

Where an employee acquires shares and makes no immediate payment for them, or only pays a part of the acquisition price, the logic of the employment-related securities regime is that the employee has received value and should be treated as having received taxable employment income equal to that value.

The principal charge will arise under ITEPA 2003, Pt. 3, Chapter 1. However, these provisions look at the consideration that an employee may give for his or her securities; where an employee acquires securities, and agrees to pay their full value in the future, he or she will have given consideration for the securities (i.e. the promise to pay), which means that no charge to tax would arise under ITEPA 2003, Pt. 3, Chapter 1.

Although it might have been possible to undertake a valuation exercise to establish the time value of the consideration given by the employee, this was one situation where the legislature opted to eschew complexity.

The legislation in ITEPA 2003, Pt. 7, Chapter 3C provides that where an employee pays less for securities than their market value, the difference between what has been paid upfront and the securities' market value will be deemed to be a beneficial loan advanced to the employee.

Example: shares acquired for less than market value

Charles is offered 5,000 shares in his employer company, Cauliflower Limited, where he works as an assistant in the marketing department. The terms of the offer are that Charles has nothing to pay when he acquires them, but will have to pay £5 per share before he sells them.

The company undertakes a valuation exercise and establishes that the value of the shares is £6 per share.

Charles will be treated as if his employer had made him a loan of £5 per share and the £1 balance of the shares' value that Charles does not have to pay for will be treated as taxable employment income.

3.4.2   Unpaid consideration treated as beneficial loan

ITEPA 2003, s. 446S treats any unpaid consideration for employees' securities as a beneficial employment-related loan and applies the provisions in ITEPA 2003, Pt. 3, Chapter 7 to the deemed loan.

This means that the employee will be potentially taxed on the benefit of the deemed loan unless he or she falls within one of the exemptions in the legislation. The "benefit" of the loan is the annual value of the interest that would be charged on it at the official rate of interest published by HMRC; at the time of writing this is 2.5% per annum.

Example: beneficial loan

The aggregate value of the loan that Charles is deemed to have is £25,000. Charles will be taxed on the benefit of the loan under ITEPA 2003, s. 175. The benefit taxable on Charles will be £625 per year (i.e. £25,000 @ 2.5%).

3.4.3 Partly paid shares

Companies, including listed companies, can issue shares with some part of the nominal value or share premium unpaid, to be paid up at a later date. These shares are called "partly paid" and usually command a lower price than "fully paid" shares, because a potential purchaser can be called to pay up the outstanding subscription monies.

Where shares are partly paid, their holder will always be potentially exposed to a claim for the unpaid monies and can be pursued for them even if the issuing company goes into liquidation.

ITEPA 2003, s. 446Q provides that Chapter 3C applies to partly paid shares, as if they were fully paid shares acquired for less than their market value.

3.4.4 Exemptions

The employment-related loans legislation envisions a number of exemptions to the benefit-in kind charge on the benefit of the loan and these apply equally to the deemed loan arising under Chapter 3C.

The most straightforward of these exemptions is ITEPA 2003, s. 180, which exempts employment-related loans from tax if they are below a *de minimis* value, currently £10,000. This exemption is designed to be a cliff-edge: if the value of the loan (or deemed loan) remains below £10,000 then the loan is exempt from the annual benefit in kind charge; if the loan exceeds £10,000 at any point in the tax year then the whole value of the loan will fall within the charge.

A more complicated relief, which may be applicable to higher-value deemed loans, is that set out in ITEPA 2003, s. 178: if the deemed loan had been a real, interest-bearing loan, and the interest would have qualified for tax relief, then the annual benefit of the loan will be exempt from tax.

The most commonly encountered exemption under s. 178 is that provided in s. 178(a), where the deemed loan falls within ITA 2007, s. 383. The only part of ITA 2007, s. 383 that will be relevant in relation to a deemed loan under Chapter 3C is the exemption for loans to acquire an interest in a close company, which is elaborated at ITA 2007, s. 392.

The combined effect of the legislation is to give employees an exemption from the annual charge on the benefit of the loan if their employer company is under the control of five or fewer shareholders and the person acquiring the shares is either employed in a role which involves him or her in the actual management or conduct of the company or where that person is acquiring more than 5% of the company's ordinary share capital.

HMRC interpret this exemption narrowly; in order to qualify for the relief an employee must be in a position equivalent to that of a main board member with oversight of at least one aspect of the company's business as a whole; it is not sufficient for someone to have oversight of a division or subsidiary (unless it is the subsidiary's shares that he or she is acquiring).

Example: exemption from charge

Charles works with Costas at Cauliflower Limited, where Costas is the marketing director. Costas is offered a share award over a larger number of shares, but on the same terms as Charles.

Because Costas is at board level in Cauliflower and has a hand in the overall direction and control of the company as a whole, the loan that he is deemed to have will not be treated as giving rise to annual income tax charge on the benefit of the loan.

These exemptions give relief from the annual benefit in kind charge on the deemed loan that the employee is treated as having, but they do not exempt the employee from the other charges that can arise if the deemed loan is treated as released or discharged. The final relief that needs to be considered is that set out in ITEPA 2003, s. 446R, which potentially exempts an employee from the entire range of charges under Chapter 3C.

The relief in s. 446R provides that an employee's shares will fall outside the regime in Chapter 3C where the whole class of shares is partly paid and either the company is employee-controlled or the class of partly paid shares controls the company. The relief will not be available if the arrangements are part of a tax avoidance scheme.

It is hard to envision a scenario in which the exemption could practically apply and it is possible that the draftsman had a hypothetical situation in mind when these provisions were inserted into the Act.

3.4.5 Subsequent tax charges

The legislation provides for a tax charge to arise when securities are sold before the deemed loan is discharged or if the employee is released from the obligation to pay up the outstanding amounts on the securities. These provisions are dealt with at **5.4** below.

3.5 Share options

3.5.1 The common law position

The common-law rules on the tax-treatment of share options are set out in the House of Lords decision in *Abbott v Philbin*. In that case it was decided that options granted to an employee were a perquisite of his employment and that the employee should be taxed on the market value of the options on the date that the options were granted.

The court explicitly rejected the argument advanced by the Inland Revenue, that the options should be taxed when they were exercised and that the amount subject to income tax should be the options' "spread" at the exercise date ("spread" being the difference between the option exercise price and the market value of the option shares on the date of exercise).

The effect of the decision was that the taxpayer was taxed under the income tax rules when the option was granted, but would only suffer further taxation if the option was sold or the option shares were eventually sold; any profit arising to the employee would be a capital gain which, at the time, would have been outside the scope of taxation (CGT was introduced after the case was decided).

Following the decision in *Abbott v Philbin*, legislation was passed in FA 1966 to reverse the position for what was then Sch. E income: for the employment taxes purposes, the point at which a securities option will be taxed will be the date on which it was exercised. This is the same legislative scheme that has been re-enacted in ITEPA 2003.

While the common law rules are no longer relevant to employment-related securities options, they are arguably still good law with regard to the taxation of share options granted to partnerships or the self-employed.

As set out at **1.3.2** above, a securities option is not treated as a "security" for the purposes of the legislation. Other types of option, for example an option to acquire commodities or real property, will be taxed as if they were securities. This means that there is a potential tax charge on the date that such options are acquired by an employee and then a second income tax charge on the date that the options are exercised under the rules on convertible securities (see **4.3** below).

Law: FA 1966, s. 25; ITEPA 2003, Pt. 7, Ch. 5
Case: *Abbott v Philbin* (1960) UKHL 1

3.5.2 Scope of the statutory scheme

The rules on employment-related securities options are set out in ITEPA 2003, Pt. 7, Chapter 5.

Section 471 of ITEPA 2003 contains similar deeming provisions to those at s. 421B: a securities option that is acquired by reason of a current, former or prospective employment will be treated as an employment-related securities option. Similarly, an option made available to someone by his or her employer will always be deemed to be employment-related securities unless the option is made between individuals in the ordinary course of the family, domestic or personal relationships of those persons.

The statutory provisions extend to all options to acquire securities except for options that have been granted for the purposes of avoiding tax or NIC. Such "avoidance options" are taxed as if they were securities and fall outside the scope of Chapter 5.

3.5.3 Grant of options

Subject to one rare exception, the grant of an employment-related securities option will not give rise to a tax charge.

The exception is where the option is granted under the rules of a Sch. 4 CSOP, and the option is inadvertently granted at a discount. This exception is discussed in more detail at **14.3.1** below.

Historically, options with a life of more than 10 years, or discounted options, were treated as giving rise to a tax charge when they were granted, but these rules fell away after FA 2003 came into force, and ITEPA 2003, s. 475 now explicitly enacts that the grant of an employment-related securities option is not treated as giving rise to taxable employment income.

3.5.4   Chargeable events relating to options – exercise

The principle underlying the taxation of options is that they give rise to tax charges at the point that they deliver something of tangible value to the employee: when the employee exercises the options and receives the securities over which the option was granted (or the proceeds of selling those securities); or when the securities are "bought out" for cash or another asset.

In each case, the amount subject to tax will be the difference between the value received by the employee and "deductible amounts" (i.e. the costs to the employee of the option).

ITEPA 2003, sections 480 and 481 provide that the following are "deductible amounts" for these purposes:

- anything that the employee has paid in consideration for the grant of the option – this is rarely encountered, but sometimes employers do ask employees to "buy" their share options;
- the consideration, if any, that the employee has given for the exercise of the option (i.e. the "exercise price" or "strike price");
- amounts that have already been taxed under another provision of ITEPA 2003 – for example, under the rules on disguised remuneration in ITEPA 2003, Pt. 7A;
- The value of any employer NIC that has been borne by the employee (this is discussed in more detail below).

Example: options exercised

Paul is granted an option to acquire 1,000 shares in Bibulous plc, his employer. The shares are worth £7 each when the option is granted and the option's exercise price is £1 per share. Paul does not pay anything to acquire the option.

Two years later Paul exercises the option, paying his employer £1 per share to acquire all 1,000 shares. At this time the shares are worth £12 each.

Paul will be treated as having received taxable employment income of £11,000 when he exercises the option (i.e. the difference between the shares' value of £12 each and the exercise price of £1 each, multiplied by the number of option shares).

Paul is granted a separate option by Bibulous plc on the same day to acquire another 1,000 shares, with the same £1 exercise price. However, it is a condition of the grant of this option that Paul enters into an agreement with his employer to bear the cost of the employer NIC.

Paul exercises this option at the same time as the other option. This gives rise to a gain subject to NIC of £11,000 and Paul pays £1,518 to his employer to meet the cost of the employer NIC (i.e. £11,000 @ 13.8%). The amount of taxable employment income that Paul is treated as having is therefore £9,482 (£11,000 minus £1,518).

3.5.5 Chargeable events relating to options – release for consideration

If the employee does not exercise his or her option, but instead allows it to be cancelled in exchange for a payment, that will also give rise to a tax charge, with the value received by the employee treated as taxable employment income.

In the UK it is quite unusual to "cash-cancel" options in this way, but it is more common in the US and other jurisdictions. This can lead to difficulties where UK companies are being acquired by US buyers, who will often propose that employee share options are cash-cancelled without regard to the UK tax consequences, which can be negative for both the company and the employer. The following example is based on a situation that the author encountered far too late to remedy:

Example: cash cancellation

Biscuits Ltd is a subsidiary of a US corporation. The parent company, Biscuits Inc., approached Gravy Ltd and offered £10m to acquire the entire share capital of the company. Gravy Ltd had granted a number of its employees EMI options (see **Chapter 13** below) when the company was originally established; the employees held EMI options constituting 20% of the fully diluted share capital of the company.

Instead of allowing the employees to exercise their EMI options, Biscuits Inc. arranged for Biscuits Ltd to cash-cancel their options, so that the consideration for buying Gravy Ltd was split £8m to the founder shareholders and £2m to the holders of the EMI options.

The employees were treated as if they had received taxable employment income of £2m between them and most of them were charged to tax at the additional rate of 45% and NIC was also due. Their employer was obliged to operate PAYE on the tax liability and account for employer NIC. The cost of cancelling the options was a capital cost in the books of Biscuits Ltd, which was not deductible for corporation tax purposes.

If the employees had been allowed to exercise their EMI options, they would have paid CGT at 10% instead and their employer company would have been entitled to claim corporation tax relief on the value of their option shares (see **Chapter 6** below).

These rules apply irrespective of whether an option is released in exchange for cash or some other asset. The only exception to this is where an option is exchanged for another option. In that case the legislation contains a specific exemption in ITEPA 2003, s. 483, which effectively ignores the exchange of options, simply deferring the tax point until the replacement option is exercised.

4. Post-acquisition changes

4.1 The legislative objective

As was set out in **Chapter 1** above, the objective of the legislation in ITEPA 2003, Pt. 7 is to treat value "gifted" to an employee as taxable employment income, while organic growth in the value of securities will be treated as capital, subject to the capital gains tax regime.

In order to achieve this objective, the legislation seeks to capture non-organic changes in the value of employees' securities after they have been acquired by the employees. The result has been to create a structure of anti-avoidance rules that overlap with the other charging sections in Part 7.

The legislation is daunting at first, but it largely achieves the objectives of the draftsman, albeit with some unpleasant quirks that arise from the labyrinthine drafting.

4.2 Chapters 3A and 3B – non-commercial changes in value

4.2.1 The mischief

ITEPA 2003, Pt. 7, Chapters 3A (Non-commercial reductions in market value) and 3B (Non-commercial increases in market value) are both intended to capture tax that might have been avoided by allowing an employee to acquire securities with a low initial value, which is then uplifted, either because the initial value was artificially depressed before the employee acquired the securities or because something was done after the employee acquired the shares which artificially increases their value.

Although, in practice, these provisions are rarely raised by HMRC, they have a high profile when transactions are being analysed and in due diligence processes that potential company buyers may undertake; as happens so often with ITEPA 2003, Pt. 7, much of the enforcement of the legislation is actually done by parties undertaking transactions, rather than by HMRC.

4.2.2 Non-commercial

At the heart of both Chapter 3A and 3B is the concept that "...things done otherwise than for genuine commercial purposes..." will be treated as giving rise to taxable employment income.

The legislation cites two particular situations where a transaction is to be regarded as non-commercial:

- if it can be shown that the main purpose, or one of the main purposes, of a transaction was avoidance of tax or National Insurance contributions; or
- transactions between companies in the same group on non-arm's length terms (other than a payment for group relief).

This list is not intended to be exhaustive, which means that transactions that are not intra-group transactions (for example, transactions between shareholders) or which might be motivated by something other than a desire to avoid tax are still within the scope of the legislation.

Where a transaction is motivated by evident and transparently commercial purposes, the risks of this anti-avoidance legislation applying are reduced. However, companies and advisers should bear in mind that HMRC and a future buyer may be sceptical about the degree to which a transaction is commercial, if the main result of the transaction is that the value of shares held by employees changes significantly.

Law: ITEPA 2003, s. 446A, 446K

4.2.3 Tax charge on acquisition

The tax charge in the first part of Chapter 3A is intended to prevent companies from manipulating the value on which an employee will be charged to tax by undertaking a transaction that takes value out of the employee's shares, perhaps by temporarily diverting an income stream from the company to another group entity.

Such a transaction would not necessarily be caught by Chapter 3B, as it might be designed to "unwind" after the employee acquired his or her securities, although it could be argued that most "reversible" transactions of this sort would be taken fully into account in

Part 2: Taxation of employee securities

arriving at the market value of the securities for the purposes of TCGA 1992, Part VIII.

Where there has been a non-commercial transaction in the seven years preceding the date on which an employee acquires shares or securities, and that transaction has reduced the value of the employment-related securities by more than 10%, the employee will suffer an additional tax charge when he or she acquires them.

Where this applies, ITEPA 2003, s. 446C effectively re-writes history by treating as taxable employment income the difference between the amount that the employee was actually taxed on when he acquired his securities and the value on which he would have paid tax if the non-commercial transaction had not taken place (referred to in the rest of this section as the "hypothetical value").

Example – value artificially depressed

John and Isobel work for Trifle Corp. In 2017 Trifle Corp undertook a transaction with another group company that artificially shifted costs into the company and reduced the value of its shares from £10 per share to £5. Later that year John and Isobel are invited to acquire shares in Trifle Corp; John is asked to pay £6 per share, while Isobel is given shares for free.

Isobel is charged to tax on £5 per share under the usual rules in ITEPA 2003, but will have tax on an additional £5 per share to pay by virtue of s. 446C (i.e. £10 minus £5).

John does not suffer a charge to tax under the normal ITEPA 2003 rules, but will be treated as having received taxable employment income of £4 under s. 446C (i.e. £10 minus £6).

Where there is a tax charge under these provisions, the restricted securities rules are partially disapplied by ITEPA 2003, s. 446D, although the forfeitable securities regime set out in s. 425 will still apply. This means that the tax charge on the acquisition of non-forfeitable restricted securities will be on the hypothetical unrestricted value of the securities, but that no further charges will arise under the restricted securities rules.

Where the securities in question are convertible securities, s. 446D stipulates that the hypothetical value is to be calculated as if the securities were not convertible securities.

4.2.4 Market value manipulation to reduce post-acquisition tax charges

The rules in Chapter 3A also make provision for adjustments to be made to tax charges under the restricted securities rules and the convertible securities rules where something has been done to depress the market value of the securities artificially before restrictions are lifted or securities are converted.

In each case, sections 446E to 446I substitute the hypothetical value of the securities (i.e. the value of the securities but for the thing done to reduce their market value artificially) for their actual value on the date that the tax charge arises in calculating the value of the taxable employment income arising on each chargeable event.

4.2.5 Non-commercial increases in market value

Chapter 3B applies where there has been a non-commercial increase in the market value of securities, which uplifts the market value of the securities by more than 10%.

ITEPA 2003, s. 446K defines a non-commercial increase as "an increase in the market value [...of the securities...] as a result of anything done otherwise than for genuine commercial purposes".

The charge operates by comparing the market value of employment-related securities on the last day of each tax year (or the date that they are disposed of by the employee, if that is earlier) with their hypothetical value (in this case, what their market value would have been if there had not been a non-commercial increase).

Example 1: non-commercial increases in market value (1)

Trifle Corp undertakes a second transaction with a group company, which diverts costs away into another group company. Because of this transaction, the shares owned by John and Isobel are worth £25 each on the following 5 April; if the transaction had not taken place the shares would only have been worth £15 per share.

As a result of this transaction, both John and Isobel are treated as having received taxable employment income of £10 per share.

It is possible for there to be multiple tax charges arising if the securities' market value increases between successive "valuation dates".

Part 2: Taxation of employee securities

The legislation focuses on the timing of non-commercial increases in market value, not on the timing of the actions which have been taken to give effect to the non-commercial increase; the increase in value may happen a period of years after the transaction which gives rise to it and still potentially fall within Chapter 3B.

Example 2: non-commercial increases in market value (2)

Trifle Corp is bought by Syllabub Private Equity LLP for £10m. The deal is heavily leveraged, which means that (after deal fees) bank loans and loan notes with a face value of £11m will need to be paid off before shareholders receive anything on selling the company. In the language of the private equity industry, the company's shares are "underwater" after the deal (i.e. if the company was sold the day after the transaction, shareholders would receive nothing, because the combined value of the loans and loan notes is greater than the value of the company).

John and Isobel are both allowed to subscribe at par for a new class of "B" shares in Trifle Corp's new parent company, which they value at par value for tax purposes. No tax charges will arise on John or Isobel at this point, as they will have paid up the market value of the "B" shares that they receive.

Three years later, Trifle Corp is struggling: profitability has declined and the value of its indebtedness has increased. Syllabub Private Equity LLP decides that a change in management is needed and John and Isobel are promoted.

In order to incentivise the new management of the company, Syllabub arranges to cancel some of its loan notes, reducing the company's indebtedness to £8m; although the shares held by John and Isobel are still underwater, the difference between the value of the company and the value of the debt owed by Trifle Corp is far smaller.

Three years later, the change in management is a success and Trifle Corp is sold for £15m. John and Isobel share in the equity value of £7m (i.e. the £15m of sale proceeds minus the debt of £8m). Because John and Isobel are sharing in a greater value of proceeds than they would have if Syllabub had not cancelled some of the loan notes, it is arguable that the uplift in the value of their shares due to the loan cancellation should be treated as taxable employment income if HMRC do not accept that the transaction was undertaken for genuine commercial purposes.

In practice, this legislation seems to be rarely considered by companies and equally rarely picked up by HMRC. However, non-commercial changes in share values are often highlighted in due-diligence processes, leading purchasers to seek price reductions and retentions of proceeds against possible HMRC challenge; employers and their advisers should be conscious of this legislation wherever a proposed transaction in shares or a change in share rights is contemplated and also wherever there are arrangements to divert costs or profits between group entities.

4.3 Convertible securities

4.3.1 *An introduction to convertible securities*

The rules on convertible securities in ITEPA 2003, Pt. 7, Chapter 3 are intended to capture the situation where an employee acquires securities of one type, that are converted into another, more valuable type.

Common examples of convertible securities would be some types of loan notes and preference shares, which give their holder the right to convert them into ordinary shares.

The rules on convertible securities are, in part, an anti-avoidance measure, intended to capture value that might otherwise be "lost" in the valuation process. But they are also a tax relief: the legislation prevents the employee from being taxed on value that he will only benefit from contingently, postponing the tax point to the time the employee actually receives the more valuable securities that he has an entitlement to acquire from holding the convertible securities.

4.3.2 *Do the shares have to change their name? "Flowering" shares*

The wording of the legislation is intended to capture situations where a share might accrue additional rights without actually changing its name. A common example of this is where a share class has rights that "flower" if conditions are met.

Example – flowering shares

Trifle Corp arranges for John to subscribe for shares in one of its subsidiaries. The articles of association ascribe no rights to the shares until an EBITDA (earnings before interest, tax, depreciation and amortization) target is met, at which point the shares will participate in 10% of the capital value of the company.

Because John's shares have no rights to start with, but acquire rights on the occurrence of a future event, his shares will be treated as convertible securities, with the point at which they acquire rights being treated as the conversion of the securities.

Trifle Corp invites Isobel to subscribe for shares in a different subsidiary, the articles of which provide that Isobel's shares will benefit from 10% of the capital value of the company in excess of the company's current market value of £5m (i.e. if the company is worth £5m, Isobel's shares are worthless, but if the company is worth £6m, Isobel will share in 10% of the £1m excess above £5m).

Isobel's shares will not be treated as convertible securities, because they have rights immediately.

HMRC's position on "flowering shares" is set out in the *Employment Related Securities Manual* at ERSM 40020 and 40030.

4.3.3 The tax charge on acquisition

As was set out at **3.2** above, the convertible securities regime changes the rules on valuing shares or securities at the time that they are acquired by an employee – the employee is taxed on the difference between the price, if any, that he or she pays to acquire the securities and the securities' market value calculated as if the securities did not carry the conversion right.

Example: convertible securities valuation

Trifle Corp allows Isobel to subscribe at par for 100 convertible preference shares of £1.00 each. The convertible preference shares do not carry voting or dividend rights and, on a return of capital, entitle their holders to proceeds equal to the shares' nominal value. The shares also carry the right to be converted into ordinary shares on a 1:1 basis; when the shares are issued to Isobel, the ordinary shares in Trifle Corp are valued at £20.00 each.

When Isobel subscribes for the shares, ITEPA 2003, s. 437 provides that the conversion right into ordinary shares must be disregarded for tax purposes; as the other rights attaching to the convertible preference shares give the shares minimal economic participation in the capital or revenues of the company, they are initially valued at their par value of £1.00 per share.

There is a targeted anti-avoidance rule ("TAAR") set out in the legislation: if there is a tax-avoidance motive underlying the award of convertible securities, then the amount treated as taxable employment income when the convertible securities are acquired will be the difference between the consideration, if any, given by the employee to acquire them and the market value of the securities into which they could be converted. If, in the example given above, there was shown to be a tax avoidance motive underlying the issue of the convertible preference shares to Isobel, then she would be taxed as if she had received ordinary shares instead.

4.3.4 Later tax charges – chargeable events

ITEPA 2003, s. 439 sets out a number of chargeable events which are treated as giving rise to taxable employment income in connection with convertible securities if the TAAR has not been invoked.

Where a chargeable event occurs, the employee will be treated as having received taxable employment income equal to the difference between the "gain" that he or she realises and the consideration, if any, that he or she gave for the conversion right.

The consideration for the conversion right is calculated by deducting the price, if any, paid by the employee from market value of the securities at the time that they were acquired, calculated by ignoring the conversion right.

Example 1: consideration for the conversion right

In addition to the convertible preference shares that Isobel subscribed for at par, she also purchased some convertible preference shares from John for £1.30 per share.

As the convertible preference shares' market value, ignoring the conversion right, is £1.00 Isobel will be treated as not having given any consideration for the conversion right in respect of the shares that she subscribes for.

Isobel will, however, be treated as having given consideration of £0.30 per share for the conversion right attaching to the shares that she buys from John.

Where the TAAR has been invoked on the acquisition of the convertible securities, the amount subject to tax on a later chargeable event will be reduced by the value that was taxed by virtue of the operation of the TAAR.

Example 2: convertible securities – effect of the TAAR

John also receives an award of convertible preference shares from Trifle Corp., but this was part of an elaborate arrangement that HMRC determined was motivated by tax avoidance and the TAAR was invoked. Instead of paying tax on the £1 value of the convertible preference shares, John pays tax on the £20 value of the ordinary shares at that time.

A subsequent chargeable event occurs in relation to John's convertible preference shares and he is treated as having made a gain of £30 per share. Because the TAAR was invoked when John acquired the shares, the amount that will be treated as taxable employment income in relation to the later chargeable event will be £10 per share (i.e. the £30 that is treated as a gain minus the £20 on which John has already paid tax).

4.3.5 Gain where securities are converted into securities of another description

Where the conversion right attaching to convertible securities is exercised, the value of the taxable employment income will be calculated by deducting the price, if any, paid to effect the conversion from the difference between the market value of the securities into which the original securities were converted and the market value of the original securities. As with the tax charge on acquisition, the market value of the original convertible securities is calculated ignoring the conversion right and is referred to in the legislation as the CMVERS.

Example: conversion of securities

Isobel pays £1 per share to convert her convertible preference shares into ordinary shares in Trifle Corp. When she does so, the Trifle Corp ordinary shares are valued at £40 per share.

The amount of gain that Isobel is treated as realising will be calculated by deducting the £1 per share that Isobel paid from the difference between the £40 per share value of the ordinary shares immediately after the conversion takes place and the CMVERS of the convertible preference shares, which will be £1 per share, given their lack of other share rights.

Isobel's gain is therefore 100 x ((40-1)-1) = £3,800.

Because Isobel incurred no other costs associated with the conversion, there are no other deductions to make from this gain and Isobel will be treated as having received taxable employment income equal to £3,800.

4.3.6 Gain where securities are sold to a third party before conversion

Where an employee sells convertible securities before they are converted into other shares, he will be treated as having realised a gain equal to the difference between the consideration that he receives for them and the CMVERS of the convertible securities.

4.3.7 Gain where conversion right is given up for consideration

Where an employee gives up the conversion right attaching to his or her securities in exchange for consideration, the legislation provides that the value of the consideration will be treated as a gain for the purposes of s. 440.

4.3.8 Gain where a benefit is received

Where the employee or one of his or her associated persons receives a benefit in money or money's worth arising from the convertible securities, then the value of the benefit will be treated as a gain for the purposes of ITEPA 2003, s. 440.

4.4 Chapter 4 – post-acquisition benefits

4.4.1 Introduction

ITEPA 2003, Pt. 7, Chapter 4 is intended to tax any benefits received "in connection with employment-related securities" either by the employee or his or her associated persons, that would not otherwise be subject to income tax.

In the context of Part 7, Chapter 4 is intended to be the other tine of Morton's Fork: it is there to catch any benefits that are not taxed by the other provisions of Part 7. In practice, its scope is more limited, as most of the other benefits of share ownership can be captured by the charge on acquisition or by Chapter 3B.

4.4.2 Exemptions from charge

ITEPA 2003, s. 449 restricts the application of Chapter 4 by exempting any benefits received in connection with shares if all of the shareholders holding shares of that class benefit and either:

- the majority of the shares are not employment-related securities; or
- the company is "employee controlled" by virtue of shares of that class.

These exemptions are subject to the proviso that anything done with a tax avoidance motive will not benefit from s. 449 and will be subject to tax.

It is quite common for quoted companies to offer shareholders vouchers and discounts that would fall within the scope of Chapter 4 if employees held shares in them, but as the majority of a quoted company's shares are likely to be held by institutional investors and the public, the exemption in s. 449 will apply.

4.4.3 Application to dividends

The one area where there is a modicum of clarity is the application of Chapter 4 to dividend payments, in that the policy has been and remains that dividend payments do not normally fall within Chapter 4. This position was set out to Parliament in 2005 by the then Paymaster General, Dawn Primarolo:

> "The purpose test introduced in Section 447 of the 2003 Act has been carefully designed to target complex, contrived avoidance arrangements that are used mainly to disguise cash bonuses. If taxpayers use contrived arrangements to get round anti- avoidance legislation – to avoid paying the proper amount of tax and National Insurance – they cannot expect to be excluded from the charge. However, it will be absolutely clear from what I say about the purpose test that this measure will not affect the taxation of those small businesses that do not use contrived schemes to disguise remuneration to avoid tax and National Insurance."

HMRC's guidance at ERSM 90060 succinctly sets out the policy:

> "Where an owner-managed company, run as a genuine business, pays dividends out of company profits and there is no contrived scheme to avoid Income Tax or NIC on remuneration or to avoid the IR35 rules, HMRC will not seek to argue that a Chapter 4 benefit has been received by the directors because of the exclusion provided by ITEPA03/s. 447 (4) – see ERSM 90200."

Even where dividends have been used in substitution for earnings, it seems unlikely that Chapter 4 will be invoked – the cases of *James H Donald (Darvel) Ltd* and *P A Holdings Limited* were both won on the basis that a payment that was, of its nature, earnings, should be taxed as earnings; although both cases related to periods that fell in part before FA 2003, the general principle has been established that earnings will be taxed as earnings, irrespective of the legal form that they take, without reference to Chapter 4.

Cases: *HMRC v P A Holdings Ltd* [2012] STC 582; *James H Donald (Darvel) Ltd v HMRC* [2015] UKUT 514

4.5 Chapter 4A – shares in spin-out companies

4.5.1 Spin-out companies and Part 7 – the problem

In the immediate aftermath of the enactment of FA 2003, it became apparent that there was an issue for the increasingly important university spin-out sector of the economy.

Where researchers have developed intellectual property ("IP") that may be of commercial value, the model used by universities to enable investment that would bring that IP to market is typically to allow the researchers to form a company, begin the process of speaking with potential investors, and then to transfer the IP into the company at roughly the same time as the investment is received.

Because the researchers will have developed the IP as employees of the university (or other research institution), the IP will belong to the university in the first instance. Although the university will have an interest in the spin-out company, it is usual for the researchers to have substantial shareholdings and the researchers' shares will be employment-related securities, as they would be expected either to become directors of, or be employed by, the spin-out company.

Before the IP is transferred to the spin-out company, the company's value is likely to be insignificant, but the IP is likely to have a value and the transfer of the IP into the company could be said to have materially increased the value of the company and, as a result, of the researchers' shares. This increase in value is arguably not a commercial increase or, alternatively, could be seen to be a post-acquisition benefit.

In recognition of the issues that Part 7 presents to the spin-out sector, ITEPA 2003, Pt. 7, Chapter 4A was introduced by FA 2005 where both the agreement to transfer the IP and the share acquisition took place after 2 December 2004.

Where a transaction between a university meets the requirements of Chapter 4A, a number of elements of Part 7 are heavily modified or cease to apply. It is important to note that, unlike the rest of Part 7, Chapter 4A specifically refers to "shares" and "interests in shares"; it does not apply to any other types of securities.

4.5.2 The relief – acquisition of shares

A key element of the relief afforded by Chapter 4A is that it disregards the value of the agreement to transfer the IP for most of the purposes of Part 7, reducing:

- the amount treated as taxable employment income on the acquisition of the shares by the employees;
- the charge if the shares are converted into other securities;

- the amount of any option gain arising if the employees exercise an option to acquire shares; and
- the amount treated as a beneficial loan by Chapter 3C.

Section 452 also reduces the value of any "relevant step" taken in relation to the shares for the purposes of ITEPA 2003, Pt. 7A (disguised remuneration), which may arise if shares are transferred to the employees by a third party.

The legislation also effectively "flips" the operation of the rules on restricted securities: under s. 454, the employee and the company are treated as having automatically made an election under ITEPA 2003, s. 431(1) to disapply the restricted securities rules, unless they choose to make an election within 14 days of the date of acquisition of the shares.

4.5.3 The relief – post-acquisition changes in value

The tax relief on the acquisition of the shares set out above, is only of any assistance if the agreement to transfer the IP has already been made at the time the employees acquire their shares. In the unlikely event that the agreement has not been made at that time, there would normally be a risk of a tax charge arising under Chapter 4 or Chapter 3B. Sections 453 and 455 disapply the effect of Chapter 4 and Chapter 3B in relation to the agreement to transfer the IP.

4.5.4 Qualifying for the relief – basic provisions

Chapter 4A gives relief where four key conditions are met:

- there must be an agreement that a "research institution" will transfer IP to a company (referred to as a "spin-out company" in the legislation);
- the person acquiring the shares must do so either before the agreement to transfer the IP is made or within the space of 183 days after the date of the agreement;
- the shares must be employment-related securities by reference to the person's employment with either the research institution or the spin-out company; and
- the person acquiring the shares must be involved in research into the IP, i.e. he or she must have been working for the research institution (either as an employee or in

any other capacity) on something relevant to the IP that is being transferred to the spin-out company.

An institution will count as a "research institution" if it is one of the universities or higher education institutions listed in the *Higher Education Act* 2004, s. 41(2) (albeit that this legislation has been repealed) or if it is any other institution that is carrying on research activities on a not-for-profit basis and is not controlled by a profit-making body. The second part of the definition effectively expands the relief to foreign universities and to charities that undertake research.

The IP can be transferred from the research institution itself or from a company under its control and will still benefit from relief under Chapter 4A by virtue of s. 459, provided that the other qualifying criteria are met in full.

Where a research institution is cooperating with a profit-making company, the relief may be available to employees of the research institution, provided that the research institution transfers its IP and the employees receive their shares before the profit-making company transfers any IP to the spin-out company or is issued with shares (see ERSM 100180 for an example).

As may be expected, Chapter 4A is subject to a TAAR, which means that it will not apply if the avoidance of tax or NIC is a motive underlying the transaction.

4.5.5 Qualifying for the relief – later transactions

The relief in Chapter 4A only extends to the value effect of the agreement to transfer IP to the spin-out company. In developing the IP, the company may take other steps that increase its value, for example it may develop commercial processes and systems to exploit the IP or it may secure future funding rounds to help it to develop the IP.

Any of these developments that take place before the employees acquire their shares will not benefit from relief, which will mean that their value is taken into account in calculating the amount of any taxable employment income that the employee is treated as receiving when he or she acquires the shares. Later funding rounds are likely to be treated as commercial transactions that do not give rise to chargeable events under Part 7.

Where a funding round is taking place at the same time as the issuance of shares to employees, HMRC have stated that they will treat the funding as having been received after the shares are issued to employees (see ERSM 100510). For these purposes, HMRC treat funding as having been provided at the point that it is legally committed; a non-binding understanding that funding will be provided is not sufficient to give rise to a tax charge.

Because the legislation takes as its point of reference the date of the agreement to transfer IP to the employee, the date of the actual transfer of IP to the spin-out company pursuant to that agreement is of lesser relevance: provided that later transfers of IP are made pursuant to the original agreement, they should not have any tax implications for the employees; if the research institution makes additional transfers of IP that were not covered by the original agreement, then these could, potentially, be treated as chargeable events giving rise to taxable employment income under Part 7.

5. Disposal of shares

5.1 Expectations as to treatment

The expectation of most people who sell shares will be that their gains will be subject to capital gains tax and not income tax, let alone being treated as taxable employment income, with the attendant need to consider PAYE and NIC withholding.

As set out at **1.2**, the scheme of the legislation treats value "gifted" to an employee as taxable employment income, while organic growth should fall to be taxed as capital. In the context of employment-related securities, the tax regime treats increases in value as being "gifted" in four main situations, where:

- an employee disposes of restricted securities;
- there is a disposal of convertible securities;
- an employee disposes of shares on which there is still some remaining unpaid consideration; and
- an employee receives more for his or her securities than their market value.

5.2 Restricted securities

5.2.1 Situations in which there is no risk of charge

There is no risk that an employee will be treated as having received taxable employment income under the restricted securities rules on selling shares or securities if he or she:

- made an election under ITEPA 2003, s. 431(1) either when he or she acquired the securities or following an earlier chargeable event;
- gave consideration that was at least equal to the securities' unrestricted market value on the date that they were acquired;

- was charged to tax when the securities were acquired on a "restricted value" that was greater than the securities' UMV (see **3.3** for more details); or
- disposes of the securities for no consideration.

There will also be no charge where an employee disposes of securities to one of the "associated persons" listed in ITEPA 2003, s. 421C. In broad terms, members of the same household and connected persons will be treated as "associated persons", although it should be noted that s. 421C(3) excludes companies that would otherwise be treated as connected persons if they are the employer or were otherwise involved in the employee's acquisition of shares.

5.2.2 Situations in which a charge will arise

As set out at **3.3**, where an employee acquires restricted securities for less than their unrestricted market value and does not make an election to disapply the rules in ITEPA 2003, Pt. 7, Chapter 2, he will be treated as having received taxable employment income when he sells the securities. The rationale for this is that a proportion of the value of the securities was not taxed when the securities were acquired and this proportion should be taxed when the restriction ceases to impact on the value of the securities.

The sale of securities is the most straightforward situation in which restrictions on securities cease to be relevant to their value.

Example: sale of restricted securities

Caroline and Paul are employed by Boats Limited, a start-up company that is hoping to commercialise an invention. Caroline and Paul are each gifted 1,000 shares by the company's founder in lieu of salary.

The company has made a small amount of turnover and the shares have a restricted value of £0.08 each and a UMV of £0.10 each. The company adopted the "model articles for companies having a share capital" set out in the *Companies Act* 2006 regulations without making amendments. The shares acquired by Caroline and Paul are therefore treated as restricted securities.

Caroline makes an election under ITEPA 2003, s. 431(1) within 14 days of receiving her shares and returns share-based income of

£100 (i.e. 1,000 x £0.10) in her self-assessment return for the year in which she received her shares.

Paul forgets to sign the s. 431 election and returns taxable employment income of £80 (i.e. 1,000 x £0.80) in connection with the acquisition of the shares.

Caroline and Paul will be entitled to claim entrepreneurs' relief when they sell their shares in Boats Limited, as they each hold 5% of the company's ordinary share capital and command 5% of the voting rights.

Four years later, Boats Limited is sold to an investor for consideration of £2,000 per share.

Both Caroline and Paul have used up their CGT annual exemptions on other disposals in the year and neither has any losses brought forward to offset against their gains.

Caroline returns a chargeable gain of £1,999,900 (i.e. (£2,000 - £0.10) x 1,000) on which she is charged CGT of £199,990 (i.e. £1,999,900 @ 10%), leaving her with net proceeds of £1,800,010.

On selling his shares, Paul is treated as receiving taxable employment income of £400,000, calculated as follows:

    1,000 x £2,000 x (IUP-PCP-OP)-CE

where:

    IUP is 0.2 (i.e. (£0.10 - £0.08) ÷ £0.10

    PCP, OP and CE are nil

Paul pays income tax at his marginal rate, and employee NIC, together totalling £188,000 (i.e. £400,000 @ 45% + 2%) and his employer will also have to account for employer NIC.

Paul will also return a chargeable gain of £1,599,920. This is calculated by deducting from the proceeds of £2,000,000:

- taxable employment income arising on acquisition (£0.08 x £1,000 = £80); and
- taxable employment income arising on sale = £400,000.

Disposal of shares

Paul is charged CGT of £159,992 on this gain (i.e. £1,599,920 @ 10%).

Paul's total tax liabilities on disposing of his shares are therefore £347,992, leaving him with net proceeds of £1,652,008.

Where an employee is disposing of restricted securities for less than their market value (for example, he or she may be leaving the company as a "bad leaver"), a charge under these provisions can still arise. Section 428(9) includes provisions adjusting the charge to reflect the actual consideration received by an employee, by taking the product of the usual restricted securities charge calculation and multiplying it by the value of the consideration given for the shares and dividing it by the shares' actual market value immediately after the disposal takes place.

This last relief is subject to a TAAR: if there is shown to be a tax avoidance motive the relief will not be given.

Example: restricted securities sold for less than market value

Caroline takes up a new position at Ships Limited and is awarded 1,000 shares with a UMV of £5 per share and an AMV of £4 per share. One of the conditions of the award is that if Caroline leaves as a bad leaver, she will have to offer the shares for sale at 25% of their market value at that date.

The restriction is not time limited, meaning that the shares are not within the special tax regime of ITEPA 2003, s. 425, and Caroline does not make any elections when she acquires the shares. Caroline is treated as having received taxable employment income of £4,000 when the shares are awarded to her (i.e. 1,000 x £4, being the shares' restricted value).

Two years later there is a disagreement between members of the senior team and Caroline resigns, which means that she is treated as a bad leaver. At the time of her resignation, her shares are worth £10 each and have an AMV of £8 each. Caroline receives proceeds of £2,500 for the shares (i.e. 1,000 x £10 x 25%) and, on the basis that:

- UMV is £10.00
- IUP is 0.2 (i.e. (£5-£4)/£5)
- PCP, OP and CE are nil

the amount of taxable employment income is calculated as follows:

1,000 x £10.00 x 0.2 x £2.50 ÷ £8.00 = £625

Even though Caroline would be treated as having realised a loss for CGT purposes, Part 7 treats her as having realised taxable employment income in these circumstances.

5.2.3 Reorganisations and restricted securities

Before 17 July 2014, a company reorganisation would be seen as a disposal of restricted securities for the purposes of ITEPA 2003, s. 427, which would mean that an employee who held restricted securities may have been treated as having received taxable employment income on a share-for-share exchange, even where that share-for-share exchange had no cash element.

Finance Act 2014 introduced into the restricted securities regime a new relief for company reorganisations. In outline, the rules, now set out in ITEPA 2003, s. 430A, mean that employees will only be treated as having received taxable employment income if they receive cash on a transaction or if the new securities that they receive in exchange for their original holdings of restricted securities are unrestricted.

The relief given by s. 430A effectively disregards the disposal of the old restricted securities and the acquisition of the new securities, treating the new securities as if they were the original securities, acquired at the time that the original securities were acquired.

The conditions for the relief to apply are that:

- the new securities received by the employee must also be restricted securities;
- the UMV of the consideration given for the old securities (i.e. the value of the new securities plus any cash that the employee receives) must not exceed the UMV of the old securities; and
- there must not be a tax avoidance motive underlying the transaction.

If the employee does receive any element of cash consideration, he or she will be treated as having disposed of a proportion of the original restricted securities calculated by the following formula, set out in s. 430A(4):

$$OS \times OC \div TC$$

where:

OS is the number of original securities held by the employee;

OC is the value of any consideration that he or she receives that is not made up of the new restricted securities; and

TC is the total value of the consideration received.

Example: reorganisation involving restricted securities

Caroline returns to Boats and is awarded new restricted securities in Boats Limited by the investor. She does not make an election to disregard the restricted securities rules. The AMV of the shares is £8 per share when Caroline acquires them and their UMV is £10. Caroline receives 100 shares in total and is treated as having received taxable employment income of £800 (i.e. 100 x £8), which will constitute her base cost for CGT purposes.

As part of the preparations for a transaction, a new holding company, Boats NewCo Limited is inserted in the group structure above Boats Limited. All of the shareholders of Boats Limited receive shares in Boats NewCo Limited in exchange for their holdings in Boats Limited and the new shares have identical rights and restrictions to their original shareholdings.

This transaction would not have tax implications for Caroline; her new shares are treated as if they were the old shares for the purposes of ITEPA 2003, Pt. 7, Chapter 2.

A second transaction is undertaken a month later, as part of a refinancing transaction, and the Boats NewCo Limited shares are exchanged for a mixture of cash and new shares in a new holding company, Boats TopCo Limited.

Caroline receives £4,000 in cash and 100 shares, which are valued at £6,000.

Section 430A treats Caroline as if she had disposed of 40 of her shares (i.e. 100 x 4,000 ÷ 10,000), which means that Caroline is treated as if she had received taxable employment income of £800 on the basis that, per share notionally disposed of:

- UMV is £100.00
- IUP is 0.2 (i.e. (£10-£8)/£10)
- PCP, OP and CE are nil

Which means that the taxable employment income is calculated as £100 x 0.2 x 40 = 800. Caroline pays income tax and NIC at a combined rate of 47% on this amount, which comes to £376.

For CGT purposes, Caroline has made a part disposal of her shares and her base cost of £800 will be apportioned in accordance with TCGA 1992, s. 28, by comparing the total value of the consideration with the cash proceeds that Caroline receives (i.e. A/(A+B), in this case £4,000 ÷ (£4,000 + £6,000) = 40%), which gives a base cost of £320 (i.e. £800 x 40%).

Caroline's chargeable gain on the disposal will be £2,880 (i.e. the £4,000 of proceeds minus her base cost of £320 and the amount treated as taxable employment income of £800), on which she will pay CGT at the standard rate of 20% unless she has brought forward losses or unused annual exemption that she can offset against her gain.

Where an employee holds restricted securities and has made an election under either s. 431(1) or s. 430(1), then the election will be treated by s. 430A(7) as applying to new securities acquired on a reorganisation as well as the old securities.

Where s. 430A applies it is not necessary to enter into new elections when there is a paper for paper transaction.

5.3 Convertible securities

5.3.1 *Disposals giving rise to taxable employment income*

As set out at **4.3** above, the disposal of convertible securities can give rise to a tax charge where the consideration received for the disposal (referred to as "DC" in the legislation) is greater than the value that would be attributed to the securities if they did not carry the conversion right. (As set out at **4.3.5** above, this value is referred to as the CMVERS in ITEPA 2003.) The difference between these two values is treated as taxable employment income.

Example 1: disposal of convertible securities

Caroline is given 1,000 convertible preference shares of £1 each in Boats Limited, which have the following rights:

- a cumulative dividend calculated at LIBOR + 2% per annum;
- on a sale, winding-up or other return of capital, their holders are entitled to receive a capital amount equal to the shares' nominal value plus any unpaid dividends; and
- the right, at any time, to convert the preference shares into ordinary shares on a 1:1 basis.

At the time that Caroline is given the shares, ordinary shares in Boats Limited are valued at £5.00 each. Ignoring the right to convert the preference shares into ordinary shares, they are valued at par when Caroline acquires them; Caroline includes this value on her self-assessment form for the year that she acquires the shares.

Two years later, the ordinary shares in Boats Limited are valued at £7.00 each and Caroline is given the opportunity to sell the convertible preference shares for this price without converting them into ordinary shares. Ignoring the conversion right, the convertible preference shares are still valued at £1.00 each (this is the CMVERS).

Caroline is treated as having received taxable employment income of £6,000 (i.e. 1,000 x (£7.00 - £1.00)), on which the company has an obligation to withhold PAYE and operate NIC.

Where an employee pays to acquire convertible securities, it is important to note that the calculation of the amount of taxable employment income on a sale of convertible securities only gives the employee a limited degree of recognition for the price paid.

Example 2: disposal of convertible securities acquired for consideration

On the same day that Caroline was awarded convertible preference shares, she was also allowed to purchase a further 1,000 convertible

75

preference shares and paid £5.00 per share to do so (i.e. the same value as that attributed to the ordinary shares).

ITEPA 2003, s. 442 treats Caroline as having paid £4.00 per share for the conversion right that the shares carry. When, as set out above, Caroline sells the convertible preference shares for £7.00 per share, the amount of taxable employment income that she is treated as receiving will be adjusted by deducting the amount calculated under s. 442 from the convertible securities gain (i.e. £6 per share) that she made when she sold the shares.

This means that Caroline will be treated as having received taxable employment income of £2.00 per share on selling the convertible preference shares. Had she invested her money in buying ordinary shares in Boats Limited, her profit on selling her shares would have been subject to the CGT rules and would likely have fallen outside the scope of income tax and NIC.

5.3.2 Situations in which there is no risk of charge

In broad terms there are two situations where the disposal of convertible securities will not give rise to a tax charge under the rules in Chapter 3:

- where the securities can be converted into less valuable securities; or
- where the securities fall within the special rules in ITEPA 2003, s. 443.

The first exception is quite commonly encountered: often employees' shares will be convertible into worthless deferred shares if they leave the company as "bad leavers" or if targets are not met (this is often called a "reverse ratchet"). The value effect of the conversion right would be to depress the value of the employees' securities, but ITEPA 2003, s. 437 instructs us to disregard the value effect of the conversion right for the purposes of ITEPA 2003, Pt. 7. This means that the market value of the securities when they are sold will be equal their CMVERS, meaning that no charges can arise under the convertible securities rules in this situation.

The second exception applies when the securities meet the conditions set out in ITEPA 2003, s. 443. In outline, these conditions are aimed at situations where employees are not being singled out for exceptional benefit. In order to meet the conditions:

- the convertible securities must be shares of a distinct class (other types of security, like loan notes, are excluded);
- all of the shares of that class must be convertible securities;
- the requirements of the usual TAAR, that there must not be a tax avoidance motive underlying the arrangements, must be met;
- all of the shares of that class are equally affected by the chargeable event (in this case, all of the shares of that class must be sold at the same time); and
- either (i) employees control the company by virtue of holdings of shares of that class, or (ii) the majority of that class of shares are held by persons who are not employees.

In essence this exemption is intended to prevent charges arising where employees are receiving something that is freely available to other shareholders and which does not constitute a carefully concealed way to gift value to employees by virtue of their employment relationship.

5.3.3   Effect of company reorganisations

In most cases, a share-for-share exchange as part of a company reorganisation will be treated as the disposal of shares to a company that is not an "associated person", which means that there is a risk of tax charges arising under Chapter 3.

If, on a share-for-share exchange, the new securities that the employees receive are not convertible securities in their own right, then any charges under Chapter 3 will be calculated by taking the aggregate value of the new securities as DC in the calculation set out in ITEPA 2003, s. 441.

The legislation contains what appears to be a glitch or oversight, in that ITEPA 2003, s. 437 does not apply for the purposes of determining what DC should be if employees receive new convertible securities in exchange for their old holdings of convertible securities. This means that, on a strict reading of the legislation, DC will be calculated by reference to the market value of the new securities taking into account their conversion right, and not their CMVERS.

The effect of the rules on disposals of convertible securities is that, where employees hold convertible securities, it may be difficult to undertake a company reorganisation without the employees being treated as if they had received taxable employment income.

5.3.4 Interaction with NIC charge

As set out at **7.6**, the NIC legislation allows the cost of employer NIC to be passed to employees in a restricted number of cases linked to the charges on employment-related securities set out in Part 7. The convertible securities rules fall within this list, meaning that an employer may choose to pass on to the employee the cost of any employer NIC arising on the disposal of convertible securities.

The employer NIC cost borne by the employee is treated as a deduction from the amount of taxable employment income received by the employee for the purposes of the income tax rules. The legislation does not permit any similar deduction for NIC purposes.

Example: convertible securities NIC transfer

Paul entered into an agreement under SSCBA 1992, Sch. 1, para. 3B to bear the cost of any employer NIC arising on his convertible shares in Boats Limited.

Paul sells some of the convertible shares, and the gain calculated for the purposes of ITEPA 2003, s. 441 is £10,000, which is the value subject to NIC. The employer NIC is calculated as being £1,380, which Paul pays over to Boats Limited.

The amount of taxable employment income that Paul is treated as having realised on selling his shares is reduced by the employer NIC that he has borne, which means that the amount subject to income tax is £8,620.

Law: ITEPA 2003, s. 442A

5.4 Chapter 3C – securities acquired at less than market value

5.4.1 The tax charge and the exemptions

As set out at **3.4**, where shares are acquired for less than their market value in situations where an employee has an obligation to pay for them at a point in the future (for example, if the shares were issued to the employee partly paid), the employee would be treated as if he or she had received an employment-related loan.

The normal rules on employment-related loans impose a tax charge on the outstanding value of the loan when the loan is discharged (for example, if the loan is forgiven). ITEPA 2003, s. 446U treats the deemed loan as having been discharged if the securities are transferred to someone who is not an associated person.

The employee would normally be treated as receiving taxable employment income equal to the value of the deemed loan on such a disposal, but s. 446U provides relief to the employee on the disposal of securities if one of the following two conditions are met:

- at the time that the employee disposes of the securities, he or she still has an obligation to pay off the outstanding amounts; or
- the consideration received by the employee is reduced to reflect the outstanding consideration.

Where either of these conditions is met, the employee will not be treated as having received taxable employment income.

Example: disposals where Chapter 3C is in point

In 2014, Paul, Caroline and Kevin are each issued with 1,000 partly-paid shares in Boats Limited. When they subscribe for the shares they are worth £5.00 per share. The terms of the subscription are that they pay nothing up-front for the shares, but will have to pay up £5.00 per share on the earlier of the date of sale of the shares and the fifth anniversary of the issue date.

In 2016, Paul retires from Boats Limited and is allowed to sell his shares for their market value of £10.00 per share. As a goodwill gesture, Boats Limited does not enforce Paul's obligation to pay the outstanding call of £5.00 per share. Paul receives total proceeds of

£10,000. Under s. 446U, Paul is treated as having received taxable employment income of £5,000 (i.e. 1,000 x £5.00). The balance of his proceeds will be taxed under the CGT rules.

In 2017, Caroline leaves Boats Limited and is obliged to sell her shares for the issue price of £5.00 per share, and to pay up the outstanding £5.00 per share consideration by Boats Limited out of her sale proceeds. Caroline is not treated as having received taxable employment income on the sale of her shares, as she still has an obligation to pay up the outstanding consideration.

In 2018, Kevin is given the opportunity to sell his shares to a third party purchaser. The price that the purchaser is paying for fully-paid shares is £15.00, and the price that the purchaser offers to Kevin is £10.00 per share. Kevin will not be treated as having received taxable employment income in this case, as his disposal proceeds reflect the value of the outstanding call that Kevin would otherwise be obliged to pay.

5.4.2   Impact of reorganisations

Any company reorganisation that involves the shareholders exchanging securities for new securities in a new holding company will usually constitute the disposal of securities.

The new holding company is unlikely to be treated as an associated person for the purposes of the legislation, which means that charges could arise under s. 446U.

Provided that the reorganisation is structured so that either the employees continue to have an obligation to pay up the outstanding amounts on their securities or the new securities that they receive are also issued with amounts outstanding on them, the reorganisation should not crystallise a tax charge under Chapter 3C.

5.5   Chapter 3D – disposal of securities for more than market value

5.5.1   The tax charge

Chapter 3D is the shortest chapter in ITEPA 2003, Pt. 7 and is in point where an employee disposes of securities for more than their market value.

Where an employee disposes of employment-related securities, the difference between the consideration that he or she receives, their market value and expenses incurred by the employee in connection with disposing of the securities will be treated as taxable employment income.

Example 1: sale at more than market value (1)

Kevin holds 1,000 shares in Boats Limited, which he originally purchased for £5.00 per share, which was their unrestricted market value at that time.

Kevin is allowed to sell his shares to the company's employee benefit trust for £10.00 per share. At the time of the sale, the shares are valued at £8.00 per share. Kevin bears costs of £200.00 to effect the transaction.

Kevin is treated as having received taxable employment income of £1,800 in total (i.e. (1,000 x (10.00-8.00)) - £200). The balance of his proceeds will be subject to taxation under the CGT rules.

The tax charge does not take into account the base cost of the employee's shares – if they are standing at a loss and are sold for more than their market value, then the employee will still be taxed under Chapter 3C.

Example 2: sale at more than market value (2)

Caroline holds 1,000 shares in Fleet Limited, which she originally purchased for £15.00 per share, which was their unrestricted market value at that time.

Caroline leaves Fleet Limited and is compelled by the articles of association to offer her shares for sale to the other shareholders at the price that she originally paid to acquire them. At this time the shares are valued at £7.00 each.

Caroline is treated as having received taxable employment income of £8,000 in total (i.e. 1,000 x (15.00-7.00)).

For CGT purposes, Caroline will be treated as having made a loss, of £8,000, on the basis that her base cost of £15,000 would be augmented by the amount of taxable employment income that Caroline had been treated as realising, i.e. £8,000.

5.5.2 What counts as market value?

As set out in **Chapter 2**, ITEPA 2003, s. 421 provides that the basis for valuing employment-related securities is the valuation standard used to value securities for CGT purposes, which has its legislative basis in TCGA 1992, Part VIII.

The body of law and practice that has grown up around this valuation standard has tripped up advisers and companies on a number of occasions, especially where one of the shareholders is leaving the business and seeking to dispose of his or her shareholding.

5.5.3 Stumbling blocks – 1 – information standards

The approach mandated in TCGA 1992, Part VIII instructs the valuer only to take into account information to which a hypothetical vendor and third party acquirer would have access.

The extent of the information available to them is usually determined by looking at the size of the shareholding that is being valued: in his or her capacity as a shareholder, a small minority shareholder would have access to far less information than a controlling shareholder; an unconnected third party purchaser of a small minority holding would be granted access to far less information about the company's affairs than someone wishing to acquire a controlling interest in a company.

Very often, in a private company context, the shareholders will also be the directors of a company, meaning that they will be privy to information about the performance of a company that would be unlikely to be disclosed to anyone other than a controlling shareholder. For example, in their capacity as directors, minority shareholders would have access to management accounts and details of forward contracts that are unlikely to be shared with shareholders.

This creates a difficulty in that deals to acquire a director's shares are often struck on the basis of the information that the director actually possesses, which can lead to prices being paid for shares that exceed the value that would be calculated in accordance with TCGA 1992, Part VIII.

Example: information standards

Kevin is a director of Boats Limited and has a 5% shareholding in the company.

The company has been loss-making for a number of years, but Kevin has led a team that negotiated a deal with Armada Inc. to exploit intellectual property that Boats Limited has developed.

The terms of the deal are highly confidential and would see Boats Limited receive annual payments of tens of millions of pounds each year for five years. This revenue stream is expected to begin in 18 months' time.

Kevin decides that the time has come to retire and sells his shares to Paul, a fellow director who is also aware of the deal with Armada, Inc.; the price agreed between them reflects the value of the future revenue stream that Boats Limited will enjoy from the deal with Armada, Inc.

A person holding 5% of the shares in Boats Limited would be unlikely to be briefed on the terms of the deal with Armada, Inc. and it is very unlikely that a third party purchaser of 5% of the company's shares would be given any access to information about a confidential contract.

Based on publicly available information about Boats Limited's financial performance, a valuer may put a significantly lower value on Kevin's shares than that which he has agreed with Paul. If HMRC took the point, it would be open to them to argue that an element of the price paid to Kevin constituted taxable employment income on which PAYE and NIC should have been operated by Boats Limited.

5.5.4 Stumbling blocks – 2 – share rights

As was set out in **Chapter 2**, it is only possible to take into account rights that attach to charges, not to persons, in valuing employee securities for tax purposes.

As in the *Grays Timber* case, which is described in more detail at **2.5** above, this means that a valuation will have regard to the rights of securities set out in the constitutional documents of a company, but rights set out in a shareholders' agreement are likely to be ignored.

This is because the rights set out in a contract tend to be personal to the contracting parties – as a matter of contract law third parties are unable to rely on contractual agreements entered into by other people. (There are some limited exceptions provided in the *Contracts (Rights of Third Parties) Act* 1999, but these are unlikely to be relevant to a valuation.)

In *Grays Timber* a shareholders' agreement conferred greater rights on an individual shareholder to participate in the proceeds of the sale of the company than were conferred on his shares by the articles of association. In considering the value of the shares the court assessed what rights a third party would have if he or she acquired the shares without becoming party to the shareholders' agreement; the difference between the proceeds received by the shareholder and the rights conferred on him by his shares was taxable employment income.

This problem is very commonly encountered, as many lawyers will include rights to fixed values of proceeds in shareholders' agreements, without mirroring provisions in the articles (for example, in provisions dealing with leavers) where there is a perception of commercial sensitivity; this can result in the shareholder suffering PAYE and NIC when he or she was expecting to realise a capital gain.

Case: *Grays Timber Products Ltd v HMRC (Scotland)* [2010] UKSC 4

5.5.5 Stumbling blocks – 2 – minority status

In valuing anything less than a controlling interest in a company, it is necessary to adjust the valuation to reflect the fact that the shareholding lacks influence. For example, if a company had a high net asset value, the owner of a 5% shareholdings would not be able to vote to liquidate the company to realise those assets, with the result that a third party would not pay a price based on a straight, pro-rata split of those assets; the price would include an assessment of the likelihood of being able to realise a return on the assets, which would lead to a substantial discount being given.

Similarly, if there is no market in the shares, that lack of liquidity would be reflected in the price offered by a third party purchaser.

This point is often heartily embraced when businesses are considering awards of shares to employees, but entirely overlooked when buying out shareholders. Unless the company's articles of association make some provision to ignore discounts for minority status, transactions in shares at their undiscounted value will lead to employee shareholders being treated as having received taxable employment income. The only exception to this is if a substantial part of the company's share capital is being transferred as part of the same transaction, in which case there would be no discount applicable.

5.6 CGT on disposing of securities

5.6.1 Interaction with employment income tax charges

The disposal of securities by an employee has the potential to give rise to tax charges under both the CGT and employment-related securities rules. The income tax rules effectively take precedence, but the employee should not pay tax twice on the same amount, because TCGA 1992, sections 119A to 120 allow amounts treated as taxable employment income to be added to the base cost of employment-related securities for the purposes of calculating the CGT charge.

Example 1

Kevin is awarded 10,000 free shares in Boats Limited. The shares are restricted securities for the purposes of ITEPA 2003, Pt. 7, Chapter 2, Kevin does not make an election under ITEPA 2003, s. 431(1) when he acquires them. On the date that he acquired the shares, the shares' UMV was £1.00 each and their restricted value was £0.90 each.

On acquiring the shares Kevin is treated as having received taxable employment income of £9,000 (i.e. 10,000 x £0.90).

When he sells the shares, Kevin receives proceeds of £75,000, i.e. £7.50 per share.

Kevin is treated as receiving taxable employment income of £7,500 on the sale of the shares (i.e. £75,000 x (IUP-PCP-OP)-CE; in this case IUP will be (£1.00-£0.90) ÷ £1.00, PCP, OP and CE will each be nil).

Kevin will calculate his chargeable gains as follows:

	£
Sale proceeds	75,000
Price paid for the shares	0.00
Amount treated as taxable employment income on acquisition	9,000
Amount treated as taxable employment income on disposal	7,500
Total base cost:	16,500
Chargeable gain	58,500

Sections 119A and 120 comprehensively list the charging provisions that are treated as giving rise to additional base cost. There is one omission that seems surprising: the tax charge under Chapter 3D. The rationale for this is that a transaction in securities that takes place for more than market value is unlikely to be treated as a bargain at arm's length, which would mean that TCGA 1992, s. 17 would be in point, substituting the market value of the securities disposed of for the actual proceeds received in the CGT calculation.

Example 2: sale of shares at over-value

Caroline acquires 100,000 shares in Boats Limited for their UMV of £1.00 per share and makes an election under ITEPA 2003, s. 431.

Two years later the shares are valued at £7.50 per share, but the company arranges for its employee benefit trust to buy the shares from Caroline at £10.00 per share.

For CGT purposes the transaction between Caroline and the employee benefit trust is treated as a non-arm's length disposal and, in compliance with s. 17, the market value of £7.50 per share is substituted for the proceeds that Caroline received in her CGT calculations.

Caroline's chargeable gain under the CGT rules is £650,000 (i.e. (£7.50-£1.00) x 100,000).

The balance of the proceeds, £250,000 (i.e. (£10.00-£7.50) x 100,000) is treated as taxable employment income and Boats Limited will be obliged to operate PAYE and NIC on that amount.

5.6.2 Company purchase of own shares

An important point to note is that the legislation governing the income tax treatment of company purchases of own shares does not contain parallel provisions on the treatment of amounts treated as taxable employment income.

If a company repurchases its own shares from an employee, and that transaction does not meet the criteria set out in CTA 2010, s. 1033-1043, that proportion of the proceeds which exceeds the amount paid up on the shares (i.e. the nominal value and any share premium), will be taxable as a dividend distribution. No allowance is made in the legislation for any amounts charged to income tax under other provisions.

This has the result that an employee could be subject to income tax twice, on the same amount.

Example: purchase of own shares

Paul is granted an option to acquire 100 ordinary shares in Boats Limited that are currently held by the company's employee trust. The option's exercise price is set at the shares' nominal value of £0.01 each, which was the price at which the employee trust subscribed for the shares.

Paul exercises the option when the market value of each share is £5.00 and is treated as having taxable employment income of £499 (i.e. (£5.00 - £0.01) x 100).

A week later, Paul is allowed to sell the shares to the company's employee benefit trust at their market value. Paul has only paid up the nominal value of the shares, and the difference between the proceeds that he receives and the nominal value will be treated as a taxable dividend distribution in Paul's hands.

There is no mechanism to offset the first tax charge against the second; if Paul has other dividends and is an additional rate taxpayer, his effective tax rate could be 85.1% on the two transactions (i.e. PAYE at 45%, NIC at 2% plus dividend tax at 38.1%).

5.7 Entrepreneurs' relief

5.7.1 Qualifying for the relief

The following sections highlight some common issues with employee shares. A comprehensive discussion of entrepreneurs' relief ("ER") is beyond the scope of this book (but see *Entrepreneurs' Relief*, available from Claritax Books).

Employees are able to qualify for ER provided that they hold shares in a qualifying company for at least a year ending on the date of sale and, throughout that time, they meet the following conditions:

- they hold at least 5% of the company's ordinary share capital; and
- they are able to exercise 5% of the voting rights in the company by virtue of their shareholdings.

The term "ordinary share capital" means any share capital other than shares that have a fixed entitlement to participate in the company's profits (for example, a fixed-rate preference share). This means that shares with a variable rate of dividend or even no right to receive dividends at all will be treated as forming part of a company's ordinary share capital.

The 5% holding test is calculated by reference to the aggregate nominal value of the shares.

Example: ordinary share capital

Kevin holds 10,000 ordinary shares of £0.01 each in Boats Limited and meets all of the other criteria for ER, but would like to know if he holds enough of the company's ordinary share capital.

Boats Limited has the following share classes in issue:

- 40,000 ordinary shares of £0.01 each – the same class as those held by Kevin;
- 10,000 5% non-cumulative preference shares of £1.00 each – these shares have a fixed dividend entitlement and are not treated as part of the company's ordinary share capital;

- 100,000 cumulative compounding preference shares of £1.00 each, which pay a dividend of LIBOR+1% – these shares are also part of the company's ordinary share capital, because they have a variable dividend entitlement.

Although Kevin holds 25% of the ordinary shares, these shares only constitute £400 of ordinary share capital (i.e. £0.01 x 40,000), while the cumulative compounding preference shares constitute £100,000 of ordinary share capital.

Kevin will not be entitled to claim ER on selling his shares while the cumulative compounding preference shares remain in issue.

5.7.2 EMI options

Finance Act 2013 introduced new reliefs for holders of shares acquired by exercising EMI options. In summary, the effect of these provisions, which are discussed in more detail at **13.5.5**, is to allow employees who would not otherwise meet the criteria for ER to benefit from it; an employee who holds a very small percentage of the company's ordinary share capital, or who holds non-voting shares, can qualify for ER if the shares were acquired on the exercise of a qualifying EMI option and at least a year had passed between the date of grant of the option and the date of the sale of the shares.

This means that it is possible for an EMI option-holder to exercise his or her options and sell the EMI shares on the same day and still claim ER.

Part 3: Company considerations

6. Corporation tax

6.1 CTA 2009, Part 12 – introduction

The key provisions governing the corporation tax ("CT") treatment of employment-related securities were originally enacted as Sch. 23 of FA 2003 and are now enacted in CTA 2009, Pt. 12.

Historically, companies would seek relief for the cost of making employee share awards by operating their share schemes through an employee benefit trust which would make recharges to the employer entities within a group of companies. These transactions resulted in P&L charges in the employing entities' accounts, which formed the basis for claiming CT relief on normal principles.

Sch. 23 of FA 2003 simplified this by introducing a general principle that, provided that the shares acquired by an employee met the qualifying criteria, an employer company would be entitled to claim CT relief on the difference between the value of shares acquired by an employee and the price, if any, paid to acquire them. The relief is given in the accounting period in which the shares are acquired.

Where a deduction can potentially be claimed under CTA 2009, Pt. 12, no other deduction may be claimed: CTA 2009, s. 1038 precludes any other relief where Part 12 is in point and s. 1038A prevents any relief being allowed, based on entries in a company's accounts, where a share option or other award has lapsed.

The only exception to this priority for deductions under CTA 2009, Pt. 12 is where the scheme in question is a qualifying Sch. 2 SIP, in which case deductions under the SIP Code – specifically CTA 2009, Part 11, Chapter 1 – will take priority. This is discussed in more detail at **15.5** below.

6.2 Basic qualification conditions

CTA 2009, Pt. 12 is divided into four chapters, dealing respectively with share acquisitions, share options, restricted securities and convertible securities. There are significant commonalities between the four chapters, and the basic requirements for relief are the same; the relief may be claimed by the employer company where:

Company considerations

- the employer company carries on a business within the charge to UK corporation tax;
- the shares or interest in shares constitute employment-related securities;
- the securities qualify for relief; and
- the employee is chargeable to tax under ITEPA 2003 on any taxable employment income arising from the shares, or would be if the employee were UK resident and the duties of the employment had been carried on in the UK.

In order to qualify for relief, the securities must be:

- non-redeemable, fully paid ordinary shares (meaning that they are shares of any class or type so long as they do not carry a fixed right to receive dividends);
- either of a class listed on a recognised stock exchange, shares in a company that is not under the control of another company, or shares in a company that is under the control of a listed company (i.e. the parent company is listed on a recognised stock exchange and is not a close company); and
- issued by:
    - the employer company,
    - the employer company's 51% parent company,
    - a member of a consortium that owns the employer company, or
    - a company owned by a consortium of which the employer, or employer's parent company, is a member, provided that the employer and the issuing company are members of the same commercial association of companies.

For these purposes a company will fall within the consortium rules if no more than five companies hold 10% of the share capital each and between them hold at least 75%.

A commercial association of companies is a number of associated companies (as defined in CTA 2010, s. 449) who carry on businesses that, taken together, it would be reasonable to view as a single, composite undertaking.

The relief is given as a deduction in the corporation tax computations of the employer entity. Any charges to the company's income statement that have been made in respect of the share awards should be disallowed for these purposes.

Where an individual's role with a group of companies serves more than one business, and some of those businesses are outside the scope of UK corporation tax, the value of the relief will be apportioned between the businesses and only that portion attributable to the UK business will be deductible.

Example: qualifying for corporation tax relief

Jeroboam is employed by Dillpickle International plc ("PLC"), a company quoted on AIM. As part of his role, Jeroboam sits on the board of Dillpickle SARL, a subsidiary based in France; this takes up two days per week of Jeroboam's time.

In the current accounting period Jeroboam has received the following securities from his employer:

- ordinary shares in PLC;
- fixed rate corporate bonds issued by PLC;
- ordinary shares in Dillpickle Ventures Limited, a subsidiary of PLC.

Provided that the ordinary shares in PLC are fully paid up and are not redeemable, and that PLC is not under the control of another company, then this award will give rise to relief under Part 12.

The fixed rate corporate bonds are not shares, and, as such, do not meet the basic requirements for relief.

The shares in Dillpickle Ventures Limited will also fail to qualify for relief, as Jeroboam is employed by its parent company and the qualification criteria looks "upwards" at group structures (i.e. shares in a parent company acquired by an employee of a subsidiary qualify for relief, but shares in a subsidiary acquired by an employee of its parent company do not).

Even if Jeroboam held office or had an employment with Dillpickle Ventures Limited, the shares would not be eligible for relief, as the company is under the control of another company and, although

PLC is listed on AIM, it does not qualify as a "listed company" for the purposes of Part 12, because AIM is not a recognised stock exchange for tax purposes.

As Jeroboam divides his time between working for a business within the charge to UK corporation tax and working for a business that is not, the value of the relief needs to be apportioned between the two businesses.

6.3 Relief on acquisition of shares (Chapter 2)

When an employee acquires shares then, provided that the criteria set out above are met, the employer company will be entitled to claim relief under Part 12 on the difference between the shares' market value and the price, if any, paid to acquire them by the employee.

In this case, the term "market value" follows the rules governing ITEPA 2003, Pt. 7. If the shares are restricted or convertible securities, then the valuation rules in Chapter 2 and Chapter 3 respectively will apply: if the shares are restricted securities, the market value will be the restricted value if no elections are made (if elections are made, then the market value will be UMV); shares that are convertible securities are valued as if they did not have the right to be converted into any other type of security.

Law: ITEPA 2003, s. 421

6.4 Relief for share options (Chapter 3)

Relief for employee share options is triggered at the time that the options are exercised: there is no relief available for the grant or vesting of share options. The relief is given on the difference between the market value of the option shares at the date of exercise and the price, if any, paid to acquire them.

The requirement with regard to the employee's tax position is modified slightly, in that the requirement is that the exercise of the option is a chargeable event within ITEPA 2003, s. 476, irrespective of whether any taxable employment income is treated as arising when the option is exercised. For example, the employee might exercise a qualifying EMI option, which would be a chargeable event for the purposes of s. 476, but which nonetheless does not give rise to taxable employment income.

Example: exercise of options

Jeroboam is granted qualifying Sch. 4 CSOP options over 10,000 shares in Dillpickle Industries plc and, at the same time, is granted non-qualifying options over 100 shares. In each case the exercise price of the options is set at £1.00 per share.

Four years later, Jeroboam exercises both sets of options, when the market value of the shares is £5.00 per share. Jeroboam is not treated as having realised any taxable employment income in respect of the CSOP options but is taxed on taxable employment income of £40,000 in respect of the non-qualifying options (i.e. (£5.00-£1.00) x 10,000).

Provided that the other conditions of Part 12 are met, Dillpickle Industries plc will be entitled to claim relief totalling £80,000 (i.e. (£5.00-£1.00) x 20,000) in respect of both the CSOP options and the non-qualifying options: although the exercise of the CSOP options did not give rise to taxable employment income, it still constituted a chargeable event within the scope of ITEPA 2003, s. 476.

Where there is a takeover after an option has been granted, but before it is exercised:

- if the option is exercised within 90 days following the takeover, and shares in the original grantor company are acquired, then the qualification tests in s. 1016 will be applied as if the takeover had not happened and the option may still qualify for relief when it is exercised;
- if the option is exchanged for a new option over shares issued by the acquirer (or the acquirer's parent or certain consortium companies – see s. 1023), the new option may qualify for relief when it is exercised.

A difficulty with claiming relief for share options arises if the business in respect of which the options were originally granted has been transferred to a different group company before the options are exercised. CTA 2009, s. 1024 allows the relief to be claimed by the company within the group to which the business has been transferred. The relief under s. 1024 will only apply if substantially the whole business is transferred and both the transferor and transferee are members of the same group of companies.

6.5 Restricted securities (Chapter 4)

Where the shares in question are restricted securities, and no elections are made under ITEPA 2003, s. 431, then there may be additional relief to be claimed when restrictions are lifted, varied or the shares are sold giving rise to chargeable events under ITEPA 2003, s. 426.

As set out above, on the acquisition of the shares (either through the award of shares or the exercise of options) the amount of relief that can be claimed by a company under Part 12 will be calculated by reference to the shares' restricted value.

On the occurrence of a chargeable event, the amount of relief that can be claimed will be calculated as the amount of taxable employment income that the employee is treated as receiving, with the following adjustments:

- any relief for the cost of employer NIC borne by the employee will be disregarded;
- any charges in respect of a non-commercial uplift in value arising by the operation of ITEPA 2003, Pt. 7, Chapter 3A or 3B will be ignored.

Where an employee dies holding restricted securities, then, for the purposes of Part 12, s. 1027 treats him as disposing of the restricted securities and the company will be able to claim relief for the notional amount of taxable employment income that would have arisen if the employee had been alive and had sold his shares.

Similar provisions to those in Chapter 3 of Part 12 apply where the business in respect of which the shares were originally acquired is transferred to another group entity between the acquisition date and the date of the lifting or variation of the restrictions, meaning that the relief effectively follows the business, rather than "sticking" with the employer company.

6.6 Convertible securities (Chapter 5)

The rules applicable to convertible securities follow a similar pattern to those that apply to restricted securities. In essence, the rules allow companies to claim additional relief as and when convertible securities held by employees are converted into securities of a different description.

Provided that the shares that the existing securities are converted into would be eligible for relief under Chapter 2 or Chapter 3 of Part 12, then the employer company will be able to claim relief equal to the amount of taxable employment income that the employee is treated as having received (as before, writing back any relief for employer NIC borne by the employee and ignoring any amounts taxed through the rules on artificial changes in value).

Example: convertible securities

Jeroboam is awarded convertible bonds in Dillpickle International plc. The bonds have a face value of £1,000, but can be converted into 1,000 ordinary shares on the third anniversary of issue.

On acquiring the bonds, Jeroboam pays tax on their face value, which ignores the value of their conversion right into ordinary shares.

On the third anniversary, Jeroboam's bonds are converted into 1,000 ordinary shares which have a market value of £10.00 each. Jeroboam is treated as having received taxable employment income of £9,000 (i.e. (10.00-£1.00) x 1,000).

Dillpickle International plc is entitled to claim a deduction under CTA 2009, Pt. 12 equal to the £9,000 of taxable employment income that Jeroboam is treated as having received.

If an employee dies while holding convertible securities, then the employer company will be entitled to claim relief under Part 12 as if the conversion had taken place on the date of death.

Law: ITEPA 2003, s. 438; CTA 2009, s. 1034

6.7 Mobile employees

Where an employee is employed by an overseas company, which is outside the charge to UK corporation tax, but performs some of his or her duties in the UK for a different UK company (described in the legislation as the "host employer"), then the UK company will be treated as the employer for the purposes of Part 12. Similarly, where an employee is granted an option by an overseas employer, but takes up employment with a company within the charge to UK corporation tax, that UK employer may be entitled to claim relief under Part 12.

Provided that the other requirements relating to the shares acquired by an employee are met, the host employer will be entitled to claim relief under Part 12 based on the value of the taxable employment income chargeable to tax under ITEPA 2003 in respect of the employee's UK workdays when he or she acquires shares or exercises options.

Similar rules permit relief to be given where restrictions are lifted or varied or securities are converted into qualifying shares.

Law: CTA 2009, s. 1007A, 1015A, 1025A, 1030A

6.8 Other corporation tax reliefs

As was set out above, no other reliefs can be given where Part 12 is potentially in point. Where share awards are settled out of assets held by an employee trust, the rules in CTA 2009, Pt. 20 may allow deductions to be claimed if the share award itself does not meet the criteria for relief under Part 12. These rules are considered in more detail at **11.7** below.

Law: CTA 2009, s. 1290

6.9 Relief for the costs of establishing a share scheme

Specific statutory provision is made for allowing the costs of establishing a Sch. 3 SAYE scheme or a Sch. 4 CSOP.

The costs of establishing any other type of scheme will need to meet the usual criteria if they are to be deducted. The main problem that companies have with claiming the costs of establishing a scheme is demonstrating that the expenditure that has been incurred is revenue and not capital spend. HMRC's view is set out at BIM 44020 and clearly states that the costs of establishing a share scheme should be viewed as a non-deductible capital cost.

The point for advisers to consider is whether all of the costs relate to the establishment of the plan or if the implementation costs include other costs that may be deductible – for example, the costs of any valuation work undertaken or tax advice given on the implications of establishing a scheme.

Law: CTA 2009, Pt. 11, Ch. 2

7. Operation of PAYE and NIC

7.1 Basic principles

There are a number of basic principles to be borne in mind with regard to the operation of PAYE and NIC on taxable employment income arising from employment-related securities:

- If the taxable employment income takes the form of cash or of "readily convertible assets" ("RCAs") (see **7.4** below), there will be an obligation to operate PAYE.
- Where there is an obligation to operate PAYE, NIC will also be in point.
- If the taxable employment income does not take the form of cash or RCAs, the employee will have to return it in his or her self-assessment.
- If an employee does not "make good" a PAYE liability, he or she will incur an extra liability under ITEPA 2003, s. 222.

7.2 PAYE on acquisition of securities

Under ITEPA 2003, s. 696 where an employee receives an RCA and is treated as having received taxable employment income, the receipt of the asset will be treated as if it were a payment of PAYE income. This treatment is extended to gains on the exercise of options by ITEPA 2003, s. 700.

7.3 PAYE on post-acquisition charges

The basic position is that PAYE must be operated on post-acquisition charges if:

- the employment-related securities are RCAs before the chargeable event that gives rise to taxable employment income; or
- the consideration received by the employee as a result of the chargeable event takes the form of cash or RCAs.

In practical terms, this means that tax charges arising on shares in listed companies will always be subject to PAYE and NIC.

Assuming that private company shares are not RCAs, then tax charges arising before the final disposal of the shares will be self-assessment matters, while charges arising on disposal will be subject to PAYE and NIC.

Example: PAYE on post-acquisition charges

Jeroboam is awarded shares in Dillpickle Industries plc that are subject to a forfeiture condition that lifts on the third anniversary of award. Jeroboam does not make an election to disapply the rules on forfeitable securities.

On the third anniversary of the award, the forfeiture condition lifts and Jeroboam is treated as having received taxable employment income of £100,000. As the shares in Dillpickle Industries plc are traded they will be RCAs and the company will have the obligation to operate PAYE and NIC on the amount treated as taxable employment income.

At the same time, Jeroboam is awarded shares in Jalfrezi International Limited, an unconnected company of which he is a director. These shares are forfeitable if the company does not hit a profit target in the next year and are also subject to restrictions on transfer.

The profit target is met in the following year, the forfeiture condition falls away and Jeroboam is treated as having received taxable employment income of £20,000, which is the shares' restricted value at that time. Jeroboam does not make an election to disregard the other restrictions on his shares.

As the shares in Jalfrezi International Limited are not RCAs at this point, PAYE will not be in point and NIC will not be levied. Jeroboam will include the taxable employment income on his tax return and pay the tax on the usual self-assessment timetable.

The following year Jalfrezi International Limited is acquired by a private buyer and Jeroboam receives £100,000 for his shares. As the shares are restricted securities, a proportion of the proceeds, £10,000, is treated as taxable employment income. Because Jeroboam received cash for his shares, this transaction will be subject to PAYE withholding and a charge to NIC will also arise.

Law: ITEPA 2003, s. 698

Company considerations

7.4   Readily convertible assets

The term "readily convertible assets" ("RCAs") is defined by ITEPA 2003, s. 702 and, in essence, it refers to any asset which can be easily converted into cash. This includes assets that can be used to realise a cash sum (e.g. if the asset can be used as collateral to secure a loan or advance).

The legislation treats securities as being convertible into cash if they are listed on recognised exchanges or if "trading arrangements" exist or are likely to come into existence at a point in the future. Examples of trading arrangements include listing on a non-recognised exchange, for example AIM, or the company being in the process of acquisition.

This can lead to difficulties if securities are acquired by employees and subsequently a company is sold. HMRC's view is set out in EIM11913, which states that:

> "It is important to remember that if, at the time the asset was awarded, there were no trading arrangements in place, nor an understanding or arrangement likely to lead to trading arrangements in future, the employer is not obliged to operate PAYE. *That remains the case even if trading arrangements subsequently come into existence.* Whether an asset is a readily convertible asset can only be considered on the basis of the facts at the time the asset is provided." (Added emphasis.)

This means that, in the context of a private company, if shares are awarded before a transaction is in prospect, then those shares may not be treated as RCAs. If, however, steps have been taken to dispose of the company – for example, if an sale instruction has been given to a corporate financier – then the shares will be within the scope of PAYE as RCAs, because trading arrangements are likely to come into existence in the future.

Example: transactions

Jeroboam is awarded shares for free in Jalfrezi International Limited. They are ordinary shares and, at that time, there are no plans to sell the business. Two months later, Jeroboam is awarded further ordinary shares, but the shareholders have, unknown to Jeroboam, given a sale mandate to a corporate financier.

Operation of PAYE and NIC

The first award of shares will not be treated as an award of RCAs, as there are no trading arrangements in existence and, at the time that the shares are awarded, it is not foreseen that trading arrangements will come into existence. Jeroboam should include any taxable employment income in his self-assessment and pay tax himself under the usual self-assessment timetable.

The second award of shares will be treated as an award of RCAs. Any taxable employment income will be subject to PAYE withholding, and NIC will also arise.

Where there is some sort of internal market in shares, often facilitated through an employee trust, this can cause securities to be treated as RCAs, as there will be a ready purchaser. However, the mere existence of an employee trust will not, of itself, lead to securities being treated as RCAs: if the trust has funds to draw on and has previously acted as a ready purchaser, then securities will be treated as RCAs; if trust funding is arranged *ad hoc*, or there is a fundraising process involved in funding an employee trust to buy securities, HMRC may be willing to accept that the securities are not RCAs.

In 2003 changes were made to the legislation as an anti-avoidance measure, with the result that securities may still be treated as RCAs even if no trading arrangements, or other means to convert them into cash, are in place.

The new provisions, in subsections 702(5A) to (5D), treat securities as RCAs if they are not "corporation tax deductible". Subsection (5B) defines this as meaning that the employer company was entitled to claim corporation tax relief under CTA 2009, Pt. 12 when the securities were originally acquired.

Example: corporation tax deductible

For his role as a director, Jeroboam receives the following share awards in March 2018. There are no trading arrangements in place for any of the securities:

- ordinary shares in Jalfrezi International Limited;
- fixed-rate preference shares in Jalfrezi International Limited;

105

- ordinary shares in Jalfrezi Limited, a wholly-owned subsidiary of Jalfrezi International Limited.

The award of ordinary shares in Jalfrezi International Limited will qualify for relief under Part 12 and will not constitute RCAs; Jeroboam will return any taxable employment income arising in his self-assessment return and pay over the tax by 31 January 2019.

The fixed-rate preference shares are not ordinary share capital and will not qualify for relief under Part 12. The ordinary shares in Jalfrezi Limited will also fail to meet the requirements of Part 12, as they are shares in a company that is under the control of another company.

Jalfrezi International Limited will need to include any taxable employment income arising in connection with the fixed-rate preference shares and the shares in Jalfrezi Limited in its RTI submission for March 2018, to operate PAYE and primary Class 1 NIC withholding, and to account for secondary Class 1 NIC.

The obvious issue with the drafting of s. 702(5B) is that it seems to suggest that shares will be RCAs if an employee pays full market value to acquire them, meaning that no relief under CTA 2009, Pt. 12 will arise. Given the intention of the legislation, it seems that the proper reading of this provision is to consider whether relief could be claimed, even if it would have been a zero amount.

7.5 Section 222

Where an employee is treated as receiving taxable employment income under the rules on employment-related securities, very often this will constitute a "dry" tax-charge, meaning that the employee will suffer tax without there being any liquidity in the shares to pay the tax.

Where a "dry" tax-charge arises and the securities in question are RCAs, the employer will need to account for PAYE to HMRC but may not be able to withhold the PAYE from amounts owed to the employee. In this situation, it will be up to the employer to chase the employee to "make good" the liability.

The legislative regime imposes a penalty on employees if they do not "make good" the tax paid over by the employer within 90 days of the end of the tax year in which the original taxable employment income arose. Under ITEPA 2003, s. 222 the amount that the employee fails to "make good" within the time limit will be treated as earnings – if the employee reimburses the employer after the time limit has expired, s. 222 will still be in point and the employee will be liable to pay the tax due.

The charge under s. 222 is not itself subject to PAYE withholding – the employee is obliged to include it in his or her self-assessment for the relevant tax year. However, a charge to Class 1 NIC does arise in respect of earnings treated as having arisen by s. 222.

It is important to distinguish between cases in which an employee fails to make good a PAYE liability and cases in which an employer fails to operate PAYE. No liability under s. 222 should arise if:

- an employer could have withheld the PAYE from amounts that it owed to the employee, but failed to do so;
- an employer did not realise or understand that PAYE withholding should have taken place and failed to act (although HMRC may wish to argue that the employer was making a net payment to the employee and gross up the amount of tax not accounted for).

As EIM 11964 makes clear, the obligation to make good an amount to an employer will usually be satisfied by making a cash payment, but it is possible to make good in other ways:

> "The requirement for the employee to 'make good' the 'due amount' to the employer indicates that the employee must provide to the employer something of value. This envisages that the employee can satisfy the requirement in a non-monetary form. However, because the due amount is calculated as a monetary figure, whatever arrangement is adopted, the value of the item provided must be quantifiable in financial terms and be at least equivalent to the due amount."

HMRC's guidance is that a mere indemnity given by an employee is unlikely to constitute "making good", but a more concrete arrangement – for example, giving the employer rights over specified assets held by an employee – would be acceptable.

7.6 Transferring NIC liabilities

As has been mentioned above, there is an exception to the general rule that an employer cannot make an employee bear the cost of secondary, employer NIC.

The exception is for a small number of tax charges connected with employment-related securities and is set out in SSCBA 1992, Sch. 1:

- paragraph 3A allows an employer to agree with an employee that the employee will bear the cost of secondary NIC;
- paragraph 3B provides for an employer and employee to enter into a joint election to make a formal transfer of the liability for the secondary NIC to the employee.

In practice, the paragraph 3B election is seen less frequently: the form of election must be approved in advance by HMRC and HMRC's practice has been to insist that the forms of election give the employer the responsibility to pay over the secondary NIC and then seek reimbursement from the employee. This practice has had the effect of eliminating any practical difference between para. 3A and 3B, leading to many employers opting for the less bureaucratic para. 3A route instead.

Within the last few years HMRC have consulted on abolishing para. 3B elections, but it is understood that there is an accounting benefit for US corporations, who still favour the formal election route.

The tax charges to which an indemnity or election can apply are limited to taxable employment income treated as arising under:

- ITEPA 2003, s. 426 (restricted securities: charge on certain post-acquisition events);
- ITEPA 2003, s. 438 (convertible securities: charge on certain post-acquisition events); or
- ITEPA 2003, s. 476 (charge on acquisition of securities pursuant to option etc.).

(The elections can also be made in respect of payments under certain restrictive covenants, governed by ITEPA 2003, sections 225 and 226, but these are beyond the scope of this book.)

The effect of the transfer of employer NIC to an employee is to reduce the value that is chargeable to income tax; in effect, the employer NIC is treated as an expense for income tax purposes.

Example: NIC transfer

Jeroboam exercises an option over shares in Dillpickle Industries plc and has entered into an agreement with the company under para. 3A to bear the cost of the secondary Class 1 NIC that arises. Jeroboam's option gain is £100,000.

	£
Value subject to NIC	100,000
Employee primary Class 1 NIC at 2%	2,000
Employer secondary Class 1 NIC at 13.8%	13,800
Value subject to income tax: (i.e. £100,000-£13,800)	86,200
Income tax at 45%:	38,790
Total tax cost borne by Jeroboam: (i.e. £38,790 + £2,000 + £13,800)	£54,590

As the example shows, the NIC transfer leaves the employee with a high effective tax rate (even greater if the employee's option gains straddle the "zone of doom" in which the personal allowance is tapered), but employers often take the view that the tax rate is acceptable, as the employee is only paying tax because he or she has received something valuable in exchange.

8. Reporting and accounting

8.1 The reporting regime

8.1.1 Introduction

One of the most visible changes to the treatment of employment-related securities following FA 2003 was the strengthened reporting regime introduced by the Act, which found many employers puzzling over a complex paper form, the (in)famous Form 42, and fearing a beefy penalty regime associated with the form.

Before FA 2003 there had been a reporting system for employee share transactions, but compliance and enforcement were patchy at best. FA 2003 introduced new, more comprehensive forms and a clear regime of penalty charges.

Further changes to the regime were introduced in FA 2014, which made online filing of employment-related securities returns compulsory, broadened the scope of the information required and introduced an automatic penalty regime for non-compliance.

The regime now provides that a return in the prescribed form must be submitted for each fiscal year (i.e. the year to 5 April) that a "scheme" is open on HMRC's system, whether or not there have been any reportable transactions in the year. The reports must be filed no later than 6 July following the end of each fiscal year. Failure to comply results in an automatic penalty of £100, followed by later penalties of £300 each if the filing remains outstanding at the three and six month mark – a daily penalty of £10 per day can be applied if the compliance failure continues past that point.

A similar system now also applies to the various statutory share schemes, which each have their own reporting regime.

8.1.2 Who needs to report

ITEPA 2003, s. 421L gives a list of persons liable to report employment-related securities transactions:

- the employer;
- the "host employer" if the person in question is employed by an overseas company but provides services in the UK to a UK company;
- the "relevant person" for the purposes of the PAYE rules on continental shelf workers;
- the person who made the securities available or who granted the option; and
- the issuer of the securities (unless the securities are government or local government bonds).

Provided that one of these persons files a report, the reporting obligation will be discharged for all of the others.

There is a limited exemption from online filing, set out in *Employment-Related Securities Bulletin* no. 20, where all of the following conditions apply:

- neither the company, nor any other company in the same group or under the same ownership, is registered for PAYE;
- the arrangements are not statutory share schemes;
- the company has no obligations to operate PAYE in respect of the reportable event; and
- the company has no obligation to operate PAYE in respect of anything else it does.

8.1.3 Reportable events

Most acquisitions of employment-related securities will be reportable. HMRC have published a list of limited exceptions to this basic rule in ERSM 140040 and 140070, which include:

- shares acquired on the incorporation of a company (or shortly after incorporation), provided that the company is "bare" (i.e. without assets other than its share capital) at the time that the shares are acquired;
- transfers of shares in the normal course of domestic, family or personal relationships;

Company considerations

- flat management companies and members' clubs – there is generally no need to report the acquisition or disposal of shares in flat management companies unless the transaction has some element of "bounty" in it (for example, the shares are sold at over-value) or the shares are restricted securities;
- although share-for-share exchanges, rights issues, bonus issues, scrip dividends, dividend reinvestment plans and independent transactions undertaken by employees or directors on their own account will usually need to be reported, no report will need to be made where the following conditions apply:
    - the employer is a company or part of a group listed on a recognised stock exchange;
    - the opportunity to acquire unrestricted securities is made available to all shareholders, including director and employee shareholders; and
    - the unrestricted securities are acquired independently of the company, for example through a broker at full market value;
- there is no need to report acquisitions by employees who are not UK resident and do not have any UK duties in the year of the award, as long as they are not likely to become UK resident or work in the UK during the vesting period of the award.

Example: reporting employment-related securities

Jeroboam owns all of the shares in Bhuna Ventures Limited, a company that he incorporated with one share in 2007. Jeroboam decides that he would like his wife to benefit from some of the dividend income from Bhuna Ventures Limited and arranges for a further share issue. Jeroboam receives 98 shares and his wife receives one share.

The issuance of a share to his wife is not reportable – the share will not be an employment-related security in her hands, as she received it in the ordinary course of her domestic or family relationship with Jeroboam.

However, the other shares issued to Jeroboam will be employment-related securities and their issuance will need to be reported to HMRC.

Most post-transaction events in relation to options or securities will need to be included in the form, for example, the exercise of an option, the release of an option for consideration, the conversion of securities, their disposal for more than market value or artificial variations in the shares' rights or values.

The reporting on restricted securities can be simplified if elections under ITEPA 2003, s. 431(1) are entered into when the securities are acquired (see **3.3.8**). If elections are not entered into then the lifting of restrictions or the sale of the securities will need to be reported even if these events do not give rise to any charge to tax.

8.1.4 Practicalities of reporting

The reporting system that has been adopted is, to be frank, a messy encumbrance for employers.

To make a report, the employer will need to go into its "PAYE for employers" account on the HMRC website and then access the section marked "ERS for employers" to set up a "scheme". This can only be done using the employer's log-in credentials; an agent cannot establish a scheme on an employer's behalf.

A scheme will need to be set up even if an employer simply wishes to report a share transaction (like the issuance of shares to Jeroboam in the example above) that does not fit within a conventional employees' share scheme.

Once the scheme has been established (which must be identified as a SIP, CSOP, SAYE, EMI or unapproved arrangement) the employer or its agent can then upload information using spreadsheets saved in the .ods format. The system is finicky and will reject minor alterations to the form or information not presented in exactly the right format.

Once all of the transactions under a scheme have been completed, the scheme will need to be closed (again, this can only be done by the employer). If a scheme is not closed, the employer must continue to file returns and will be liable for penalties if the returns are not made.

8.2 Accounting for employee share awards

8.2.1 Background

The following is intended to be an outline of the accounting principles currently set out in s. 26 of FRS102 and IFRS2.

Changes to the accounting rules for transactions in a company's own shares were introduced after a series of scandals at the time of the dot-com boom of the late 1990s / early 2000s, as it was felt that awards of share options, often to suppliers, were being used to disguise the costs of doing business, flattering profit lines.

This coincided with the wider movement by the various accounting standard setters to re-assess the value of assets and liabilities in a company's books by reference to market mechanisms.

8.2.2 Valuation and amortisation

The basic premise of the accounting standards is that the value of a share award should be assessed and then that value should be amortised over the expected life of the award.

The value of the share award is relatively straightforward in the case of a simple gift of shares – the start point will be the difference between the value of the shares at the date of gift and the value of any monetary consideration given for them.

The position is more complex for options and option-like instruments, where an option pricing methodology will have to be used. The main methodologies that readers may have heard of are Black-Scholes option pricing, binomial modelling and Monte-Carlo simulations. Given the complexity of building a Monte-Carlo simulation or binomial model, these are approaches that are more often discussed than implemented, with businesses falling back onto Black-Scholes modelling. This is on the basis that, even if the mathematics are convoluted, Black-Scholes calculators are freely available online and, for what might be a small number that is below the company's materiality level, offer a relatively painless way to derive a value for employee share options.

For a quoted company operating a standard share plan, option pricing can be relatively straightforward:

- there will be a quoted share price, which will give the accountant the most fundamental element of any assessment of the value of an employee share award – namely the value of a share;
- most plc plans have a three-year vesting period, after which most employees tend to liquidate their awards;
- there will be available measures of the volatility of the company's share price;
- there will be a clearly defined dividend history that is not muddled by owner-managers effectively remunerating themselves with dividends.

For private companies, the position is often more difficult, but if a value has been agreed with HMRC for the shares (where the options have been granted under one of the statutory share schemes), then this would seem to be the most rational start-point for the exercise.

The period over which to amortise the share awards is also often more complex for private companies, as many options will be designed to be geared to an exit; companies will need to make a realistic assessment of their commercial expectations as to when options will be exercised.

8.2.3 Accounting entries

Once a company has established the value of its share awards and the period over which they should be amortised, the amortised value for each accounting period should be charged to the company's income statement, with the other side of the transaction being a credit to an employee share reserve in the balance sheet.

The accounting standards do not call for the share awards to be revalued each year; once a value has been arrived at on grant, that will be the basis for all of the subsequent accounting entries.

If an employee's share award lapses during the amortisation period, the value of his or her award will be taken out of the annual amortisation charge; it does not get written back to the income statement.

When share awards vest, or options are exercised, the employee share reserve is written back to the retained earnings reserve through the balance sheet.

Company considerations

8.2.4 *Interaction with the tax rules*

As set out above, the company tax position is that where relief is potentially available under CTA 2009, Pt. 12, no other relief can be claimed in respect of employee share awards. This means that any entries made in the books of the company in respect of the accounting rules on share-based payments must be disallowed for tax purposes.

Part 4: Implementing share schemes

9. Designing an employee share scheme

9.1 The basic elements of a share scheme

There are two elements to any employee share scheme, the shares (or other securities) themselves and the means to get them into the employees' hands. Both elements need to be considered to ensure that they deliver the commercial objectives of the share scheme; a well-designed option plan that delivers valueless shares is unlikely to satisfy the objectives of either the employees or the shareholders.

In a listed company, the scope to tailor the rights of the employee shares is likely to be curtailed and it is unusual for such a company to have more than one class of shares in issue. In a private company, there is far greater flexibility and it is possible to tailor share rights to deliver very specific economic goals, as will be shown in more detail in **Chapter 10** below.

The means to deliver shares to employees can take a number of forms and those most commonly encountered are:

- the grant of share options;
- an immediate award of shares, which may be subject to forfeiture in certain situations; and
- a promise to deliver shares at a time in the future.

The first two of these structures should be relatively familiar to most practitioners, and are described in more detail below, but the third structure is less commonly encountered in a UK context.

US companies often structure their share schemes as a promise to deliver shares at a fixed date in the future because of the combined peculiarities of the US tax code and US accounting standards, which conspire to make share options unattractive. These awards are often labelled "restricted stock units" ("RSUs") and, although they are amenable to different legal analyses from a UK perspective, depending on the drafting (which makes reporting them to HMRC a challenge) their effect is to deliver a number of shares at a date in the future.

A less frequently encountered structure, which is in use both in the UK and the US, is known as stock appreciation rights or SARs. SARs are essentially a promise to an employee that he or she will benefit from the growth in value of a specified number of shares, which may be settled in equity or in cash.

A cash-settled SAR is also known as a phantom share option. The principle behind an equity-settled SAR is best illustrated with an example:

Example: stock appreciation rights

Juliet is awarded an equity-settled SAR over 1,000 shares in Hand Holdings Inc. when the share price is USD 1.00 per share. Her SAR vests the following year, when the shares are worth USD 1.50. The growth in the value of the 1,000 shares is USD 500 (i.e. (1.50-1.00) x 1,000), which means that Juliet will receive 333 shares in Hand Holdings Inc. (i.e. 500 ÷ 1.50).

9.2 Immediate ownership v options

9.2.1 Overview

Whether a share scheme is structured to provide immediate share ownership or to defer share ownership will depend on the strategic objectives of the company and whether it is able to benefit from the statutory share schemes set out in the schedules to ITEPA 2003 and the benefits code.

In simple terms, where the owners of a company intend to sell the company in the medium term, don't want to pay dividends to employees and qualify to grant enterprise management incentive ("EMI") options or company share option plan ("CSOP") options, it is very unlikely that an award of shares will fit the company's commercial objectives as well as a grant of qualifying options.

In the alternative, if the company is not heading towards a sale, or the owners would like to pay dividends to key employees, or the company does not qualify for any of the statutory share option plans, then an immediate share award may be more commercially effective.

9.2.2 Private companies

Private companies tend to be quite resistant to immediate share ownership for employees. Although business owners are often keen on reducing costs by topping up key employees' earnings with dividend payments, they are much less keen on allowing employees to vote or on the myriad complications of corporate governance that leavers can present.

Factors in favour of the grant of options:

- The shareholders do not want the complication of minority employee shareholders before an exit takes place – share options can be a means to give employees a stake in the equity of a company without immediate ownership.
- If there is no ready market in the shares tax charges arising on an award of shares will be "dry" charges – in other words, the employee will have tax to pay without the means to realise value from the shares to meet the tax liability.
- Where the value of the shares is expected to increase significantly, the value of the CT deduction arising on the exercise of the option may be material, whereas the relief available on the making of a share award would be limited to the lesser value at grant.
- Where the company is able to grant qualifying EMI options, the employee may benefit from a more generous tax treatment than an employee receiving an immediate award of shares (this is discussed in more detail in **Chapter 13**).
- It is far easier to deal with leavers – their options will simply lapse, there is no need to consider buying back shares from leavers or keep in contact with a minority shareholder who no longer has any other connection with the company.

The factors favouring immediate share ownership are:

- Employees may be permitted to benefit from dividend payments, which may reduce the costs of remunerating them.

- The company may wish to tie in key employees by making them shareholders with the right to vote and take decisions about the company's future.
- The company, or the employees, may not qualify for awards of options under the statutory share schemes and the board may consider it better to take an immediate "hit" by awarding shares to employees, which could then benefit from capital treatment on any growth in their value.
- The employees may wish to purchase shares, possibly as part of a wider buy-out.

9.2.3 Public companies

For quoted companies, the considerations will be quite different, as there is a market in their shares and, outside of the statutory share schemes, both share awards and share options are likely to give rise to similar tax charges, the timing of which may differ.

The issues that will impact on a quoted company's choice between some sort of option plan and a share award scheme are most likely to be those of dilution – as companies often limit the number of new shares that can be issued in employee share schemes – and accounting: the requirements of IFRS 2 can make outright share awards significantly less attractive than share options.

There are also company law considerations that skew public companies towards share option awards; in the UK it is quite difficult for a company to make awards of forfeitable securities without incurring the cost of an additional structure, like an EBT to hold those securities as a nominee; such a structure also has negative implications for a company's all-important earnings-per-share metrics, as companies have to have more shares in issue for use in such structures.

For these reasons, public companies favour share options over structures giving immediate ownership to employees, with the honourable exception of shares awarded pursuant to an all-employee share incentive plan ("SIP").

9.3 "Vesting" and performance conditions

To the irritation of many lawyers, in the arcane language of share schemes the term "vest" is used to describe the point at which an employee share award crystallises: either the point at which the employee becomes entitled to exercise an option or when a forfeiture condition lifts.

The vesting of awards granted under an employee share scheme is often made subject to conditions, which can vary from something as basic as an obligation to enter into an election under ITEPA 2003, s. 431 (see **3.3.8**) to performance conditions that measure a metric like total shareholder return against a basket of comparator companies.

In a quoted company context, institutional investors demand that performance measures are attached to awards made to senior management to ensure that shareholders are getting value for their money.

For private companies, the issues are slightly different: smaller companies are often on a growth trajectory, meaning that the value of awards under an employee share scheme will have an intrinsic link to the performance of the company; and shareholders will often be heavily involved in the management of the company, which will mean that under-performing employees will rarely stay long enough to be able to benefit from share awards.

In a private company context, it is important to ensure that any performance or exercise conditions do not get in the way of the commercial intention of the shareholders and that they retain the ability to provide rewards to employees whether or not they have met conditions that seemed wildly important when the scheme was in the design phase. For this reason, it is usually recommended that any performance conditions are made subject to the discretion of the board to over-ride them on an exit.

9.4 Treatment of leavers

9.4.1 A crucial issue

The earliest stages of the planning of a share scheme will need to include the planning of the treatment of leavers; this is often the single most important and contentious part of any share plan.

There is little point in allowing a leaver to hold shares in a company, but there will always be situations where an individual leaver may have contributed to a company and its success and will be justifiably upset if his share scheme does not yield value to him. It must also be borne in mind that the incentive effect of the scheme will be diminished if employees perceive unfairness or bias against them in this element of scheme design.

A further point to consider is that some of the statutory share schemes – particularly share incentive plans ("SIPs"), Save As You Earn ("SAYE" or "Sharesave") and CSOPs – stipulate that people leaving for certain defined reasons must be allowed to exercise options / withdraw shares when they leave.

Where an employee has been granted share options, the usual position will be that a "good leaver" may be allowed to exercise his or her options, while options held by a "bad leaver" will lapse.

For quoted companies, the company's stock exchange listing will give leavers the opportunity to sell their shares and the organisation of the share capital will be well adapted to mass share ownership – there should be few governance complications associated by allowing leavers to acquire or hold shares.

In a private company setting, allowing leavers to acquire or hold shares can create complications; the shares acquired by a leaver on the exercise of his or her options will need to be dealt with. This may be achieved either by allowing the leaver to sell the shares or by making special provision for the leaver to hold them without causing complexities for the running of the company. For example, a share scheme may make the exercise of a share option by a leaver conditional on his or her entry into a power of attorney over those shares in favour of the directors.

As there is no external market in private company shares, there can be complexities associated with arranging for leavers to sell their shares. Unless there is a shareholder with funds who is willing to acquire leavers' shares, or some sort of informal "over the counter" market in the shares (which a small minority of private companies do facilitate for their employees), the company will usually have to facilitate the disposal of a leaver's shares, often by buying back the shares or by arranging for an employee benefit trust ("EBT") to acquire them. Each alternative has its own problems and both will impact on the company's cash-flow.

9.4.2 Company purchase of own shares

A buy-back by the company has superficial attractions: no new structures have to be set up, and it is a process which is well understood by companies and advisers. The downsides of such an approach are that the company will usually need to have sufficient distributable reserves to allow the buy-back to be completed and, for the employee, the tax consequences can be quite adverse.

Unless a leaver meets the conditions set out in CTA 2010 (starting at s. 1033), he or she will be treated as receiving a taxable dividend distribution. The detailed requirements of this legislation are beyond the scope of this book, but often employees will not have held their shares for the minimum five years stipulated by the legislation and will not qualify for capital treatment on their proceeds.

The amount subject to tax will be the difference between the sale proceeds and the amount of capital represented by the shares (i.e. the nominal value of the shares plus any share premium attaching to them). This can potentially result in significant double taxation for the employee, as very often he or she will have acquired the shares at par or for a very small amount of premium.

Example: purchase of own shares

Ian is granted a non-qualifying option over 10,000 shares with an exercise price of £0.01 per share, which is the shares' nominal value. Ian leaves the company on good terms and is allowed to exercise his option – the company issues new shares to satisfy the exercise of Ian's option – and Ian is allowed to sell his shares back to the company that day for their market value of £10.00 per share.

Part 4: Implementing share schemes

Ian will be treated as having received taxable employment income of £9.99 per share when he exercises his option (the difference between the exercise price of the option and the market value of the shares that he receives) and is taxable at his marginal rate on £99,900.

Under the CGT rules, Ian would not be treated as having realised a taxable gain – the rules in TCGA, s. 119A mean that his base cost would be his exercise price plus the amount on which he had paid income tax (i.e. £0.01 x 10,000 plus £99,900), meaning that there would be no gain.

However, the rules in CTA 2010 will only give Ian credit for the amount paid up on his shares, in this case their £0.01 of nominal value. In short, Ian will suffer a second income tax charge on £99,900, this time under the rules on dividends.

Assuming that Ian is an additional rate taxpayer, his position is as follows:

> Income tax and employee NIC on exercise of the option (£99,900 x (45% + 2%)) = £46,953.
>
> Income tax on deemed distribution (£99,900 x 38.1%) = £38,062.
>
> Total tax = £85,015.
>
> Net (£99,900 minus £85,015) = £14,885.

9.4.3 Buy back by an EBT

Instead of having the company repurchase shares from leavers, the company could establish an EBT to buy back and hold leavers' shares. The company would establish an EBT and make contributions, which would then be used to buy the shares. The shares held by the EBT could then be "recycled" – used to satisfy other employee share awards.

While such an approach would ensure that the rules on company purchases of own shares are not in point, the purchase of shares by the EBT would constitute a "transaction in securities" and have the potential to be the subject matter of a counteraction notice under ITA 2007, s. 698 if HMRC believed that the transaction had an avoidance motive, although, in practice, HMRC rarely (if ever) take this point.

The major complications with such an approach are that the company will need to have a strategy for dealing with the shares held by the EBT – if the EBT has a large shareholding at the point that the company is sold, the value represented by those shares would be lost to the shareholders, who would, in all likelihood, be barred from benefiting from the EBT's assets.

If the shares are sold by the EBT trustee there could be a significant capital gains tax charge (unless the company is willing to meet the expense of appointing trustees in an offshore jurisdiction). If the trustees then used the net funds to pay bonuses to employees, this would be treated as a payment of general earnings, subject to PAYE and NIC. The company may also miss out on getting the full benefit of corporation tax relief, because of the operation of the rules in CTA 2009, Pt. 20; these rules limit the corporation tax deductions that can be claimed by companies to the value of the original contributions to the EBT.

Example: sale to an EBT

Biscuit Brokers Limited made several employees redundant in 2009 and allowed them to sell 100,000 shares in total to a UK resident EBT for their market value of £3 per share. The company funded this transaction by making a contribution of £300,000 to the EBT.

In 2017 Tea Time Industries plc acquired Biscuit Brokers for consideration that equated to £10 per share. The EBT trustees sold their holdings as part of the transaction and, after setting aside an amount to cover their CGT liability, used the balance of the funds to pay bonuses to the employees of Biscuit Brokers.

The trustees' share of the consideration is £1,000,000 on which they will have CGT of £198,890 to pay (i.e. £1,000,000-£5,550 (the trust annual exempt amount) @ 20%). This leaves the trustees with £801,110 to distribute to the employees.

Biscuit Brokers will have an obligation to withhold PAYE and operate NIC on the amounts distributed by the trustees. Assuming that all of the employees are subject to tax at the additional rate of 45%, the net amount received by the employees will be around

Part 4: Implementing share schemes

£424,588 (i.e. £801,110 net of income tax at 45% and employee NIC at 2%).

The company will incur employer NIC of £110,553 in total and will be entitled to CT relief on £410,553 (i.e. the value of the original contribution of £300,000 plus the value of the employer NIC of £110,533).

If, in the run-up to the deal, Biscuit Brokers had arranged for the trustees to grant nil cost options to the employees, which were exercisable on an exit, the trustees would be treated as having made a disposal for no value by TCGA 1992, s. 144ZA. The employees would have received shares worth £1,000,000 on which PAYE and NIC would be due (because of the proximity to the transaction, the shares will be RCAs), which would mean that their net proceeds would have been £530,000 in aggregate. The company itself would have a higher employer NIC bill (£138,000), but would entitled to claim CT relief on the full value of the shares under CTA 2009, Pt. 12.

Assuming that the rate of corporation tax is 19%, and that Biscuit Brokers is able to utilise the relief, the difference between these approaches in cash terms for the company would be as follows:

Bonus distribution after sale of shares: (£410,553 x 19%)-£110,553 = (£32,548) cost to the company.

Nil cost options (£1,000,000 x 19%)-£138,000 = £52,000 cash benefit to the company.

A further consideration is that the assets held by the EBT trustees would be within the scope of the disguised remuneration rules in ITEPA 2003, Pt. 7A, which could accelerate tax charges for employees if shares or assets are "earmarked" by the trustees for specific employees. Although there are specific exemptions for employee share schemes, they are complex and it is easy to fail to comply with them. These rules are dealt with in more detail below.

9.4.4   Other choices

Another route that the owners of a company may wish to explore would be to allow leavers who hold options to retain some or all of their share options, so that they would be allowed to exercise them alongside their colleagues on an exit or when performance conditions are met.

The attraction of this route is that it defers the point at which the leaver becomes a shareholder and also does away with the need for the company or shareholders to expend cash buying out leavers.

Where a leaver holds a non-qualifying option, the tax treatment will be unchanged; all of his or her option gains will be subject to income tax. Where a leaver holds qualifying EMI options, the position is more complex, and it is likely that the leaver will suffer some degree of tax penalty when he is finally permitted to exercise his options, but this might be seen as a reasonable consequence of his having left the company and being permitted to benefit from the company's share option plans.

The rules for CSOPs are more restrictive, meaning that this approach is unlikely to be employed.

9.4.5 Interaction with provisions in the articles

The provisions of the articles will also need to be considered: company articles usually make some provision for dealing with leavers; they are often forced to offer shares for sale. The provisions of the articles will need to be considered carefully where employees who hold shares or share options become leavers.

In particular, where an employee is being allowed to exercise an option early as a leaver, the default treatment of leavers in the articles will need to be evaluated and decisions taken as to whether to exercise any rights or discretions that the articles confer on the board with regard to the leaver's shares.

9.5 Exit strategy

The purpose of implementing a share scheme is usually to motivate employees to perform well in the future and to reward that good performance (although some private company share schemes are often implemented to reward past performance with a share of the capital value of the company).

Just holding a share in a company is unlikely to be seen as a material benefit by most employees; employees need to be able to see a route to realising value from their shares for them to be seen as a valuable reward.

In a quoted company context, employees will usually be able to sell shares on the stock market and should be able to realise value for their shares very easily. In a private company, there will not usually be a ready market for the shares and it can be hard for employees to see how they will benefit from holding them.

For this reason, share schemes often work best where a company has a clear route to an exit in mind. The exit could take the form of a sale to a third party or some other opportunity to sell shares in the future. If a sale is not in prospect, the possibility that the employees will be able to participate in significant dividend distributions may be enough to persuade employees that there is a positive benefit to them of being rewarded in shares.

Being able to show employees that the company has positive forward plans, and is helping the employees to participate in those plans by holding shares, is crucial to the success of a share scheme.

Any private company share scheme will need to be designed with terms of the proposed exit in mind: if the objective is a sale to a third party, the share awards or options will often be geared to "vest" shortly before the sale; if some other form of exit is planned (for example, the sale to an EBT or some other market-maker), the share scheme will need to take those plans into account. Many of the problems with selling shares to an EBT or other market-maker are set out in the section on leavers at **9.4** above.

The recent changes to the rules on EBTs, especially the introduction of the rules on disguised remuneration, have highlighted the need for flexibility where the owners of a company ultimately plan to allow employees to sell shares to an EBT: share scheme rules and company articles of association should ensure that they do not bind the employees to sell shares only to one identified purchaser; future rule changes could render it unattractive to sell to that particular purchaser.

9.6 Dilution

Awarding shares to employees will usually result in the dilution of the existing shareholders' interests in the company. In a quoted company, the dilutive effect of a share scheme can be managed by buying shares in the market to recycle in the company's share schemes. Share awards that dilute the existing shareholders are always subject to close scrutiny by shareholders, and company secretarial departments can end up devoting significant time and resources to managing and minimising the dilutive effect of share schemes.

In a private company context, dilution can pose different problems: there may be shareholders for whom any dilution may not be acceptable, for example, minority shareholders, investors or the holders of existing employee share awards.

There are three broad approaches to dealing with dilution:

- warehousing shares in an EBT for use in the company's share schemes (the problems with this approach are dealt with in more detail above);
- granting options over shares held by shareholders who are willing to suffer dilution; and
- amending the company's articles of association so that new shares issued under the share scheme have rights that only economically impact classes of shares held by shareholders willing to suffer dilution.

Of these three approaches, the third has a number of attractions, as it doesn't require new structures or entities to be established, it doesn't result in the risk that shareholders' value could be trapped in an EBT if the share awards do not vest, there is no risk from the rules on disguised remuneration, and none of the shareholders would be treated as having made a disposal for CGT purposes when share awards vest.

The downside of the third approach is that it would need changes to be made to the company's articles of association and would add a small amount of complexity to the rights of the shares.

The source of shares to be used in an employee share scheme needs to be considered at the outset and will impact on the design of the scheme because of the risk that the awards could be treated as the disposal of shares under the CGT rules, which has the potential to give rise to capital gains tax charges on the disposing shareholders.

This last issue was highlighted by the case of *Mansworth v Jelley*, in which it was held that the exercise of an option was a non-arm's-length transaction to which TCGA 1992, s. 17 applied. This decision would mean that if a shareholder or an EBT granted options over shares and those options were exercised, the disposal of shares by that shareholder to satisfy the option would be taxed as if the shareholder had sold the shares for market value, even if the shareholder had received little or nothing when the option was exercised.

To prevent this perverse result, two new provisions were enacted in TCGA 1992:

- section 144ZA, which treats the grantor of an option as having disposed of shares for the option price receivable when the option is granted; and
- section 239ZA, which provides that an award of shares for no consideration will not be treated as a disposal within s. 17.

There are peculiarities associated with both provisions.

The wording of s. 144ZA only seems to give protection to the grantor of an option. This means that if a company grants an option which is satisfied out of shares held by an EBT or by an individual shareholder, then the EBT or the shareholder would not seem to benefit from the relief in s. 144ZA. It is understood that HMRC do not take this point and accept that an individual satisfying an option granted by a company may still benefit from the relief. However, to avoid the ambiguity inherent in this situation, it is often considered better to arrange for options to be granted by the person whose shares will ultimately be used to satisfy the option.

The relief given by s. 239ZA only applies to the trustees of an EBT and can only be claimed where the employee is fully taxable on the value of the shares that he or she receives and where the employee does not give any consideration for the shares. The particular difficulty with this provision is the wide meaning given to the term "consideration" in English law; if the terms of a share award are such that an employee agrees to bear the cost of employer NIC under SSCBA 1992, Sch. 1, para. 3B then he or she could be seen to have given consideration for the shares and more nebulous undertakings could also be treated as giving rise to consideration. In practice HMRC do not take this point, but it should be borne in mind that even a nominal amount of consideration for share awards could potentially deprive the protection of this relief from an EBT trustee.

Case: *Mansworth (HMIT) v Jelley* [2003] BTC 3, STC 53

9.7 Communication

This last consideration is, in some ways, the most important of all: the most carefully designed share scheme will be ineffective if it is not clearly communicated to the potential participants.

Anyone designing a share scheme should consider carefully how the plan will be communicated to participants and should do so at an early stage in the design of a scheme. Scheme communication is too often treated as an after-thought by advisers, whose idea of scheme communication might be a densely worded leaflet for participants focusing on technical areas of the planning, rather than the commercial objectives of the scheme and its benefits to the participants.

Early thought about scheme communication can have a direct impact on the design of the scheme, as an employer faced with the realisation that he will have to explain the plan to his employees may be inclined to simplify his plans or to drop performance conditions that require a post-graduate qualification in financial modelling to calculate.

10. What shares to use in the plan

10.1 The basics

It is an old but accurate cliché that a share is simply a bundle of rights. Those rights are determined by a company's constitutional documents with some minor interventions from statute, most of which are aimed at the governance of companies, not the rights of individual shareholders.

There are few fixed characteristics: different classes of shares within the same company may or may not have voting rights; dividend rights may be fixed or variable (or there may be no right to a dividend at all); the capital rights of different share classes may vary considerably, or be capped.

The rights that an individual may have in his capacity as a shareholder may be augmented or restricted by other rights conferred by shareholders' agreements that he has entered into.

It is important to bear in mind that parties to a shareholders' agreement have their rights or obligations under the agreements in their personal capacities as signatories to the agreements, not because they hold shares; as set out at **5.5.4** above, this can have significant tax implications for employees who hold shares.

Depending on the age of the company, the articles of association will often be drafted to supplement one of the statutory forms of model articles of association: for pre-2008 companies, this will be "Table A", a set of regulations that have their origin in the *Joint Stock Companies Act* 1856; for post-2008 companies, this will be the Model Articles set out in the *Companies (Model Articles) Regulations* 2008 (SI 2008/3229). Where this is the case, the articles need to be read in tandem with the relevant regulations.

Some post-2008 companies disapply the model articles in their entirety, but this may often be "gold plating" by incorporation agents, rather than a response to the commercial needs of the investors.

10.2 Employee classes

In private companies, it is not uncommon for business owners to wish to make employee share awards over a new class of shares, specifically designed for employees. There are a number of factors in favour of a separate class for employees:

- the employer may not want to confer voting rights on the employees;
- it may be the intention that different rates of dividends might be declared on the shares held by employees to those held by other shareholders;
- an employer may wish to set out terms on which leavers are obliged to dispose of their shares;
- the shareholders may not wish to be subject to the same restrictions on transferring shares as those that they need to impose on the employees;
- owners may wish to reserve to themselves the right to appoint directors; or
- the commercial intention may be to define or limit the rights to capital that an employee's shares enjoy.

Company law in England and Wales allows companies to "customise" their share capital to a high degree. The only real constraints are those imposed by the tax code; for example, redeemable shares rarely qualify for reliefs and convertible or "flowering" shares give rise to significant income tax charges for shareholders.

Another tax-geared limitation on a company's freedom to design the shares that it wants to use in its share schemes are the restrictions set out in the statutory share schemes: all four schemes impose minimum requirements on the nature of shares that can be used in a qualifying scheme; these range from minimal specifications in the EMI Code to more onerous requirements about the ownership of the shares as a class in the CSOP and SAYE codes.

10.3 Growth shares

10.3.1 What are growth shares and why are they used?

The term "growth shares" refers to a special class of shares that has no right to participate in the current equity value of a company (i.e. the proportion of the company's value that would be returned to shareholders after debt has been repaid), but only have an interest in the company's future growth.

Example: growth shares

PatCo Limited has two classes of shares, ordinary shares that participate in the whole capital value of the company and ordinary A shares that only participate in that part of the value of the company that exceeds £5m ("the Threshold").

Pat, who founded the company, holds 90 ordinary shares and her employee, George, holds 10 ordinary A shares.

The company is sold for £7m and the proceeds are distributed as follows:

>**Pat:**
>Share of proceeds up to the Threshold –
>90/90 = 100%   £5,000,000
>Share of proceeds above the Threshold –
>90/100 = 90%   £1,800,000
>
>**George:**
>Share of proceeds up to the Threshold –
>0/90 = 0%   £0
>Share of proceeds above the Threshold –
>10/100 = 10%   £200,000

Growth shares are often used by mature businesses, which have a significant equity value. This can make it difficult for businesses to make significant share awards without employees bearing large tax costs when shares are awarded to them.

Alternatively, a business owner may wish to ring-fence the equity value that has been built up to date for him or herself, wishing to give management a stake in future value.

Growth shares may be awarded to, or purchased by, employees. Alternatively it is possible to grant options over growth shares (this can even be possible in the context of options granted under one of the statutory share schemes).

10.3.2 Tax analysis of growth shares

Growth shares awarded to employees will be treated in the same way as any other employment-related securities:

- on acquisition, the employees will be treated as having received taxable employment income equal to the difference between the market value of the growth shares and the consideration, if any, given by the employees;
- the growth shares are likely to constitute restricted securities, which means that the employees and employer may wish to enter into an election under ITEPA 2003, s. 431(1) when the shares are acquired;
- provided that the growth shares are not structured so as to constitute "flowering shares" (see **4.3.2** above), if they are subsequently sold for their market value, any uplift in value should fall within the CGT regime.

If the growth shares do not give their holders an interest in the current equity value of a company, they are unlikely to have a significant market value for tax purposes. This means that growth shares that are "out of the money" can be awarded to employees with only negligible up-front tax consequences.

Assuming that s. 431(1) elections have been entered into when the shares were acquired, and that the shares are sold for no more than their market value, any growth in their value will be subject to CGT. If the employee meets the requirements for entrepreneurs' relief ("ER"), the gain on the growth shares will qualify for the relief.

Example: acquisition and disposal of growth shares

George pays nominal value to acquire 10 growth shares in PatCo Limited and makes an election under ITEPA 2003, s. 431(1). The growth shares participate in equity value in excess of £5m, but at the time that they are awarded to George, the value of PatCo Limited is only £4m. The shares are "out of the money" and have no current value for tax purposes.

The shares carry one vote each and represent 10% of the ordinary share capital of the company and 10% of the voting power.

George has no tax to pay on acquiring his shares, as he has paid more than the shares' market value to acquire them.

Three years later, PatCo Limited is sold to a third party for £7m. George receives proceeds of £200,000.

Provided that PatCo Limited qualifies for ER and George continues to be employed by the company, he will be able to claim ER on his gains and will pay tax at 10% on any value in excess of his annual exemption for the year.

Following FA 2003, the Inland Revenue (as was) published a paper suggesting that growth share mechanisms could be treated as giving rise to taxable employment income under ITEPA 2003, Pt. 7, Chapter 4, using a thin capitalisation analysis. This opinion was subsequently withdrawn and HMRC have adopted a more favourable view of growth shares, as is evidenced by the fairly positive views of growth shares set out in HM Revenue and Customs *Research Report* 372, published in 2015.

10.3.3 Joint share ownership plans

Joint share ownership plans (or JSOPs) are a form of growth share planning that is used by quoted companies and companies that, for whatever reason, are unable or unwilling to introduce additional share classes.

The basic principle of a JSOP is that shares are acquired jointly by an employee and a counterparty (often an employee share trust). The shares are registered in the names of both parties, which defines the legal ownership of the shares, and then the parties enter into an agreement which sets out the extent of their equitable ownership in the shares. Typically, this results in the employee having only a future interest in the value of the shares, while the counterparty has an entitlement to all of the current value.

Example: JSOP awards

PatCo plc's shares are priced at £2.50 per share. The company invites an employee, George, to subscribe for shares jointly with the company's EBT. George pays 20p per share and the EBT pays £2.30 per share. The shares are registered in the EBT's and George's joint

What shares to use in the plan

names and they enter into an agreement setting out their respective rights in the JSOP shares: the EBT will be entitled to the first £3.00 per share of any sale proceeds that they receive, and the balance will belong to George.

Three years later, the JSOP shares are sold for £5.00 per share. The EBT takes its entitlement of £3.00 per share and George receives his entitlement of £2.00 per share.

This arrangement constitutes an "interest in securities" for the purposes of ITEPA 2003, meaning that the employees will be taxed on their interests in the JSOP shares under the same rules as apply to holding entire shares.

At the time that the employee acquires his or her interest in the shares, it will be "underwater", meaning that, at the date of acquisition, the counterparty is entitled to all of the value of the shares and the employee will only receive any value from the shares if their value grows significantly.

For this reason, the initial value of the employee's interest in the shares is usually quite low when compared to the value of the underlying shares, meaning that they can be acquired by the employees for a low price without taxable employment income being deemed to arise at that point.

When the employees and counterparties liquidate their interests in the shares, provided that there has been no value shifting between the joint owners (and assuming that the employee has entered into a joint election to disapply the restricted securities rules), then any uplift in the value of the shares attributable to the employee will be taxed under the CGT rules.

The main difficulty with JSOP arrangements is in valuing the employees' interests. This has proven to be quite difficult in a quoted company context, as market volatility makes it far easier to impute a meaningful hope value to the employees' interests. For illiquid private company shares, the position is far more straightforward, with valuations for JSOP shares being in line with standard growth share valuations.

10.3.4 Freezer shares

So-called "freezer shares" are a structure that is a mirror image of growth shares – these are shares that have their right to participate in the value of a company capped.

This is a mechanism that is often used in IHT planning, as it can allow parents to cap their interests in a company, allowing the children to benefit from future growth, but can also be seen in the context of employee share awards.

Example: freezer shares

George holds shares in his employer, PatCo Limited. George wishes to retire and, under the leavers' provisions in the articles of association of the company, would normally be obliged to offer his shares for sale to Pat, the main shareholder.

On a pro-rata basis, George's shares are worth £10.00 each, but after taking into account discounts for minority status and lack of marketability, the shares would only be worth £5.00 each.

Pat plans to start the process of putting the company up for sale over the course of the next year and is personally short of cash and would struggle to fund the purchase of George's shares.

George and Pat agree between them to vary the articles of association of the company, so that George does not have to sell his shares immediately, but such that their participation in the value of the company will be capped at their current undiscounted value of £10.00 per share.

The following year, PatCo Limited is sold at double the price, George receives £10.00 per share, while Pat receives the balance of the proceeds.

10.4 Company law considerations

10.4.1 Role of company law in employee share schemes

The following sections are intended to provide an overview of the company law issues that employee share schemes can give rise to. As is the case elsewhere in this book, the emphasis is on the issues facing private companies; the regime that public companies are subject to is more onerous, and the points of differentiation are flagged below.

10.4.2 Making changes to the company constitution

In preparation for the award of shares to employees a number of steps are likely to be needed, in particular:

- new articles of association, to ensure that employees' shares are subject to leavers' provisions, drag-along and tag-along (see below);
- the share capital of the company may need to be sub-divided, so that there are numerically enough shares to satisfy share awards (for example, a company may be incorporated with a single share with a £1.00 nominal value, which could be subdivided into 1,000 shares of £0.001 to allow new awards to be made over, say, 10% of the company's fully-diluted share capital);
- the shares held by the existing shareholders may be re-designated into separate classes of, say, A, B and C shares, with a view to making awards over a new class of D shares;
- redundant classes of shares (e.g. deferred shares) may be repurchased.

(Drag-along is the right of the majority shareholders to compel minority shareholders to join in a sale transaction with them. Tag-along gives the minority shareholders the means to ensure that they have the right to join in any sale, rather than be left behind by the majority shareholders.)

Changes to the company's share capital will usually require a special resolution of the shareholders, which must be passed by shareholders holding at least 75% of the voting rights in the company. Additional authorities may be required if the articles give classes of shares the right to veto changes to the articles.

In a private company context, these resolutions are typically passed as written resolutions of the members, which will have the same effect as if they had been passed at a general meeting of the company by virtue of CA 2006, s. 288.

141

10.4.3 Authority to issue shares

Before CA 2006 came into force, companies had an "authorised share capital", which set a cap on the number of shares that could be issued by the company and could only be varied by way of shareholders' resolution.

CA 2006 abolished the concept of "authorised share capital", but the Act still limits the rights of a company's directors to issue shares. As a minimum, newly issued shares are usually subject to pre-emption rights, meaning that they must first be offered to existing shareholders before they can be issued to new shareholders.

CA 2006, s. 566 disapplies pre-emption provisions when shares are being issued under an employees' share scheme, which is defined in CA 2006, s. 1166 as follows:

> "**1166 Employees' share scheme**
>
> For the purposes of the Companies Acts an employees' share scheme is a scheme for encouraging or facilitating the holding of shares in or debentures of a company by or for the benefit of—
>
> > (a) the bona fide employees or former employees of—
> >
> > > (i) the company,
> > >
> > > (ii) any subsidiary of the company, or
> > >
> > > (iii) the company's holding company or any subsidiary of the company's holding company, or
> >
> > (b) the spouses, civil partners, surviving spouses, surviving civil partners, or minor children or step-children of such employees or former employees."

The term "scheme" is not defined in the legislation, but is generally taken to mean an arrangement that could be extended to more than one employee on more than one occasion; a one-off arrangement between a company and a single employee is unlikely to meet the definition in the Act.

In a quoted company context, the rules under which the company is listed may stipulate that any employee share scheme is adopted by the shareholders before it is implemented and the directors may need specific authority allowing them to issue shares under the scheme.

Quoted companies also need to consider whether the exemptions from issuing a prospectus set out in the *European Prospectus Directive* (Directive 2003/71/EC) apply.

10.4.4 Financial assistance

The term "financial assistance" means any assistance given by a company to a person to purchase its own shares or shares in its parent undertaking. Examples of financial assistance that are relevant to employee share schemes include making contributions to an EBT to allow it to acquire shares for use in its share schemes or advancing loans to employees to allow them to buy shares.

Until CA 2006, both public and private companies needed to consider whether a share offer to employees constituted unlawful financial assistance; this constraint has been removed from private companies (i.e. companies that are not registered as "plc", irrespective of whether the shares are listed or not).

For public companies there is an exemption from the prohibition on financial assistance set out in CA 2006, s. 682, which allows companies acting in good faith to provide financial assistance for the purposes of an employees' share scheme.

10.4.5 Nominal value

Under UK company law, shares in a company will have a nominal or par value (in other jurisdictions, including the US and Jersey, it is possible for companies to issue shares that have a nil par value). When shares are issued, this par value must be paid up; if it is left outstanding or unpaid, in many cases the shares will not enjoy their full rights and in every case, the unpaid amount is treated as a debt owed to the company.

The statutory share schemes all demand that the shares acquired by employees are fully paid up. Where shares are newly issued shares, and the share awards or options carry a price that is at least equal to the shares' nominal value, then this presents few problems.

However, if options over new shares are granted at nil cost, either under the rules on EMI or under a non-qualifying option plan, then the company will have to find an alternative way to credit the shares as fully paid. This is typically done by capitalising some of the company's distributable reserves.

Example: issuing shares fully paid

PatCo Limited grants EMI options over newly issued £1 ordinary shares to George and to Philip. In recognition of George's long service with the company, he is granted nil-cost options. Philip is granted options with an exercise price of £5.00 per share – the shares' current market value.

Three years later, both George and Philip exercise their options and 5,000 shares are issued to each of them.

Philip will have paid his exercise price of £5 per share, of which £1 per share will be treated as paying up the shares' nominal value.

George will not have paid anything to exercise his options, which means that PatCo will need to capitalise £5,000 of its distributable reserves in order to treat the shares as fully paid.

Other approaches that can be adopted would be to use the proceeds of a new issuance of shares to fund the nominal value of shares or, in a private company context, it is relatively easy to point to non-cash consideration (for example, services provided) as paying up the nominal value of the shares. In such a case, the board could determine that it has received non-cash consideration equal to the nominal value of the shares (if, for example, the board determined that the services rendered by an employee were equal to the value of the nominal value to be paid up on shares, the accounting entries would be a debit to the employment cost account and a credit to share capital). This is, of course, entirely separate to the employment taxes analysis of the issuance of shares, which does not recognise anything except cash consideration.

11. Employee share schemes and employee trusts

11.1 Employee trusts and share schemes in general

It is not uncommon for companies to use employee trusts, commonly referred to as employee benefit trusts or EBTs, in their employee share schemes.

The term "EBT" has acquired a rather unfortunate association with aggressive and unsuccessful tax planning following the introduction of the disguised remuneration legislation in 2011 and the unwinding of the litigation involving Rangers Football Club. Because of this murky association, many advisers, including the author, are increasingly looking to other ways to describe employee trusts used in conjunction with employee share schemes, but for the purposes of the present work, the term EBT has largely been used.

An EBT can serve a number of purposes for the company:

- The EBT can act as a "buyer", to give shareholder liquidity in the shares, particularly for employees who may be exercising options or acquiring shares under employee share schemes.
- The EBT can also act as a "warehouse" to hold the shares that it has bought from other shareholders and to use them to satisfy employee share awards and options – this can be attractive where there are concerns about the dilutive effect of employee share schemes.

In order to qualify for most of the tax reliefs set out in the legislation, an EBT would need to exclude the company itself from benefiting. This means that the trust would be unable to settle the company's own liabilities, which can cause problems where an EBT is asked to settle existing awards made by the company.

However, where a new EBT is being established, its funding can be made contingent upon an agreement to settle pre-existing share options and share awards. Where it is proposed that existing share awards are settled by an EBT it would be necessary to check the terms under which the award has been made to ensure that there is nothing in the share scheme terms that would prevent the awards being settled in this way.

One point that will need to be considered is the potential income tax exposures that the trustees can face if they are in receipt of dividends. Although the legislation and ESCs allow either the trustees or beneficiaries some degree of relief for the double taxation, there can be a timing delay and possibly tax leakage.

Example: dividends received by EBT trustees

Philly Factors Limited establishes an employee share trust, which holds shares on behalf of its employees. The company pays a dividend to the EBT of £101,000. The trustees pay tax at the trust dividend rate of 38.1% on all of its income in excess of the first £1,000, which means that the trustees have a liability of £38,100.

The next tax year the trustees resolve to distribute the net value of the dividend, £62,900, to Sammy and Charlie, the company's senior engineers. As Sammy and Charlie are higher rate taxpayers, the trustees withhold tax and NIC at a combined rate of 42% from the payment, leaving Sammy and Charlie with £36,482 between them.

If the employee share trust is resident in the UK, it will be able to claim relief for the taxes borne by Sammy and Charlie under ITA 2007, s. 496A after the end of the tax year in which it makes the distribution. Section 496B quantifies that relief as the lesser of (i) the trust's s. 497 tax pool and (ii) the amount treated as taxable employment income multiplied by the trust tax rate – currently 45%. This amount is then deducted from the trust's tax pool.

In this example, the trustees would be able to reclaim the lesser of the value of the tax pool and £28,305 (i.e. £62,900 x 45%). Assuming that there have been no other distributions and no other income, this would leave the tax pool of the trust at £9,795 – enough to "frank" distributions of £21,767.

It would be possible for the trustees to use the refunded monies to make further distributions to Sammy and Charlie that would result in their receiving net amounts that equate to 58% of the gross dividend received by the trustees, but there would, at the minimum, be a cash flow/timing issue for the trustees to contend with.

If the trust is an offshore trust, then Sammy and Charlie would, after the end of the tax year, be able to claim relief under ESC B18, which is explained in more detail in TSEM 10440.

Under ESC B18, Sammy and Charlie would claim credit for the tax that had been paid by the trustee on the basis that the gross amount of taxable employment income that they received was "franked" by the trustee's tax payments at the rate of tax that the original income had been taxed in the hands of the trustees. In this case, Sammy and Charlie would apply to HMRC for relief at the dividend trust rate of 38.1% on £69,200.

This will mean that unless there is a dividend waiver in place, the trustees will have a tax liability whenever a dividend is paid on the class of shares held by the trustees.

The nature of trustees' fiduciary duties generally precludes them from waiving dividends. For this reason, many EBT deeds contain a waiver of dividend rights, often with the proviso that the trustees will be able to receive dividends if requested to do so by the board of directors of the company.

11.2 Establishing an employee trust

11.2.1 *Formalities*

An EBT will require an instrument to define who the settlor, trustees and beneficiaries will be. The employee trusts are structured as discretionary trusts for the benefit of the past, present or future employees of a particular company and its subsidiaries.

The trustees will be the legal owners and have control of any assets held within the trust. Many companies use dormant subsidiaries to act as trustee, the prohibition on subsidiaries owning shares in their parent undertaking only applies to beneficial ownership; as the trustee is acting in a fiduciary capacity, the prohibition does not apply. Alternatively, a professional trustee could be appointed.

Any shareholders' or investment agreements will need to be reviewed to see whether the directors have an obligation to seek shareholder or lender consent before establishing an EBT.

11.2.2 Situs

A UK resident trust must register with HMRC using the online trust registration service for self-assessment. New trusts will need to register online by 5 October following the end of tax year following the later of:

- the date that the trust has been set up; and
- the date that it starts to make income or chargeable gains.

For ease of compliance it may be easier to register a trust at the point when it is set up.

A UK resident trust will be subject to UK taxes on any worldwide income or gains generated within the trust (subject to double tax relief) all of which should be reported on a self-assessment trust tax return.

If all of the trustees are resident outside the UK, the trust would be treated as an offshore trust. The offshore trust would not need to register with HMRC for self-assessment, provided that there are no UK income or gains to report. Any professional advisers who assist in the establishment of an offshore employee trust will also have a separate obligation to notify HMRC that the trust has been established under IHTA 1984, s. 218.

11.2.3 Benefiting from IHT reliefs

IHTA 1984 provides for a number of exemptions from the normal IHT regime that applies to discretionary trusts. These exemptions are available to trusts that meet the requirements set out in IHTA 1984, s. 86.

Section 86 will apply where assets are held within a trust, either indefinitely or until the end of a period, for a class of beneficiaries defined by either their own employment with a company or the employment of a family member. An EBT will only qualify for these purposes if the class of beneficiaries comprises "all or most" of the employees or directors.

Any property settled into a qualifying EBT will not be treated as relevant property for IHT purposes and will be excluded from the ten-year anniversary charges.

Where a close company establishes an EBT, the contributions to a qualifying EBT will not be treated as a taxable transfer of value by virtue of IHTA 1984, s. 13 provided that the deed excludes the following persons from benefiting from the trust assets:

- a shareholder who is beneficially entitled to, or has rights to acquire, 5% or more of shares and on a winding up of the company is entitled to 5% or more of its assets;
- any person connected with that shareholder (as defined by IHTA 1984, s. 270); or
- any person who has been such a shareholder in the previous 10 years.

However, IHTA 1984, s. 13(4) disregards any powers that the trustees may have to make payments that will be treated as taxable employment income.

If the conditions set out in IHTA 1984, s. 13 are not met, contributions to an EBT set up by a close company could be treated as chargeable dispositions made by the company's major shareholders, although other exemptions may be available that would negate any charge (for example, payments made out of the working capital of a trading company will benefit from business property relief).

11.3 Funding an employee trust

11.3.1 Loan funding

There is an attraction to loan funding an employee trust, in that, if the EBT is left holding unallocated shares at the time of an exit, the EBT would be able to use part of all of its proceeds on disposing of its remaining shares to repay the indebtedness, which would be of benefit to the shareholders.

The difficulty with such an approach would be that the EBT, as a shareholder, would be a participator in the lender company. This would mean that the company would be obliged to account to HMRC for corporation tax under CTA 2010, s. 455 on the value of the loan. This tax charge would be repayable to the lender company when and if the loan was repaid by the EBT trustees.

In practice, if assets are left in an employee trust following a transaction, there has been an increasing willingness on the part of purchasers to recognise the value held in the employee trust in the purchase price paid for a company, on the basis that the purchaser will be able to use the trust assets to provide discretionary bonuses and other incentives to its employees.

11.3.2 Funding by way of contribution

No tax liabilities should arise if a company makes outright contributions to an employee trust, provided that the trust meets the requirements of IHTA 1984, s. 86 and s. 13.

The contributions to the employee trust would constitute "employee benefit contributions", falling within the scope of CTA 2009, Pt. 20. This means that the contributing company would be unable to deduct the contribution from its profits for corporation tax purposes. A separate corporation tax deduction may be available when shares are distributed to employees (see below), but a deduction in respect of the original contribution to the trust would only be available on the distribution of assets from the trust if:

- it can be shown that the original contributions were made wholly and exclusively for the purposes of trade; and
- the distributions are subject to PAYE and NIC.

11.3.3 Funding by way of individual gifts of assets

In the event that an individual shareholder transfers shares to an employee trust for no consideration (for example, a "bad leaver" is obliged to give up shares for no consideration), then, provided that the trust meets the conditions of IHTA 1984, s. 13, the transfer will be treated as occurring on a nil gain nil loss basis for CGT purposes. This relief does not require any claim or election.

Law: TCGA 1992, s. 239

11.4 Acquiring shares from employees or other shareholders

The acquisition of shares from employees and other shareholders by the trustees as part of a market value transaction should be treated as falling within the scope of the CGT rules.

The main exceptions to this general position are disposals that can give rise to employment taxes under one of the provisions discussed in **Chapter 5** above, and transactions that fall within the scope of the rules on transactions in securities.

The purchase of shares by an employee trust potentially falls within the scope of ITA 2007, Part 13, Chapter 1, as the transaction would be effectively funded by the sponsoring company of the trust. This means that HMRC could potentially issue counter-action notices, the effect of which would be to tax transactions between sellers of shares and an EBT as if they were dividend distributions.

In the event that a shareholder disposes of all of his or her holdings in a company by way of a sale to an employee trust, it would be unlikely that any counter-action would be issued, provided that the transaction's commercial rationale is clear. However, it may be desirable to make a clearance application under ITA 2007, s. 701 if individual shareholders are selling part of a large shareholding to an employee trust or selling in a series of transactions.

11.5 Using EBT assets to satisfy share awards – CGT

11.5.1 UK resident trust

Under TCGA 1992, s. 144(3), the grant of an option and exercise will be treated as a single transaction, by the original grantee. The grant of an option will not be treated as a disposal by the trustee of the employee trust, but the exercise of the option will be a disposal for CGT purposes.

The case of *Mansworth v Jelley* established that the exercise of an option is a transaction that is potentially within the scope of TCGA 1992, s. 17, meaning that the market value of the shares transferred to an option-holder on the exercise of an option would be substituted for the exercise price paid for the option.

In order to manage this type of exposure, TCGA 1992, s. 144ZA was introduced, which disapplies s. 17, so that when an option is exercised, the person who disposes of the shares is treated for the purposes of the CGT rules as having disposed of the shares for the exercise price paid for them.

In the context of an option granted under an EMI or other employee share scheme, when the employee exercises the option, a trustee would be treated as disposing of the shares acquired at the exercise price paid by the employee for CGT purposes.

HMRC's guidance at CG 56321 and 12397 supposes that an employee trust satisfying a share option granted by an employer company will benefit from the relief in s. 144ZA (although the wording of the section implies that only the grantor of an option can benefit from the relief).

Section 144ZA means that, in practice, an EBT's exposure to CGT can be managed, provided that the aggregate price paid by the trustees to acquire shares exceeds the exercise price of the options that those shares are intended to satisfy.

If the trust acquires a significant number of shares at a comparatively low value and future options are priced above that value, there could be a significant exposure for the trust.

Example 1: TCGA 1992, s. 144ZA

The Philly Factors Limited UK resident employee trust grants options over 10,000 shares to Sammy with a strike price of £1.00 per share. The trust acquired the shares from an outgoing employee, Charlie, for £5.00 per share.

Two years later Sammy pays the trustee £10,000 to exercise the option. At this time the shares are valued at £10.00 each.

In the trustee's tax return the transaction is recorded as having given rise to a loss of £40,000 (i.e. (£5.00-£1.00) x 10,000) by virtue of TCGA 1992, s. 144ZA.

Awards made under CSOP, SIP and SAYE schemes are also protected from CGT by a separate relief provided for in Sch. 7D to TCGA 1992, which exempts gains from charge where made by trustees satisfying awards or options under these schemes.

The final exemption for trustees is set out in TCGA 1992, s. 239ZA, which provides that qualifying free share awards to employees will be exempt from CGT. In order to qualify, a number of criteria must be met:

Employee share schemes and employee trusts

- the trust must fall within IHTA 1984, s. 86;
- no consideration of any sort may be given for the share award;
- the whole value of the shares must be treated as taxable employment income in the employee's hands; and
- the employee must not hold either 5% or more of the share capital of the company or more than 5% of any class of shares in the capital of the company.

If a share award does not fall within s. 144ZA, s. 239ZA or Sch. 7D, it will be treated as a non-arm's length transaction within the scope of TCGA 1992, s. 17 and the trustees will be taxed as if they had disposed of shares at their market value.

Example 2: qualifying and non-qualifying share awards

The Philly Factors Limited UK resident employee share trust holds 5,000 ordinary shares with a current market value of £10 per share and 2,000 B shares, which are valued at £1 each – there are no other B shares in issue. The trustees acquired the ordinary shares for £2 each and the B shares for £0.10 each.

On 1 July the trustees resolve to make the following share awards:

- To Sammy, 2,500 ordinary shares for a discounted price of £1.00 per share;
- To Charlie, 2,000 B shares for no consideration.

On 1 September the trustees resolve to distribute the remaining 2,500 ordinary shares to Charlie for no consideration.

The award of ordinary shares to Sammy is made for consideration, which means that it will not fall within TCGA 1992, s. 239ZA – the trustees will be treated as having realised a chargeable gain of £20,000 (i.e. (£10-£2) x 2,500).

The award of B shares to Charlie is made for free and meets the requirements of the legislation. The trustees are treated as having realised a gain of £1,800 (i.e. (£1-£0.10) x 2,000), but this gain is exempt from tax.

The second award of shares to Charlie is more problematic: Charlie now holds 100% of the B shares in issue, which means that the relief cannot be given to the trustees, who are treated as having realised a chargeable gain of £20,000 (i.e. (£10-£2) x 2,500).

Case: *Mansworth (HMIT) v Jelley* [2003] BTC 3, STC 53

11.5.2 Offshore trust

If an employee trust is established offshore, any gains arising in the hands of the trustees would fall outside the scope of UK CGT. HMRC accept that this type of EBT does not constitute a "settlement" and is not subject to the regime in TCGA 1992, s. 86 and s. 87, meaning that the rules that charge beneficiaries for gains made by trustees do not apply.

Against this beneficial tax regime must be set the costs of establishing and maintaining an offshore trust, which can run to several thousand pounds per annum.

11.6 Using EBT assets to satisfy share awards – disguised remuneration

11.6.1 Background to the rules

Assets held within any employee trust are potentially subject to the rules on disguised remuneration, which can be found in ITEPA 2003, Pt. 7A.

The disguised remuneration rules apply where an arrangement meets the gateway requirements set out in ITEPA 2003, s. 554A:

"(a) a person ("A") is an employee, or former or prospective employee, of another person ("B"),

(b) there is an arrangement ("the relevant arrangement") to which A is a party or which otherwise (wholly or partly) covers or relates to A,

(c) It is reasonable to suppose that, in essence–

(i) the relevant arrangement, or

(ii) the relevant arrangement so far as it covers of relates to A,

is (wholly or partly) a means of providing, or is otherwise concerned (wholly or partly) with the provision of, rewards or recognition or loans in connection with A's employment, or former or prospective employment, with B,

(d) a relevant step is taken by a relevant third person, and

(e) it is reasonable to suppose that, in essence–

    (i) the relevant step is taken (wholly or partly) in pursuance of the relevant arrangement, or

    (ii) there is some other connection (direct or indirect) between the relevant step and the relevant arrangement."

Any properly operated employee share trust will clearly fall within the criteria set out in s. 554A, as the purpose of the arrangement is to provide rewards to members of a company's staff in recognition of their employment with that company.

Where any of the following "relevant steps" are taken, the value of the "relevant step" is treated as taxable employment income and will give rise to NIC and a PAYE withholding obligation:

- earmarking a sum of money or an asset, with a view to taking a relevant step in the future;
- paying a sum of money or transferring an asset to an employee;
- making an asset available to an employee on terms similar to absolute ownership of the asset.

A standard employee share scheme, with options satisfied from trust assets, runs the risk that the trustees will be deemed to have earmarked assets on behalf of employees and will have transferred assets on satisfying the options.

These rules should not apply where the arrangements fall within the exemptions in the legislation.

11.6.2 *Exemptions for statutory share schemes*

ITEPA 2003, s. 554E makes an explicit exemption where a relevant step is taken for the sole purpose of making awards under a statutory share scheme, including granting options, acquiring or holding shares which will then be used in a statutory share scheme, or satisfying qualifying share awards.

The exemptions in s. 554E are dependent on two restrictions:

- the inevitable TAAR – there must be no direct or indirect connection between the relevant step and a tax avoidance arrangement; and
- the EBT, insofar as it relates to the statutory share scheme, must not be "over-funded", meaning that it must not hold more shares of any type than might reasonably be expected to be needed to satisfy awards in a ten-year period.

11.6.3   Exemptions for non-qualifying share incentives

Additional reliefs are available where the company has granted other forms of share incentive, for example, non-qualifying options to persons who do not meet the working time requirements of the EMI Code. They fall into two categories:

- earmarking charges are disapplied by sections 554J-554M, which apply to share awards and share options that have a realistic risk of lapsing without value being passed to the employees;
- charges under s. 554(C) on the transfer of shares pursuant to the exercise of an option are disapplied by s. 554N where the option is an employment-related securities option and tax charges arise under ITEPA 2003, s. 476 (exercise of options) when the options are exercised.

The four sections giving relief from earmarking charges deal with two types of share incentive, share options (sections 554L and 554M) and share award schemes (sections 554J and 554K, which also extend to "phantom" share arrangements). These provisions distinguish between incentives that only vest on an "exit" (sections 554K and 554M) and incentives that are not exit based (sections 554J and 554L). Other than adaptations to reflect the legal structures of the share incentives and their vesting provisions, the requirements of the four sections are essentially the same:

- The scheme itself must meet the following criteria:
    a. the main purpose of the incentive must not be to provide "relevant benefits" (meaning retirement benefits),

b. the terms of the incentive must defer the date on which the employee can benefit from it and must be at risk of forfeiture if specified conditions are not met,
   c. the vesting date must not be more than ten years after the award date, and
   d. there must be a reasonable chance that the incentive might be forfeited.
- The assets being earmarked for use in the incentive must be securities issued by the employer company (or a group company) within the definition set out in ITEPA 2003, s. 420(1)(b).
- The scheme must not be "overfunded".
- On the vesting date of a share award, or on the final date on which a share option can be exercised, either:
   a. the shares are acquired by the employee, who is taxed under the relevant section within ITEPA 2003, Pt. 7;
   b. if the award is a "phantom", the cash amount is paid out to the employee and taxed as taxable employment income; or
   c. the option or award lapses and the shares cease to be earmarked.

If the trustee earmarks securities for use in a scheme, but the proposed grants are not made within a 3-month window, then, if the securities are still earmarked, the exemption from charge will be lost. Similarly, if the trustee continues to hold earmarked shares after the termination of the employee share scheme, the exemption will cease to apply and a charge will arise.

The relief will also be lost if the trustees change the reasons for earmarking shares – for example, the share incentive lapses but the trustees continue to hold the shares earmarked for a particular employee.

Without the exclusion, income tax and NIC would be due under PAYE, irrespective of whether the shares in question were readily convertible assets, at the time that the trustees agreed to settle the options.

For most employers operating share schemes through an EBT, it should be straightforward to arrange their affairs so that the exemptions in Part 7A apply; the tax treatment of the employees should be unaffected by the use of a trust to satisfy employee share awards.

11.7 Using EBT assets to satisfy share awards – CT relief

As the assets held in the EBT will be used to satisfy share awards, the rules in CTA 2009, Pt. 12, which are discussed in detail at **Chapter 6**, will govern the availability of deductions for the employer company.

The rules in Part 12 take priority over any other basis for claiming deductions, but if relief under Part 12 is not available for any reason, any deductions will be governed by CTA 2009, Pt. 20.

Any contributions made to the trust will constitute "employee benefit contributions" for the purposes of CTA 2009, Pt. 20. This means that deductions are not be allowed for EBT contributions unless and until benefits were provided to employees out of the trust assets and unless:

- the benefits are taxable when they are received by the employees; and
- the receipt of the benefits gives rise to a liability to employer NIC.

Finance Act 2017 introduced additional conditions so that deductions will not be allowable unless qualifying benefits are provided from the EBT within five years of the end of period in which the contribution is made. If the qualifying benefits give rise to both an income tax charge and a National Insurance charge, the tax and NIC must be paid within 12 months of the period in which the deduction of tax and NIC would otherwise be allowed.

11.8 Transactions

If there are unallocated shares held within an employee trust at the time that there is a sale of the sponsoring company, the trustees would sell those shares as part of the transaction, potentially giving rise to a substantial CGT liability if the trustees are resident in the UK.

The only way that any resulting cash held by the trustees could be used would be to pay it out to beneficiaries – any such transaction would constitute a "relevant step" for the purposes of ITEPA 2003, Pt. 7A and would give rise to PAYE and NIC liabilities for both the employer and employee. No credit would be given for the CGT that the trustees had already suffered.

Example: transaction with UK resident EBT

Philly Factors Limited is sold to Liz Corp. for £15.00 per share. At the time of the transaction, the company's UK-resident employee trust holds 9,000 unallocated shares, which it acquired with third party debt funding of £18,000.

The trustees sell their shares as part of the transaction, and are left with proceeds of £135,000, from which they must settle their indebtedness of £18,000 and their CGT liability:

Proceeds	£135,000
Deduct base cost	(£18,000)
Deduct trustee annual exemption	(£5,650)
Chargeable gain	£111,350
CGT @ 20%	£22,270

The trustees have net proceeds of £94,730, which they distribute to Sammy and Charlie in equal shares, from which PAYE and NIC are deducted, leaving Sammy and Charlie with net proceeds of £54,943 in total (i.e. £94,730-42%).

The company will have an employer NIC liability of £13,073, which translates into a net liability of £10,589 after corporation tax relief at 19% has been allowed.

There is no corporation tax relief available to the company in respect of the distribution to Sammy and Charlie: the distribution was in cash, not shares, which means that CTA 2009, Pt. 12 is not in point; the company has not made any contributions to the trust that can be deducted under CTA 2009, Pt. 20.

If the trustees had, instead, granted options to Sammy and Charlie with a strike price of £18,000, no gain would have arisen in the trust, the EBT would have had sufficient funds to repay the third party debt and the employer company would have been entitled to claim relief on the share award under CTA 2009, Pt. 12.

A potential purchaser may be willing to adjust the purchase price to reflect the assets held in the EBT, which could be used to provide future benefits to employees, but in the absence of such an offer, shareholders would be unable to derive any benefit from the trust assets.

For this reason, in a private company context, consideration should always be given to the likely use of trust assets and to ensuring that they are fully distributed in the event of a transaction.

Part 5: Statutory share schemes

12. Introduction to the statutory schemes

12.1 An overview

ITEPA 2003 legislates for four types of statutory share scheme, three of which are share option schemes, while the fourth is a share award/share-holding vehicle.

The option schemes are enterprise management incentives ("EMI"), company share option plans ("CSOP") and save as you earn ("SAYE" or "Sharesave"). The fourth scheme is the share incentive plan ("SIP").

EMI and CSOP are both "discretionary" schemes, meaning that they can be offered to individual participants as a company sees fit, whilst SIP and SAYE must essentially be offered to the whole workforce on similar terms.

Each of the statutory share schemes confers tax advantages on its participants:

- the three option schemes allow employees to benefit from capital treatment on the growth in value of their option shares between the date of grant and the date of exercise;
- SIP potentially allows employees to receive awards of shares that are totally exempt from tax.

Employers benefit from the schemes because there are employer NIC savings available to them and the schemes allow the employer to access corporation tax relief. For the option schemes, this will be on the conventional basis set out in CTA 2009, Pt. 12 (see **Chapter 6** above). For SIPs, there are separate rules governing the reliefs available to the employer.

Historically, CSOP, SAYE and SIP schemes had to be pre-approved by HMRC before awards could be granted, which is why these schemes are sometimes referred to as "approved" schemes. Since FA 2014, the rules on these three schemes have been aligned with EMI: the approval process has been abolished; instead, it is up to the employer to certify that their share plan meets the requirements of the legislation and that its schemes qualify for relief. To differentiate between qualifying and non-qualifying schemes, the legislation unfortunately names qualifying schemes "Schedule 2 SIPs", "Schedule 3 SAYEs" and "Schedule 4 CSOPs". (It probably sounded better in the original Klingon.)

In each case, the statutory draftsman has helpfully set out the relevant parts of the tangled mess of statute in the first paragraph of the four schedules to ITEPA 2003 that form the legislative backbones of the statutory share schemes.

12.2 Enterprise management incentives

12.2.1 Background

EMI was introduced to support small and medium-sized enterprises ("SMEs") and has similar qualification criteria to those applying to the enterprise investment scheme (discussed in more detail in **Chapter 13** below).

Of the four schemes, EMI is probably the most flexible for both the employer and employees, and can be used as a framework to provide a variety of share awards.

Under EMI, an employer can grant options to selected employees on such terms as he or she sees fit:

- the option price, if any, can be set at a level to suit the employer's commercial objectives – there is no statutory minimum;
- options can be granted on terms that allow them to vest immediately or only on the occurrence of an exit event;
- options can be made subject to the satisfaction of performance conditions or not, as the employer determines;
- the limits on the value of options that can be granted to an individual are generous – up to £250,000 per participant;
- the overall limit on grants of £3m is also rarely problematic for qualifying companies;
- there are few limits on the type of share that can be offered to employees under EMI.

12.2.2 Outline of the tax treatment

Under the EMI Code:

- no tax charges arise on the grant of an option;
- when an EMI option is exercised then, provided it is still a qualifying option, the employee will be treated as having received taxable employment income equal to the difference, if any, between the exercise price and the AMV of the shares (see **Chapter 2**) at the date of grant;
- if at least one year passes between the date of grant of an EMI option and the date on which the shares are sold, the employee can qualify for entrepreneurs' relief.

When an EMI option is exercised, the employer will be entitled to claim corporation tax relief under CTA 2009, Pt. 12 on the difference between the market value of the option shares at the date of exercise and the price, if any, paid by the employee to exercise the options.

Example: qualifying EMI option exercise

Van Hire Limited grants a qualifying EMI option to Helen over 1,000 shares. The shares have an AMV of £5.00 per share when they are granted, and the options have an exercise price equal to the shares' par value of £0.10 per share.

Two years later, the owner of Van Hire Limited decides to sell the company to an investor for £70.00 per share and Helen exercises her option and sells her shares as part of the transaction.

On exercising her option, Helen will be treated as having received taxable employment income of £4,900 (i.e. (£5.00-£0.10) x 1,000), which will be subject to PAYE at Helen's marginal rate of 40% and employee NIC of 2%, as the options are being exercised when the shares are readily convertible assets.

Helen will be treated as having realised a chargeable gain of £65,000 (i.e. her £70,000 proceeds minus her base cost, which is made up of the exercise price of £100 plus the amount treated as taxable employment income of £4,900), on which Helen is able to claim entrepreneurs' relief.

Helen's position is as follows (ignoring any annual exemption or brought forward losses):

Proceeds	£70,000
PAYE and EE NIC (£4,900 @ 42%)	(£2,058)
CGT (£65,000 @ 10%)	(£6,500)
Exercise price (1,000 x £0.10)	(£100)
Net proceeds	**£61,342**

From the perspective of the other shareholders, the position is as follows (assuming that the purchaser gives the shareholders credit for the CT relief generated and that the company is able to utilise it):

Proceeds forgone	£70,000
Exercise price	(£100)
Employer NIC (£4,900 @ 13.8%)	£676
CT relief (£676 + £70,000-£100 @ 19%)	(£13,409)
Total cost to employer	**£57,167**

In this example, it has cost the owners of Van Hire Limited around £0.93 to provide Helen with £1.00 of net proceeds (i.e. £57,167 ÷ £61,342).

By way of a comparison, assuming that Helen was an additional rate taxpayer, if she had received a bonus of the same gross value, she would have received net proceeds of £37,100 (i.e. £70,000-47%), while the cost to Van Hire Limited would have been c.£64,525 (i.e. (£70,000 + 13.8%)-19%), a cost of about £1.74 to deliver £1 of net value to Helen.

For more detail on the tax treatment of EMI options, please see **13.5** below.

12.3 Company share option plans

12.3.1 Background

CSOP is one of the older statutory share schemes, and had largely fallen out of favour with businesses for a number of reasons:

- the scheme limits are comparatively ungenerous – an employee may only hold options over shares valued at £30,000 at the date of grant;

Introduction to the statutory schemes

- the rules were rigid – options exercised before the third anniversary of grant did not qualify for relief unless the option-holder was one of a limited class of "good leavers";
- there were strict limits on the types of shares that could be used in the scheme (these have been largely relaxed);
- the approval process that existed before 2014 was slow and, at times, tortuous; and
- before the changes to CGT in 2008 and the introduction of lower tax rates, CSOP only offered employers and employees an NIC saving.

All of these factors made CSOP unattractive to companies, especially smaller, unquoted companies.

Over successive Finance Acts, the rules on CSOP have been relaxed and the scheme is far more attractive to companies:

- there is no need to have a CSOP plan pre-approved; instead companies notify HMRC that a qualifying scheme has been established;
- the tax rules have been relaxed, so that employees can still benefit from income tax relief if an option is exercised early in the context of the sale of the company;
- the limitations on the rights of the shares that can be offered to employees have been relaxed, although there is still a requirement about how the shares are held (explained in more detail at **14.1.1** below);
- the option price must at least equal the market value of the shares at the date of grant and, for an unquoted company, must be agreed in advance with HMRC;
- options can be granted on terms that allow them to vest immediately or only on the occurrence of an exit event;
- options can be made subject to the satisfaction of performance conditions or not, as the employer determines;
- the limits on the value of options that can be granted to an individual remain at £30,000 per participant;

167

Part 5: Statutory share schemes

- there is no overall limit on the plan, nor is there any restriction on the type of trade that the company offering CSOP options may carry on.

12.3.2 Outline of the tax treatment

Under the CSOP code:

- no tax charges arise on the grant of an option (note – there is an exception, see **14.3.1** below);
- there will be no tax to pay when an option is exercised, provided that it is exercised on the latest of:
    - the third anniversary of the date of grant,
    - the date of a sale of the company, or
    - the date on which an employee becomes a "good leaver";
- if the option shares are sold, any growth in the value of the option shares will be subject to CGT at the normal rate.

When a CSOP option is exercised, the employer will be entitled to claim corporation tax relief under CTA 2009, Pt. 12 on the difference between the market value of the option shares at the date of exercise and the price paid by the employee to exercise the options.

Example: qualifying CSOP exercise

Following the acquisition of Van Hire Limited, the new investor wishes to grant options to key members of the management team. The company has grown too large to grant EMI options and so the investor establishes a Sch. 4 CSOP over shares in the new holding company, Van Hire Topco Limited.

Helen is granted CSOP options over 20,000 shares, which are valued at £1.50 per share and have a strike price equal to their market value. Four years later, the company is floated on the stock exchange, Helen exercises the options and sells her shares for £10.00 each in the flotation.

As Helen has exercised her option in a qualifying manner, she will have no income tax to pay when the option is exercised and will pay CGT on her gains on the sale of her shares. Helen's position is as follows:

Proceeds	£200,000
CGT (£170,000 @ 20%)	(£34,000)
Exercise price (20,000 x £1.50)	(£30,000)
Net proceeds	**£136,000**

From the shareholder's perspective, the position is as follows:

Proceeds forgone	£200,000
Exercise price	(£30,000)
CT relief (£200,000-£30,000 @ 19%)	(£32,300)
Total cost to employer	**£137,700**

In this example, it has cost the owners of Van Hire Limited around £0.99 to provide Helen with £1.00 of net proceeds (i.e. £136,000 ÷ £137,700).

Law: ITEPA 2003, Sch. 4

12.4 SAYE

12.4.1 Background

SAYE is an all-employee option plan that, despite some high-profile scheme closures, has continued to be used by companies to enable employees to benefit from tax-advantaged savings and share options:

- SAYE combines two elements:
    - a savings plan, that allows employees to contribute up to £500 per month from their net earnings to a savings account, and
    - share options that can be exercised on the maturity of the savings account;
- the options can be granted with a discounted exercise price – the discount can be up to 20% of the market value of the shares on the date of grant;
- the savings plan can have a 3-year or 5-year maturity (it is up to the company to decide whether to offer savings contracts over three or five years);
- the number of shares that can be acquired under the options is calculated by dividing the exercise price by the overall value of the savings account at the maturity date;

- the savings account will attract interest, expressed as additional months' savings, on the maturity date – although at the time of writing low interest rates in the economy generally mean that the "bonus rate" on the SAYE savings account is zero;
- SAYE options must be offered to the entire workforce of the companies in a group that elect to participate in a plan, so it is not possible to pick and choose between employees to participate;
- SAYE is a one-way bet for employees, who can choose not to exercise their options and who can withdraw their savings at any time.

Given the savings-linked nature of the plan, the tendency is for employees to wish to realise the value in their options when their savings accounts mature; if the company has done well over a period, the employees may have a bonanza windfall when the options are exercised and shares sold.

As with CSOP, SAYE schemes no longer need to be pre-approved by HMRC; it is instead up to employers to design qualifying plans and to register the scheme once awards have been made. If the shares in question are not quoted on a recognised stock exchange, the company will need to agree values with HMRC to use in the scheme.

12.4.2 Outline of the tax treatment

Under the SAYE code:

- no tax charges arise on the grant of an option;
- there will be no tax to pay when an option is exercised, provided that it is exercised on the latest of:
  - the third anniversary of the date of grant,
  - the date of a sale of the company, or
  - the date on which an employee becomes a "good leaver";
- if the option shares are sold, any growth in the value of the option shares will be subject to CGT at the normal rates.

When a SAYE option is exercised, the employer will be entitled to claim corporation tax relief under CTA 2009, Pt. 12 on the difference between the market value of the option shares at the date of exercise and the price paid by the employee to exercise the options.

Example: qualifying SAYE exercise

Van Hire TopCo Limited has floated on the main list of the London Stock Exchange as Van Hire plc.

In order to reward its employee group as a whole, the company establishes a Sch. 3 SAYE plan and makes an offer to its employees to participate in the plan; the company only offers 3-year savings contracts. Helen and Tom both sign up. Helen decides to save £200 per month, while Tom can only afford to save £50 per month.

At the date of grant, the market value of a share in Van Hire plc is £15.00. The company elects to offer the employees the maximum discount of 20%, meaning that the exercise price of the options is £12.00 per share.

At the maturity date of the savings contracts the share price is £20.00; both Helen and Tom elect to exercise their options. Helen receives 600 shares on the exercise of her options (i.e. £200 x 36 ÷ £12.00) and Tom receives 150 shares (i.e. £50 x 36 ÷ £12.00). They both elect to sell their shares, receiving proceeds of £12,000 and £3,000 respectively. Neither has CGT to pay, because of the combination of the exercise price (their base cost) and their annual exemptions.

Law: ITEPA 2003, Sch. 3

12.5 Share incentive plans

12.5.1 Background

Share incentive plans were introduced in FA 2000. Originally named "all employee share ownership plans" or AESOPs, they were renamed to avoid confusion with ESOPs – employee share ownership plans – a term used for share schemes more generally; the draftsman was seemingly unaware of self-invested personal pensions at the time of the change.

SIP can be best described as a tax-efficient "wrapper", like the ISA rules, that can be used to envelope a number of different types of share awards.

SIP has an undeserved reputation for complexity, which is mainly the result of the flexibility and comprehensiveness of the scheme, and, as a share award scheme and not an option scheme, it has its own very different rules to the other statutory share schemes.

The SIP regime has the following features:

- SIP is an all-employee plan – participation in SIP must be offered on "similar terms" to all employees of participating companies;
- awards under SIP can be made in four forms:
  - partnership shares – employees may be allowed to purchase shares out of their gross earnings (effectively a form of salary sacrifice in exchange for shares),
  - matching shares – an employer may choose to gift up to two additional shares for every partnership share acquired by the employees,
  - free shares – this is a simple award of shares to participants, and
  - dividend shares – employees may choose to reinvest dividends in further company shares;

  employers are not obliged to offer all of these elements to employees; it is open to them to pick and choose between the various elements of SIP;
- SIP shares are held in an employee share trust, rather than being registered in the employees' names;
- free and matching shares can be subject to performance conditions;
- shares must be held within the trust for a fixed holding period to maximise the tax savings;
- the scheme is extremely tax efficient – if the employees meet the holding criteria the shares can be sold from the trust without any taxes or social security charges arising at all;
- the rules allow SIP shares to be sold early if there is a takeover without giving rise to taxes for the employees;

Introduction to the statutory schemes

- a range of statutory corporation tax deductions are available to employers under SIP; and
- like SAYE and CSOP, the approval process for SIP has been abolished – employers just have to design a qualifying plan and register it with HMRC.

12.5.2 Outline of the tax treatment

Once shares have been awarded under SIP they are held in a dedicated employee share trust. No tax will arise while the shares are held in the SIP trust provided that the company, the employee and the SIP scheme itself continue to qualify.

The tax point for the employees will be the date on which shares are withdrawn from the SIP trust. If the shares have been held for the appropriate holding period, they can be withdrawn tax-free.

For free, partnership and matching shares, if the shares are kept in the trust for five years, they can be withdrawn without any income tax charges arising. Dividend shares can be withdrawn tax-free on the third anniversary of award.

If free, matching or partnership shares are withdrawn before the third anniversary of award, the market value of the shares on the date that they are withdrawn will constitute taxable employment income in their hands. If the shares are withdrawn between the third and fifth anniversary of the date of award, the lesser of the value of the shares on the date of withdrawal and the initial value (i.e. for free and matching shares, their market value on the date of award, for partnership shares the value of the salary sacrificed to acquire them) will count as taxable employment income.

If dividend shares are withdrawn before the third anniversary of award, the value of the dividends used to acquire them will be treated as taxable dividend income in the employee's hands.

If the company is taken over before the end of the holding period, or if the employee leaves for one of the reasons set out in the legislation, the individual may be able to withdraw the shares without tax charges arising.

For CGT purposes, the employee is treated as having acquired any shares withdrawn from a SIP at their market value on the date of

Part 5: Statutory share schemes

withdrawal. If the employee sells the shares on the date of withdrawal he or she will not suffer CGT on any gains made.

Example: SIP shares

Van Hire plc establishes a SIP and invites its employees to acquire partnership shares, which it matches 1:1 with matching shares. Van Hire plc does not offer free shares, but it does give its employees the chance to reinvest in dividend shares.

Helen and Tom both sign up – Helen contributes £1,200 per year to the plan and Tom contributes £750 per year – and both elect to reinvest their dividends. Both are higher rate taxpayers, so the annual cost to each in net terms is £696 for Helen (i.e. £1,200 – 42%) and £435 for Tom (i.e. £750-42%).

The plan is run over three years:

- Year 1: the price of the partnership shares is £5.00 per share; dividends of £0.60 per share are paid;
- Year 2: the price is £7.00 per share; dividends of £0.80 are paid;
- Year 3: the price is £10.00 per share; dividends total £1.00 per share.

Helen acquires the following shares:

- Year 1
    - Partnership – 240 (i.e. £1,200 ÷ £5.00)
    - Matching – 240
    - Dividend – 57 (i.e. 480 x £0.60 ÷ £5.00)
    - Running total – 537
- Year 2
    - Partnership – 171 (i.e. £1,200 ÷ £7.00)
    - Matching – 171
    - Dividend – 100 (i.e. (537 +342) x £0.80 ÷ £7.00)
    - Running total – 979

- Year 3
    - Partnership – 120 (i.e. £1,200 ÷ £10.00)
    - Matching – 120
    - Dividend – 121 (i.e. (979 + 240) x £1.00 ÷ £10.00)
    - Running total – 1,340

Tom's holdings are as follows:

- Year 1
    - Partnership – 150 (i.e. £750 ÷ £5.00)
    - Matching – 150
    - Dividend – 36 (i.e. 300 x £0.60 ÷ £5.00)
    - Running total – 336
- Year 2
    - Partnership – 107 (i.e. £750 ÷ £7.00)
    - Matching – 107
    - Dividend – 62 (i.e. (336 +214) x £0.80 ÷ £7.00)
    - Running total – 612
- Year 3
    - Partnership – 75 (i.e. £750 ÷ £10.00)
    - Matching – 75
    - Dividend – 76 (i.e. (612 + 150) x £1.00 ÷ £10.00)
    - Running total – 838

Neither Helen nor Tom suffers tax charges on the awards at the time that they are made.

The company enters a period of difficult trading and does not make further awards under the scheme for a period.

Tom leaves the company in Year 6 and withdraws all of his SIP shares and sells them for £12.00 per share and realises £10,056 in total. The tax consequences for Tom are as follows:

- Year 1 shares have been held for more than five years and can be withdrawn tax free;
- Year 2
  - the dividend shares have been held for more than three years and can be withdrawn tax free,
  - the partnership and matching shares have not been held for five years, but have been held for more than three years – Tom will be taxed on the lower of the value of the shares when they were originally awarded/purchased and their value when they are withdrawn,
  - Tom is treated as having received taxable employment income of £1,498 (i.e. (107 + 107) x £7.00);
- Year 3
  - the dividend shares have been held for less than three years, so the value of the dividend used to buy the dividend shares is treated as taxable dividend income (i.e. £760),
  - the partnership and matching shares have been held for less than three years, so Tom is treated as having received taxable employment income equal to the current market value of the shares, i.e. (75 + 75) x £12.00 = £1,800;
- In total, Tom is treated as having received taxable employment income of £3,298 and taxable dividend income of £760. As a higher rate taxpayer, Tom pays tax and NIC of £1,632.16 (i.e. (£3,298 x 42%) + (£760 x 32.5%)).

Helen leaves her shares in the SIP trust and does not suffer any tax charges.

Law: ITEPA 2003, Sch. 2

12.6 The statutory schemes in an OMB context

Because SAYE is really a savings vehicle, with a fixed maturity date, it is most suited to companies whose shares are listed on the stock exchange or have some other market for employees to realise the value of their shares. For this reason, and the added complexity of the linked savings arrangement, SAYE schemes are rarely seen in a private company context.

EMI is rightly seen as the "go to" share scheme for private companies, on the basis that it can be implemented easily and has significant tax advantages for both the employee and employer. The main reasons for companies to seek an alternative to EMI are:

- the commercial intention is to give the employees an immediate interest in shares, which is incompatible with an option scheme;
- there is little prospect of an exit that would allow employees to realise value from a share option;
- the company does not meet the requirements to grant qualifying EMI options; or
- the company wishes the employees to build up a significant shareholding over time, possibly with the chance to reinvest dividends.

Where a company is not able to grant qualifying EMI options, a CSOP may give the company a viable alternative route to grant tax-advantaged options to employees. The implementation process is less straightforward, but it can be a way for employees to benefit from capital treatment on their option gains, while giving the company the benefits that a share option structure confers.

In the other circumstances mentioned above, private companies tend to look to non-statutory arrangements like growth shares or partly paid shares to give employees a shareholding. Following the reforms that culminated in the abolition of the approval process in 2014, SIP is far easier for private companies to implement and could provide a vehicle to allow employees to access tax-free share rewards, without the complexity and uncertainty that is inherent in the non-statutory approaches.

Part 5: Statutory share schemes

12.7 Comparison between statutory and non-statutory remuneration – example

Example

Type of award	Cash	Non-statutory options	Growth shares	CSOP options	EMI options
Gross value of shares	-	250,000	220,000	250,000	250,000
Exercise price	-	30,000	-	30,000	30,000
Gross value of award	220,000	220,000	220,000	220,000	220,000
Value treated as taxable employment income	220,000	220,000	-	-	-
Value subject to CGT	-	-	220,000	220,000	220,000
Income tax @ 45%	99,000	99,000	-	-	-
Employee NIC @ 2%	4,400	4,400	-	-	-
CGT @ 20%	-	-	44,000	44,000	-
CGT @ 10%	-	-	-	-	22,000
Total employee taxes	103,400	103,400	44,000	44,000	22,000
Net value of award	116,600	116,600	176,000	176,000	198,000
Employer NIC @ 13.8%	30,360	30,360	-	-	-
CT relief at 17%	42,561	42,561	-	37,400	37,400

Introduction to the statutory schemes

Type of award	Cash	Non-statutory options	Growth shares	CSOP options	EMI options
Total cost to employer	207,799	207,799	220,000	182,600	182,600
Cost to employer of providing £1 of benefit to employee	1.78	1.78	1.25	1.04	0.92

The example shown above makes the following assumptions:

- The value of the awards is based on a cash bonus of £220,000, growth shares that have a hurdle of £30,000 in aggregate and options (CSOP, EMI and non-statutory) with an exercise price of £30,000 in aggregate.
- There is a 3-year performance period between the date of grant/award and the date that the awards are realised.
- There is a market for the shares, which are sold on the vesting date.
- The CSOP and EMI options continue to qualify throughout the vesting period.
- Annual exemptions and possible brought forward capital losses are ignored.
- The recipients are already additional rate taxpayers.
- The company is within the charge to corporation tax and is able to utilise its losses. (The corporation tax rate stated here is the rate that has been announced will be in force for periods commencing on or after 1 April 2020).
- The cash payment is deductible and is not treated as a capital item (a point that HMRC have raised with some exit bonuses).

Part 5: Statutory share schemes

- The cost to the employer is calculated by taking the gross value of the award (for share options, this is the value of the shares minus the exercise price paid), adding any employer NIC payable and deducting CT relief.

13. Enterprise management incentives (EMI)

13.1 Eligibility for qualifying EMI options – company

13.1.1 Outline

The qualification criteria for companies to grant qualifying EMI options are set out in Part 2 of Schedule 5 to ITEPA 2003.

EMI is a relief for small and medium sized entities ('SMEs') that meet strict qualification criteria, which are similar to those that apply to the enterprise investment scheme (known as EIS, with which EMI is often mixed up). (See *Enterprise Investment Scheme* from Claritax Books for details of that other scheme.)

Because EMI is not available for all entities to utilise, it constitutes "state aid" in the eyes of EU law, and must be specifically exempted by the EU to allow the tax reliefs to operate. Without this exemption, the EU Commission could compel HMRC to claw back any tax relief given to employees and companies under the EMI Code. At the time of writing, the state aid exemption has lapsed, meaning that no new EMI options can be granted until a new exemption has been given. It is hoped that this situation will have been resolved by the time of publication. HMRC have stated that any options granted before the state aid exemption lapsed at midnight on 6 April 2018 will continue to benefit from tax relief under the EMI Code.

In outline, to qualify to grant EMI options:

- a company must not be under the control of another company;
- any company that it controls must be a "qualifying subsidiary" or a "qualifying property managing subsidiary";
- the company must have gross assets of less than £30m;
- it must have fewer than 250 full time equivalent employee roles;

- it must undertake a qualifying trade or be preparing to do so; and
- it must have a permanent establishment in the UK.

Each of these requirements is dealt with in more detail below.

While each of the requirements must be satisfied at the date of grant, any qualifying options granted by a company that outgrows the gross assets, number of employees or qualifying subsidiaries tests will continue to be qualifying options. The company will simply not be able to grant further EMI options.

13.1.2 Independence

In order to grant qualifying EMI options, a company must not be a 51% subsidiary of another company (i.e. the other company must not hold more than 50% of the ordinary share capital of the proposed grantor company) and must not be under the control of another company.

"Control" in this context is defined at ITA 2007, s. 995, as one person's ability to direct that the affairs of the company are pursued in accordance with the wishes of that person.

The control test is added to by a requirement that the grantor company must not be controlled by a combination of a company and persons connected to that company (in this case, the term "connected" takes the meaning set out in ITA 2007, s. 993).

The rules can lead to some unexpected problems:

Example: control (1)

Puppy Ltd wishes to grant EMI options. It meets all of the conditions for EMI, but its advisers are concerned about its shareholders. Its shares are held as follows:

Rachel	50 shares
Ali	25 shares
Roddy	10 shares
Anna	10 shares
Dog Ltd	5 shares

Rachel owns 100% of the issued share capital of Dog Ltd. Under s. 993(6), Dog Ltd will be connected with Rachel as Rachel has control of Dog Ltd.

Between them, Rachel and Dog Ltd are able to control Puppy Ltd, which means that Puppy Ltd fails the independence test and is not able to grant EMI options.

Another common example of problems that companies can have with these rules is if there are a number of shareholders, including a company, that are in partnership together and between them control the proposed EMI company. This can apply where there is a formal partnership between shareholders, but also where shareholders have agreed to act together to control a company under s. 993(7).

This can cause particular problems where a company has private equity investors, because private equity structures typically involve partnerships with corporate general partners.

Example: control (2)

Puppy Limited receives a considerable investment from Canine Private Equity, which takes a 60% stake in the company. A Scottish Limited Partnership, Canine LP, holds the shares in Puppy on the private equity investors' behalf and a company, Canine General Partner Ltd, acts as the general partner of the fund.

Even if the investors are private individuals, they will be treated as connected with Canine General Partner Ltd, meaning that Puppy Ltd will continue to fail the independence test for EMI purposes.

The legislation goes on to prevent companies from granting qualifying EMI options if there are arrangements in existence for the company to fall under the control of another company. An obvious example might be where a company's majority shareholder grants an option to a minority corporate investor to allow it to take over the company at a point in the future.

This can also prove to be problematic where an institutional investor has rights to take over control of a company if the business fails to meet performance targets. These rights are often called "swamping rights" and tend to be enshrined in a company's articles of association.

Example: arrangements to take control

Puppy Ltd undergoes another management buy-out, backed by a bank. The bank takes a 20% stake in the company's share capital.

The articles of association provide that the each share in the company has one vote – meaning that the bank can normally exercise 20% of the voting rights and does not have day-to-day control of Puppy Ltd.

However, if Puppy Ltd does not meet its banking covenants the bank's shares gain an extra 1,000 votes per share, meaning that it would have near absolute control of Puppy Ltd in those circumstances.

This constitutes an arrangement for Puppy Ltd to fall under the control of another company and disqualifies Puppy Ltd from granting qualifying EMI options.

Another commonly encountered situation where this requirement has proven problematic is where shares are held by an employee benefit trust and the trustee is a corporate entity. In these cases HMRC have taken a hard line, ignoring the beneficial ownership of the shares and instead looking to the legal ownership, with the result that such companies cannot be qualifying companies for EMI purposes.

One exception is where the company is controlled by the corporate trustee of an employee ownership trust ("EOT") that meets the requirements of ITEPA 2003, Sch. 2, para. 27(4) to (6).

Law: ITEPA 2003, Sch. 5, para. 9

13.1.3 *Qualifying subsidiaries*

The legislation effectively provides that if a company has a subsidiary, but does not hold more than 51% of the ordinary share capital of that company, then the company will not be able to grant qualifying EMI options.

The EMI code defines the term "subsidiary" in an unusual way. Any company that is under the control of the proposing grantor company is defined as being a subsidiary for these purposes ("control" taking the more expansive definition in CTA 2010, s. 450 and s. 451). The definition is widened, mirroring the independence test: if the proposed grantor company collaborates with a connected person to control another company, then that company will be treated as a subsidiary of the grantor company.

This can prove troublesome where a company has entered into a joint venture or has a minority shareholding in another entity.

In a typical joint venture situation, two companies will each hold half of an entity's shares, meaning that the joint venture company will not be a 51% subsidiary of either of the joint venture partners. This gives rise to four possibilities:

- the joint venture company is under the control of the proposed EMI company;
- the proposed EMI company is acting together with its joint venture partner to secure control of the joint venture company;
- it is under the control of the joint venture partner;
- neither joint venture partner has control of the joint venture company.

The first two possibilities would disqualify the company from granting qualifying EMI options, as the joint venture company would be treated as a subsidiary for EMI purposes, but the last two would not.

Example: joint venture companies

Puppy Ltd has a joint venture, Pupper Ltd, with a Spanish Company, Cachorro SA.

Each joint venture partner holds 50 £1 ordinary shares in Pupper Ltd. There is a rudimentary shareholders' agreement which sets out that each partner is entitled to appoint a director to the board of Pupper Ltd but does not regulate how the partners will vote.

Neither Puppy Ltd nor Cachorro SA controls Pupper Ltd and it does not appear that the shareholders' agreement is evidence that they are acting together to secure control of Pupper Ltd.

On this basis, Puppy Ltd's shareholding in Pupper Ltd should not be treated as disqualifying it from granting qualifying EMI options.

The definition of a qualifying subsidiary can lead to difficulties where a company has an interest in a company that does not have a share capital, for instance a company limited by guarantee. This was recently highlighted in an EIS case, *Hunters Property plc*, in which it was held that a guarantee company could not be a qualifying subsidiary, as it did not have share capital.

Subsidiaries incorporated in other jurisdictions can also be problematic, as companies are often constituted differently elsewhere, often taking forms that are not treated as having ordinary share capital for UK tax purposes. *R&C Brief* 87/09 sets out a number of tests that should be applied in these circumstances.

If a subsidiary holds property and is treated as a "property managing subsidiary", it will only be a qualifying subsidiary if the company has control of the subsidiary, holds at least 90% of the subsidiary's shares and voting rights, and is entitled to 90% of its assets on a winding up.

The term "property managing subsidiary" is defined by ITA 2007, s. 188 as follows:

> "(2) 'Property managing subsidiary' means a subsidiary of the company whose business consists wholly or mainly in the holding or managing of land or any property deriving its value from land.
>
> (3) In subsection (2) references to property deriving its value from land include—
>
>   (a) any shareholding in a company deriving its value directly or indirectly from land,
>
>   (b) any partnership interest deriving its value directly or indirectly from land,
>
>   (c) any interest in settled property deriving its value directly or indirectly from land, and
>
>   (d) any option, consent or embargo affecting the disposition of land."

Law: ITEPA 2003, Sch. 5, para. 10
Case: *Hunters Property plc v HMRC* [2018] UKFTT 96 (TC)

13.1.4 Gross assets

In order to grant qualifying EMI options, a company's balance sheet prepared in accordance with Generally Accepted Accounting Practice ("GAAP"), as at the date of grant, must not disclose gross assets (i.e. assets before liabilities are deducted) in excess of £30m.

Where the proposed grantor company is the parent company of a group of companies, the gross assets test is applied by ignoring the group's consolidated accounts and instead following the principles set out in SP 2/06. Under these rules the balance sheets of each constituent in a group will be added together and inter-group items (like the book value of holdings of subsidiary shares and inter-company loans) will be excluded.

Law: ITEPA 2003, Sch. 5, para. 12

13.1.5 Number of employees

The maximum number of employees that a qualifying company has is 250 full time equivalent employees. This number includes all of the employees of subsidiaries and will also include overseas employees.

Example: number of employees

Puppy Ltd employs 278 people in total, of whom 50 work part-time and a further 18 are on zero-hours contracts. Full time employees at Puppy Ltd work 37.5 hours per week.

In order to determine whether the company falls within the limits to grant EMI options, the HR manager has averaged the working time of the workforce over the last three months and reports the following:

210 full time employees working 37.5 hour weeks: 210 x 37.5 =	7,875.0 hours
29 part time employees working 22.5 hour weeks: 29 x 22.5 =	652.5 hours
21 part time employees working 30 hour weeks: 21 x 30 =	630.0 hours
Average hours per week worked by all zero hours staff	180.0 hours
Total number of staff hours per week	9,337.5 hours

On this basis, the company has 249 full time equivalent roles (i.e. 9,337.5 ÷ 37.5) and qualifies to grant EMI options.

In most cases, the position will be rather more obvious than that set out in the above example.

Law: ITEPA 2003, Sch. 5, para. 12A

13.1.6 *Qualifying trade*

In order to grant EMI options, the sole purpose of the existence of a company must be to carry on a qualifying trade and it must be either actively engaged in that trade or preparing to do so. (Ancillary activities like holding assets used in the trade, and other minor matters that do not get in the way of trading, are disregarded).

Where there is a group of companies, at least one company in the group must be undertaking a qualifying trade and a substantial part of the business of the group as a whole cannot consist of non-qualifying activities.

As a matter of HMRC practice, the threshold at which an activity is treated as "substantial" is 20% of the activity of the group or company in question. There is no fixed metric for measuring the activity of the group, but tests like the number of employees engaged in a specific activity or an activity's contribution to a company's turnover are typically used.

The term "qualifying trade" is defined as an activity undertaken with a view to the realisation of profits that does not, to a substantial extent, consist of an excluded trade.

Research and development can be treated as a qualifying trade if it is being done for the purposes of a qualifying trade being undertaken by either the company undertaking the R&D or another company in its group. This provision allows technology start-up companies to qualify, as they may have very significant R&D activities in their early years that may not, of themselves, generate much profit.

Excluded trades are defined in ITEPA 2003, Sch. 5, para. 16:

"16 The following are excluded activities—
(a) dealing in land, in commodities or futures or in shares, securities or other financial instruments;
(b) dealing in goods otherwise than in the course of an ordinary trade of wholesale or retail distribution (see also paragraph 17);
(c) banking, insurance, money-lending, debt-factoring, hire-purchase financing or other financial activities;
(d) leasing, including letting ships on charter or other assets on hire (see also paragraph 18);
(e) receiving royalties or licence fees (see also paragraph 19);
(f) providing legal or accountancy services;
(g) property development (see also paragraph 20);
(h) farming or market gardening;
(i) holding, managing or occupying woodlands, any other forestry activities or timber production;
(ia) shipbuilding (see also paragraph 20A);
(ib) producing coal (see also paragraph 20B);
(ic) producing steel (see also paragraph 20C);
(j) operating or managing hotels or comparable establishments, or managing property used as a hotel or comparable establishment (see also paragraph 21);
(k) operating or managing nursing homes or residential care homes, or managing property used as a nursing home or residential care home (see also paragraph 22);
(l) any activities which are excluded activities under paragraph 23."

Other than specific prohibitions, like producing coal and steel or providing legal or accountancy services, the thrust of the exclusions is to prevent companies involved in amassing investment-grade assets from granting EMI options; the relief under EMI is intended for companies that are taking normal commercial risks and amassing value through developing their trades, not by building up large reserves of investments.

This is illustrated by paras 16(a) (investment), (b) (dealing in goods) and (c) (banking, insurance and other financial activities), which prevent businesses that trade in investment-grade assets from qualifying, but permit companies involved in trading non-investment-grade assets to qualify.

These exclusions do not extend to businesses providing support to investment businesses without taking ownership of the investments or profiting from holding them; examples of qualifying trades that might, at first sight, fall within the excluded categories, include asset management companies, independent financial advisers and insurance brokerages.

Para 16(e) (royalties and licence fees) at first sight prevents software developers from granting EMI options, as their business model is to develop a product that they then license to others. The legislation contains a specific carve-out for businesses that license or receive royalties for intangible assets (including intellectual property) that they themselves have developed (either from scratch or from fairly primitive beginnings).

To prevent companies that just acquire a portfolio of IP developer companies from qualifying for EMI, the legislation provides that the intangible assets must have been created by the proposed grantor company or a company that was a qualifying subsidiary of the grantor company throughout the period that the intangible assets were created.

This can create problems for companies that have been subject to group reorganisations, as the parent company in the group will not have held shares in the subsidiary throughout the period during which the intangible assets were created. This problem is corrected by para. 19(8), which allows a new holding company to be inserted into a group without impacting the status of the company's trade. Para. 19(8) will apply if:

- the new holding company only had subscriber shares in issue immediately before it was inserted into the group; and
- the transactions was purely a share-for-share transaction – no cash or loan notes were issued to the shareholders in the old parent company.

Para. 16(l) disqualifies companies that would otherwise qualify for EMI, but which exist to provide services to a company under common control that undertakes disqualifying activities.

Example: qualifying trade

Puppy Ltd is engaged in developing software for banks to help transition legacy systems onto more up-to-date software platforms. The company's profits are mainly derived from licensing a program that was developed in-house by the company's employees.

The company has invested its surplus cash reserves in quoted investments, which are managed by a third party asset manager. None of the company's employees are engaged in the day-to-day management of the investments, the income from which makes up less than 1% of the company's income.

Although Puppy Ltd is providing services to companies that carry on disqualifying trades, it is not controlled by them nor is it under common control – para. 16(l) does not apply in this case.

Puppy Ltd's trade is based on the exploitation of its own IP, which means that para. 16(e) does not prevent the company from qualifying for EMI.

Although Puppy Ltd is undertaking a disqualifying activity, holding investments, this does not impact on the rest of its activities and, because it does not take up any staff resources and does not significantly contribute to the company's income, it cannot be said to be a substantial part of the company's activities.

For these reasons, based on the information given, Puppy Ltd carries on a qualifying trade for EMI purposes.

Law: ITEPA 2003, Sch. 5, para. 13

13.1.7 Permanent establishment

Either the proposed grantor company or one of its subsidiaries must have a permanent establishment in the UK to grant qualifying EMI options. The term "permanent establishment" is defined in ITA 2007, s. 191A as either:

- a fixed place of business at which some or all of the company's business is conducted; or
- an agent with authority to enter into contracts on behalf of the company and who regularly acts on that authority.

Section 191A sets out a number of additional points to be considered when evaluating the test. In practice, the position will be clear for most companies seeking to grant EMI options, but these tests might require detailed consideration for some of the more diffuse business models that are adopted by web-based businesses, who may not have a "bricks and mortar" base in the UK.

Law: ITEPA 2003, Sch. 5, para. 14A

13.1.8 Advance assurance

HMRC will give companies advance assurance that they are qualifying companies for the purposes of the EMI Code; the process is currently administered by the Small Companies Enterprise Centre.

Applications are made by letter, ideally setting out the qualifying criteria and explaining how the applicant company meets them – there is no fixed form for applications.

This process is not compulsory and many companies decide not to seek advance assurance. It can, however, be useful for companies going through a due diligence process to be able to produce written confirmation from HMRC that the company was entitled to grant qualifying options.

13.2 Eligibility – shares

Qualifying EMI options may only be granted over shares that are:

- ordinary share capital (meaning that they must not be shares with a fixed right to participate in the company's income);

- non-redeemable; and
- fully paid up (meaning that there is no obligation to pay up any amounts on the shares).

Law: ITEPA 2003, Sch. 5, para. 35

13.3 Eligibility – employees

13.3.1 *Employment and working time*

A person can be granted a qualifying EMI option if he or she is an officer or employee of either the company whose shares will be subject to the option ("the issuing company") or a subsidiary of the issuing company.

Someone who works as a contractor to the company will not be able to receive qualifying EMI options.

The individual must also devote a minimum amount of working time to the business of the issuing company or its wider group, spending the lesser of:

- 25 hours per week working for the company; or
- 75% of his working time on the business of the company.

In this context "working time" means time spent on remunerative work (i.e. work that would result in pay that would be treated as taxable employment income or self-employed work undertaken with a view to realising a profit).

Example: working time requirement

Anna and Roddy are both employed part time by Puppy Ltd.

Anna works four days per week for Puppy Ltd (30 hours) and three days per week (including Sundays) working for her own business. Anna does not meet the 75% working time test; her work for her own business is undertaken with a view to realising a profit and would count as "working time" for these purposes. However, she is spending more than 25 hours per week on the business of Puppy Ltd, which means that she is eligible to receive qualifying EMI options.

Roddy spends two days each week working for Puppy Ltd (15 hours) and spends the rest of his week caring for his two children,

193

aged 8 and 5. Although Roddy is spending less than 25 hours per week, he is spending 100% of his working time on the business of Puppy Ltd and he also can be granted qualifying EMI options.

Employees do not fail the working time test if they are absent from work for the following reasons:

- injury, ill health or disability;
- parental leave;
- reasonable holiday entitlement; or
- they are on a period of garden leave (although it seems unlikely that anyone would be granted an option when they were in the process of leaving employment).

Law: ITEPA 2003, Sch. 5, para. 24-27

13.3.2   Material interest

Qualifying EMI options may only be granted to individuals who do not have a material interest in the issuing company or any subsidiary company of the issuing company.

A material interest is beneficial ownership or control (without ownership) of over 30% of the ordinary share capital of a company. In the context of a close company (i.e. a company under the control of five or fewer persons), a person will be treated as having a material interest in the company if he or she has a right to receive 30% of the assets of the company on a winding up or has the ability to acquire the right to receive 30% of those assets.

A person is treated as having a material interest in a company if:

- that person has a material interest in his or her own right;
- that person and an associate together have a material interest between them; or
- an associate of that person has a material interest.

In broad terms, an "associate" is a relative or partner of a person, the trustees of a settlement which that person has settled or the trustees of a settlement holding shares in which the person has a beneficial interest.

Enterprise management incentives

The rules are detailed and it is recommended that the legislation in paragraphs 31 to 33 are reviewed in detail if shares are held by a deceased estate, an employee trust or a discretionary trust.

Options that allow an individual to acquire shares are treated as a right to control those shares and will be counted into the material interest test. The only exceptions to this are qualifying EMI options, which are left out of the calculation (and shares held in a SIP are also disregarded).

Example: material interest

Puppy Ltd has an issued share capital of 100 shares of £1 each. Ali holds 25 shares, representing 25% of the company's ordinary share capital.

Ali is granted a qualifying EMI option over a further seven shares; on a fully diluted basis Ali will hold 32% of the ordinary share capital of the company when he exercises the option.

The company proposes to grant a further qualifying EMI option over five shares to Ali. At the time that the option is granted, Ali meets the material interest test, as the qualifying EMI options that he holds are left out of account.

Law: ITEPA 2003, Sch. 5, para. 28-33

13.3.3 Limit on qualifying EMI options held by an employee

There are two limits on the number of shares that can be granted to an employee; both are calculated by reference to the market value of the shares on the date of grant (any unexercised qualifying CSOP options are counted into these limits):

- the maximum value of shares that can be held under unexercised qualifying EMI options by one person at any one time is £250,000; and
- where an employee has been granted options over £250,000, that person cannot be granted another qualifying option for three years.

Both limits are calculated by reference to the UMV of the shares (see **3.3.6**) on the date that the options are granted. Only options granted by the same company/group of companies are counted –

unexercised options granted by an unconnected company are not counted into this limit.

Example: individual limits

Ali is granted the following qualifying EMI options:

Date	Number of shares	UMV per share	Aggregate EMI value
January 2015	1,000	£10.00	£10,000
June 2016	2,000	£20.00	£40,000
February 2017	4,000	£50.00	£200,000
Total 'headroom' used			£250,000

Even if Ali exercises some of these options and frees up "headroom" to be granted additional options, he will be unable to be granted any more qualifying EMI options until February 2020, when the three year waiting period expires.

Rachel is granted the following qualifying EMI options:

Date	Number of shares	UMV per share	Aggregate EMI value
January 2015	24,999	£10.00	£249,990
Rachel exercises these options in June 2016			
February 2017	50,000	£50.00	£250,000

It is only on the grant of the second option that Rachel has triggered the three year waiting period – the second grant of options can be made because Rachel has enough "headroom" to be granted the options and, at that point, she has not been granted £250,000 of qualifying EMI options.

If an employer grants an option that partly exceeds an individual employee's limit for holding EMI options, the legislation treats the value of the option up to the limit as a qualifying option, but the balance of the option cannot be a qualifying option. The treatment of the part of the option that exceeds the limit will depend on the scheme rules:

- some schemes are drafted so that the whole option will be void;

- the excess above the limit could be treated as void, with only a qualifying option up to the £250,000 limit treated as having been granted; or
- the excess over the £250,000 limit treated as a non-qualifying option.

Because of the three-year waiting period, it is generally advisable to scale grants of qualifying EMI options to individuals to fall just below the £250,000 limit, as this gives companies flexibility to grant further options if, for example, options lapse because performance conditions are not met and it is felt that the performance conditions were unduly restrictive.

Law: ITEPA 2003, Sch. 5, para. 5, 6

13.4 Establishing the scheme

13.4.1 Scheme requirements

The legislation sets few formal requirements on EMI schemes, the three requirements being that:

- "…options must be granted for commercial reasons in order to recruit or retain an employee in a company and not part of a scheme or arrangement the main purpose (or one of the main purposes) of which is the avoidance of tax." (para. 4)
- the employee cannot hold options in excess of the limits set out at **13.3.3** above; and
- each company can only grant qualifying options if the aggregate UMV of unexercised qualifying options (measured at their respective dates of grant) does not exceed £3m.

Although, historically, EMI options have been very rarely subject to challenge on the first of these criteria, the availability of entrepreneurs' relief for qualifying options means that there is a risk that HMRC scrutiny could significantly increase. Of particular concern are EMI options that are exercised immediately after they are granted: HMRC have, in the past, flagged this as an indicator of avoidance activity.

There are two additional requirements, that are specific to the options granted:

- the employee must sign a declaration that his or her working time meets the requirements to be granted qualifying EMI options; and
- the options must not be transferable (the only exception to this is on the death of the employee, in which case the options can be transferred to his or her estate).

Law: ITEPA 2003, Sch. 5, para. 3-7

13.4.2 Implementation process

The steps to implementing an EMI scheme are as follows:

- the company's articles of association should be reviewed to ensure that they cater for employee share ownership and that the rights of the shares under option reflect the commercial intention of the shareholders – any changes to the articles should ideally be made before the options are granted;
- the terms of the options should be determined:
  - will there be performance conditions?
  - how will leavers' options be treated?
  - what happens if there is a disqualifying event?
  - what happens if the company is taken over?
  - when will the options be exercisable?
- advance assurance can be sought from HMRC that the company is a qualifying company – there is, at the time of writing, a six-week turnaround from HMRC for qualifying options, that will need to be factored into any implementation process if advance assurance is to be applied for;
- any shareholders' agreements will need to be reviewed to ensure that the rights of other shareholders have been taken into account and that any approvals process can be fully factored into the implementation timeline;
- plan rules and ancillary documents will need to be drafted;
- the plan will need to be adopted by the company; and

Enterprise management incentives

- the scheme will need to be set up on HMRC's online reporting system.

13.4.3 Granting EMI options

The legislation on EMI sets out minimal requirements for qualifying options:

- the options must be granted over qualifying shares (see **13.2** above);
- the options must be capable of being exercised within ten years beginning on the date of grant – the options do not have to lapse after the tenth anniversary, but they lose the benefit of the tax relief after the tenth anniversary of the date of grant; and
- the terms of the option must be agreed in writing between the grantor and the employee and, as a minimum, the option agreement must set out:
    - the date of grant,
    - that it is granted under the provisions of Schedule 5 to ITEPA 2003,
    - the number or maximum number of shares that can be acquired when the option is exercised, or it must state how this number will be calculated,
    - the option exercise price (if any),
    - when and how the option can be exercised,
    - any restrictions on the shares under option,
    - any conditions on the grant of options (including performance conditions), and
    - if the shares are at risk of forfeiture.

The details of the restrictions, performance conditions or forfeiture can be included in the option documentation or, if they are set out in the articles of association or some other document, that document can be appended to the option agreement. If the company chooses to refer to a second document, then the restrictions, performance conditions etc. must be very clearly signposted for the employees and the document must be identified precisely in the option agreement (details such as the title, date of adoption and dates of any amendments applicable to the employees).

Once a plan has been established, the following steps are needed to grant options:

- The company needs to finalise to whom options will be granted and the terms on which the selected employees will benefit from the options.
- A valuation exercise should be undertaken, to determine whether the options fit within the scheme limits and also to quantify the likely future tax liabilities that will arise when the options are exercised.
- If it is considered appropriate to do so, the valuation can be submitted to HMRC Shares and Assets Valuation ("SAV") for their agreement. This step is strongly recommended, as it gives all parties certainty about the position of the options. Employers should allow between four and six weeks for SAV to respond, although in practice, they are extremely efficient, often able to respond very much more quickly.
- If values have been agreed with SAV, they remain valid for 60 days. Grants should be timed to fall within this time limit.
- Option agreements should be finalised and circulated to the employees so that, if necessary, they can seek their own advice about the terms of the options.
- The option agreements should be signed by the employees and returned to the company, which should arrange for the agreements to be executed on its behalf. (If the options are to be granted over shares held by an EBT, a parallel process of consultation with the trustees should take place and, ideally, they will be made party to the grant of options.)
- Once the option agreements have been signed by both parties, the options should be notified to HMRC using their online system within 90 days of the date of grant.

Some employers may choose to grant EMI options by deed, which has the advantage that it is guaranteed that all of the options will have been granted on the same date. Although this approach allows options to be validly granted, as it creates legally enforceable rights for the employees, the employees must still enter into written EMI option agreements for the options to be qualifying EMI options; if the deed is entered into before the written agreements are signed, the options will be non-qualifying options until the agreements are signed.

If the employer fails to notify HMRC that the options have been granted within the 90-day period, the options will not be qualifying EMI options and will not benefit from any tax advantages. It is possible to apply to HMRC for permission to make a late submission of the grant of options if the employer is able to demonstrate a "reasonable excuse" for failing to file the notice on time, but HMRC police this rigorously and are generally unwilling to allow late submissions; failure by an agent to file on a company's behalf is not generally accepted as constituting a reasonable excuse.

Law: ITEPA 2003, Sch. 5

13.4.4 Performance conditions and the exercise of discretion

HMRC's starting point in evaluating performance conditions is that an option must constitute the grant of "a right to acquire shares". If the right to exercise an option is effectively dependent on the whim of the grantor company, the option does not give the option-holder a right to acquire shares; it instead gives the grantor the right to allow an employee to acquire shares.

Any performance conditions attaching to a qualifying option must be objective and measurable and must meet the tests set out by HMRC in their interpretation of *CIR v Burton*, which can be found in the *Employee Tax Advantaged Share Scheme User Manual* at ETASSUM 47250.

HMRC's key argument in *Burton* was that an option would only be valid if it set out:

- the shares that the option-holder has the right to acquire; or
- a mechanism to determine which shares can be acquired when the option becomes exercisable.

The specific issue in *Burton* was whether a grant of options that allowed the board of directors of the company to amend or vary performance conditions after options had been granted constituted the valid creation of a right to acquire shares.

The judgment in the case held that such a structure does constitute a valid grant of rights to acquire shares and that it would be permissible to vary performance conditions where the board acted fairly and reasonably:

- the new performance conditions would be a fairer measure of an individual option-holder's performance of his or her role in the company; and
- the new conditions would reasonably be less difficult to satisfy than they would have been without the amendment.

The effect of this interpretation is that any discretion that a grantor has over the operation of an option should improve the clearly stated position of the option-holder, rather than taking rights away or creating new rights. Common examples of permissible and impermissible uses of discretion would be:

- An option that only vests at the discretion of an employer (i.e. there are no objective criteria that can be met that would allow an employee a right to exercise the option without the employer exercising discretion) would be impermissible.
- An option that allows the employer the discretion to revoke the employee's right to exercise the option would not be permissible.
- An option with clearly defined performance conditions, where the board has the discretion to waive the performance conditions, would be permissible.
- An option that, by default, lapses when an employee leaves, but that allows the board discretion to permit the leaver to retain his or her options, would also be permissible.

Case: *CIR v Burton* (1990) 63 TC 191

13.5 Employee tax treatment

13.5.1 Income tax and NIC

When an employee exercises a qualifying EMI option in a qualifying manner, the employee's maximum income tax exposure will be on the difference, if any, between:

- the exercise price paid to exercise the option; and
- the lesser of the AMV on the grant or the exercise of the option.

If the employee has paid anything to be granted the option, this amount is also deducted in arriving at his or her taxable employment income.

Any tax charges will be collected through the PAYE and NIC rules if the shares are readily convertible assets (see **7.4** above).

Example: qualifying exercise

Roddy is granted qualifying EMI options over 1,000 shares in Puppy Ltd. The options are nil-cost options (i.e. they do not have an exercise price). The shares in Puppy Ltd had an AMV of £1 each when the options were granted.

Two years later Puppy Ltd is sold, Roddy exercises the option and sells his 1,000 shares for £100 per share.

Roddy is treated as having received £1,000 of taxable employment income when he exercised his option (i.e. the AMV of £1 each on the date of grant), which will be subject to PAYE and NIC, as the Puppy Ltd shares will be RCAs when he acquires them.

The tax treatment of the options can be shown as follows:

The tax treatment can be shown as follows:

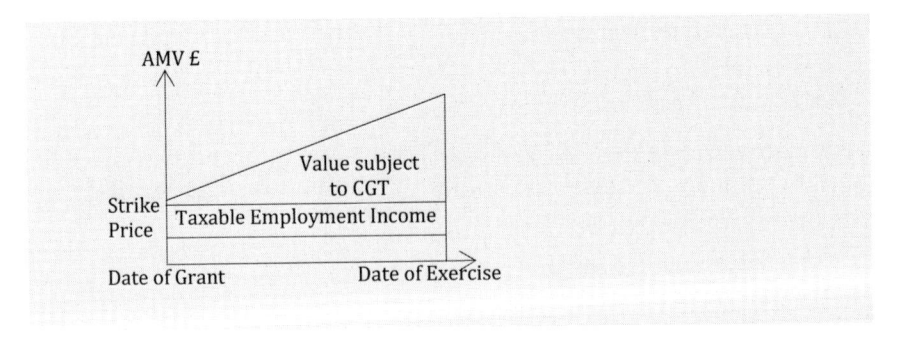

[Figure: Chart showing AMV £ on vertical axis, with Strike Price at Date of Grant rising to higher value at Date of Exercise. Area between strike price line and value line is split into "Taxable Employment Income" (lower portion up to AMV at grant) and "Value subject to CGT" (upper portion).]

Law: ITEPA 2003, s. 530, 531

13.5.2 Disqualifying events – in outline

There are a number of situations in which an EMI option can lose its qualifying status (a "disqualifying event"). In summary, the following constitute disqualifying events:

- the grantor company losing its independence and falling under the control of another company;
- the grantor company ceasing to conduct a qualifying trade (or failing to take up a qualifying trade if the options were granted in preparation for the company beginning a trade);
- the employee ceasing employment or falling below the working time requirement;
- the employee being granted a CSOP option that takes his total number of unexercised options over the £250,000 limit;
- making changes to the terms of the options, the option shares or to the share capital of the company, that increase the market value of the option shares or lead to the option itself or the option shares ceasing to be qualifying options or shares.

Where a company that is preparing to carry on a qualifying trade grants qualifying EMI options, it has two years from the date of grant to take up the trade; after that the EMI options lose their qualifying status.

If the grantor company falls under the control of a qualifying employee ownership trust (EOT) (see **13.1.2** above), this will not be treated as a disqualifying event, notwithstanding that the trustee of the EOT is a corporate entity.

When considering an employee's working time, his average working time over the whole period that he holds options during a tax year must be considered – this prevents employees from qualifying if they have a "paper" working time commitment that meets the statutory minimum, but who only work when required; equally, it may be of assistance to an employee who works irregular hours, but, taken as a whole, meets the 75% requirement.

Alterations of share capital can constitute disqualifying events in two main situations:

- if the alteration affects the value of the option shares and is the result of any changes to the rights of any of the shares in the capital of the company (i.e. it is not limited to changes just affecting the rights of the option shares), including the imposition or lifting of restrictions; or
- if the change increases the shares' market value and is not made by the company for commercial reasons or has a tax avoidance purpose.

A final possible disqualifying event is the conversion of shares of the same class as the option shares into shares of a different class. A share conversion will not give rise to a disqualifying event if it affects all of the shares of that class currently in issue and either the majority of those shares are held by non-employees or shares of that class confer control of the company on their holders.

13.5.3 Disqualifying events, tax treatment

The tax treatment of the options will differ following a disqualifying event, depending on the timing of the disqualifying event and the date of exercise of the options.

Where an option is exercised within 90 days of a disqualifying event, it will retain all of its tax advantages and will be treated as the qualifying exercise of a qualifying option.

If the option is exercised more than 90 days after the date of the disqualifying event, a different tax treatment, set out in ITEPA 2003, s. 532, will apply. The amount of taxable employment income suffered by an employee will be determined by adding together:

Part 5: Statutory share schemes

    i.   the lesser of the AMV of the option shares at the date of grant and the date of exercise; and

    ii.   the amount by which the option shares have increased in value from the date of the disqualifying event to the date of exercise;

and then deducting the sum of:

    i.   the option exercise price, and

    ii.   the consideration (if any) given for the grant of the option.

Example: exercising an option after a disqualifying event

Rachel and Anna were both granted qualifying EMI options over 1,000 shares in Puppy Ltd. Both of their options had a strike price of £1.00 per share.

When the options were granted to Rachel, the AMV of the option shares was £1.00 per share, but when they were granted to Anna the AMV was £2.00 per share. Neither of them gave any consideration for the grant of the option.

On 1 April 2017 the company was suffering significant cash flow problems and, as part of an agreement with its largest creditor, Hound Inc., the board agreed to take instructions from Hound Inc. until it had cleared its indebtedness. During the following three months the company was effectively run in accordance with Hound Inc.'s wishes, meaning that it had fallen under the control of another company – a disqualifying event for EMI purposes. After the end of this period, Puppy Ltd had repaired its cash flow and was trading profitably.

On 1 April 2017 the company's shares were valued at £4.50 each.

In the current tax year Hound Inc. has made a formal offer to buy Puppy Ltd for consideration of £10.00 per share. Rachel and Anna exercise their options and take part in the sale.

The amount treated as taxable employment income is as follows:

Rachel:

AMV on grant (£1.00 x 1,000)	£1,000	
Deduct exercise price paid	(£1,000)	
ITEPA 2003, s. 531 gain		£0
Market value on exercise (£10.00 x 1,000)	£10,000	
Deduct market value on date of disqualifying event (£4.50 x 1,000)	(£4,500)	
ITEPA 2003, s. 532 gain		£5,500
Total taxable employment income		£5,500

Rachel's base cost for CGT purposes is £6,500 (i.e. her taxable employment income of £5,500 plus the exercise price paid), meaning that the balance of her gain, £3,500, will be subject to CGT.

Anna:

AMV on grant (£2.00 x 1,000)	£2,000	
Deduct exercise price paid	(£1,000)	
ITEPA 2003, s. 531 gain		£1,000
Market value on exercise (£10.00 x 1,000)	£10,000	
Deduct market value on date of disqualifying event (£4.50 x 1,000)	(£4,500)	
ITEPA 2003, s. 532 gain		£5,500
Total taxable employment income		£6,500

Anna's base cost for CGT purposes is £7,500 (i.e. her taxable employment income of £7,500 plus the exercise price paid), meaning that the balance of her gain, £2,500, will be subject to CGT.

The tax treatment can be shown as follows:

Part 5: Statutory share schemes

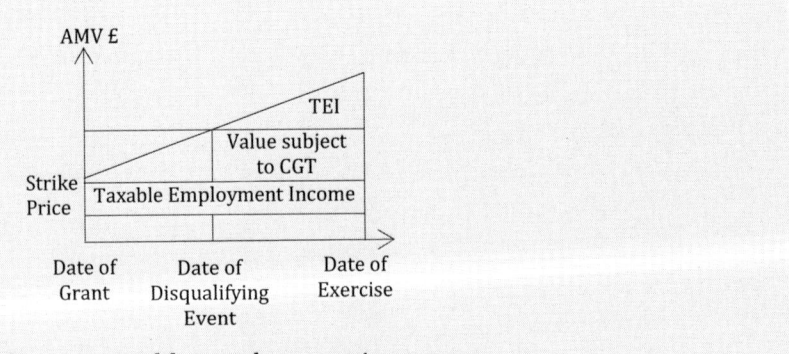

```
AMV £
        ↑
                              TEI
                        ┌─────────────┐
                       /│ Value subject│
                      / │    to CGT    │
         Strike ─────/  ├─────────────┤
         Price      │Taxable Employment Income│
                   └──────────────────────┘→
         Date of    Date of        Date of
         Grant    Disqualifying    Exercise
                    Event
```

TEI denotes taxable employment income.

13.5.4 Restricted securities and elections

Where an employee exercises a qualifying EMI option with a strike price equal to the AMV of the option shares at the date of grant, the individual is treated as having automatically made an election under ITEPA 2003, s. 431(1) to disregard the restricted securities rules (s. 431A).

If the employee has been granted an option with a strike price that is less than the AMV of the option shares, he will have a choice as to whether to make an election. If the option is exercised and the employee makes an election, then he will be taxed on the difference between the strike price and the lower of:

- the AMV at grant; and
- the UMV at exercise when the option is exercised.

There will be no exposure to tax under the restricted securities rules when the shares are sold.

Example: discounted EMI options and restricted securities

Ali is granted a qualifying EMI option over 2,000 shares in Puppy Ltd. The shares' AMV is valued at £4.50 each, but the strike price of the option is £1.00 per share.

A year later, when the AMV is £5.00 and the UMV is £6.25, Ali exercises one quarter of the option and acquires 500 shares. Ali does not make an election at this time.

When Ali exercises this part of the option, he is taxed on the difference between the strike price and the lesser of the AMV at grant and the **AMV** at exercise – i.e. on £4.50 (the AMV at grant) – minus £1.00 per share.

As he has not made an election, the restricted securities rules will apply and, when he sells these shares, the AMV and UMV on the date of exercise will be used to work out what IUP will be in calculating the charge (i.e. IUP = (£6.25-£5.00) ÷ £6.25 – see **3.3.7**).

Another year later, when the shares' AMV is £6.40 each and their UMV is £8.00, Ali exercises the balance of his option and acquires the remaining 1,500 shares. This time Ali makes an election under ITEPA 2003, s. 431(1).

This time, Ali is taxed on the difference between the strike price and the lesser of the AMV at grant and the **UMV** at exercise. Again, this translates into £4.50 (the AMV at grant) minus £1.00 per share.

The following year Ali sells his shares as part of the transaction with Hound Inc. for £10.00 per share.

Ali's tax position is as follows:

Taxable employment income arising on exercise of first half of option:

Aggregate AMV at grant (500 x £4.50)	£2,250
Aggregate strike price (500 x £1.00)	(£500)
Taxable employment income	£1,750

Taxable employment income arising on exercise of second half of option:

Aggregate AMV at grant (1,500 x £4.50)	£6,750
Aggregate strike price (1,500 x £1.00)	(£1,500)
Taxable employment income	£5,250

Taxable employment income arising on sale of shares (see **3.3.7** above for the calculation of the amount chargeable under the restricted securities rules):

500 x £10.00 x (£6.25-£5.00) ÷ £6.25	£1,000
Total taxable employment income arising on exercise of options and sale of shares	£8,000
Aggregate exercise price	£2,000
Total base cost for CGT purposes	£11,000

Although the amount of taxable employment income per share realised by Ali on the exercise of each part of the option is the same, his failure to make an election on the exercise of the first part of the option has left him with a proportion of his sale proceeds taxable under the rules on restricted securities, instead of falling to be taxed under the CGT rules.

If the employee holds an option that was granted with a strike price that was less than the shares' AMV at grant, but the share price has fallen between the date of grant and the date of exercise, the effect of an election will be to increase the value treated as taxable employment income when the option is exercised, but will prevent taxable employment income from being treated as arising when the option shares are sold.

Example: discounted EMI options and restricted securities (2)

Roddy is granted qualifying EMI options over 2,000 shares in Puppy Ltd, with a strike price of £1.00 per share. At the time that Roddy is granted the options, the shares' AMV is agreed to be £8.00 per share.

The following year, after difficult trading conditions, Roddy exercises half of his option and acquires 1,000 of the shares; he does not make an election under ITEPA 2003, s. 431(1). At this time the shares' AMV is £4.50 per share and their UMV is £5.625.

Three months later, Roddy exercises the remaining proportion of his option, and this time makes an election. At this point, the shares' AMV and UMV are unchanged.

Roddy sells his shares to Hound Inc. as part of the takeover process for £10.00 per share.

Roddy's tax position is as follows:

First option, no s. 431(1) election made		
Aggregate **AMV** at **exercise** (1,000 x £4.50)	£4,500	
Aggregate strike price (£1 x 1,000)	(£1,000)	
Taxable employment income		£3,500
Second option, s. 431(1) election made		
Aggregate **UMV** at **exercise** (1,000 x £5.625)	£5,625	
Aggregate strike price (£1 x 1,000)	(£1,000)	
Taxable employment income		£4,625
Income tax arising on the sale of Roddy's shares		
1,000 x £10.00 x (£5.625-£4.50) ÷ £5.625		£2,000
Total taxable employment income		£10,125
Aggregate exercise price		£2,000
Total base cost for CGT purposes		£12,125

13.5.5 Capital gains tax – automatic qualification for entrepreneurs' relief

One of the main benefits enjoyed by holders of qualifying EMI options is the relaxation of the rules on entrepreneurs' relief ("ER"), so that EMI option-holders can access ER even if their shareholdings are not large enough to meet the requirement set out in TCGA 1992, s. 169S(3), i.e. that they confer 5% of the voting rights and constitute 5% of the ordinary share capital of the company.

The treatment of shares acquired by exercising qualifying EMI options was changed by Sch. 24 to FA 2013; where an option is exercised on or after 6 April 2013, the shares will be treated as "relevant EMI shares" for the purposes of TCGA 1992, s. 169I(7A) and (7B), provided that:

- the option is exercised before the tenth anniversary of the date of grant; and
- the option is not exercised more than 90 days after a disqualifying event.

Provided that the company meets the qualification conditions for ER on the date of disposal of the shares, and more than a year has elapsed from the date of grant of the qualifying EMI option to the date of sale of the relevant EMI shares, then the employee will be entitled to claim ER when he or she sells them.

Example: entrepreneurs' relief

Rachel is granted a qualifying EMI option over 20,000 shares in Puppy Limited, when the shares were each valued with an AMV of £1.00 and a UMV of £1.20. The exercise price of the option is £1.00 per share, and no disqualifying events occur in relation to the option. The issued share capital of Puppy Limited is 2,500,000 ordinary shares at the date of grant, Rachel's options constitute less than 1% of the company's fully diluted share capital.

Five years later, Hound Inc. offers to buy Puppy Ltd for consideration equal to £10.00 per share. Rachel exercises her qualifying EMI option on the day of the transaction between the two companies and sells her shares.

As more than a year has elapsed between the date of grant and the date of exercise, Rachel is entitled to claim ER on the disposal of her shares. Assuming that Rachel has used up her annual exemption on other gains and has no losses brought forward, her tax position is as follows:

Total proceeds of sale (20,000 x £10.00)	£200,000
Aggregate exercise price (20,000 x £1.00)	(£20,000)
Total chargeable gain	£180,000
Tax @ 10%	(£18,000)
Net benefit to Rachel	**£162,000**

Where relevant EMI shares in one company are exchanged for new shares as part of a reorganisation or other transaction, the new shares will also be treated as relevant EMI shares provided that:

- the replacement shares are equated with the new shares by virtue of TCGA 1992, s. 127; or
- the transaction is treated as a "qualifying exchange of shares" (see **13.7.1** below) and TCGA 1992, s. 135(3) applies.

13.6 Company tax position

13.6.1 Corporation tax relief

The employer company will be entitled to claim corporation tax relief under the ordinary provisions in CTA 2009, Part 12 provided that the other conditions for relief are met (see **6.2** above for more information).

13.6.2 Operation of PAYE and NIC

Whether any tax liabilities arising under an EMI plan are subject to PAYE and NIC will depend on the status of the option shares at the time of the chargeable event: if the option shares are RCAs at the time of the chargeable event, PAYE will need to be operated and NIC will also arise. If the shares are not RCAs, any tax charges will be self-assessment matters for the employee.

The rules on RCAs and PAYE are set out in more detail at **7.4** above.

13.6.3 Deductibility of implementation costs

Unlike the other statutory share schemes, there is no specific legislative provision giving companies an automatic entitlement to claim corporation tax relief for the costs of implementing an EMI plan. Companies will be able to claim relief for costs that are demonstrably wholly and exclusively for the benefit of their trade and are revenue and not capital in nature.

13.7 Company transactions

13.7.1 Company reorganisations

Any situation in which the issuing company falls under the control of another company will normally constitute a disqualifying event for the purposes of any qualifying EMI options held by employees. This means that the insertion of a holding company can, potentially, lead to EMI options losing their qualifying status.

In order to give employers flexibility to make changes to their group structures, Part 6 of Sch. 5 contains a number of relieving provisions, allowing companies in this situation to replace qualifying EMI options with new qualifying options over shares in a new holding company.

Paragraph 39 defines a company reorganisation as a transaction in which one company:

- obtains control of the issuer company by making a general offer to acquire the whole of the issued share capital of the company or all of the shares of the same class as the option shares;
- obtains control of the company through a court-sanctioned arrangement or compromise under CA 2006, s. 899;
- becomes entitled to buy out minority shareholders under CA 2006, s. 979 to 982 (which applies where an offeror has already secured acceptances from 90% of the shareholders of the company) or is bound to buy out minority shareholders under CA 2006, s. 983 to 985 (which applies when an offeror has made a general offer to the shareholders of the company); or
- obtains all of the option shares as a result of a "qualifying exchange of shares".

A general offer is an offer made in writing to all of the shareholders (or to all shareholders holding shares of the same class as the option shares), that has a fixed time limit for responses. A general offer does not need to be made by the same means to all of the shareholders (some could receive a detailed comprehensive document, other shareholders could receive a far less detailed note). In practice, most private companies are unlikely to use such a formal process to communicate with shareholders, who are likely to be personally known to each other and more likely to speak face to face.

The term "qualifying exchange of shares" is defined in ITEPA 2003, Sch. 5, para. 40 as an arrangement under which a company acquires all of the shares in the issuing company. A number of conditions must be met:

- The transaction must be a share-for-share exchange – no other consideration can be given for the shares in the issuing company.
- The share capital of the new holding company must consist entirely of subscriber shares (or shares previously issued in exchange for shares in the issuing company).

- The share capital of the new company must replicate the issuing company's share capital, with shareholders acquiring the shares proportion of each class as they held in the issuing company.
- The transaction must not be treated as the disposal of the old shares for CGT purposes.

Where a company reorganisation within the meaning of para. 39 has taken place, the acquiring company has six months following the change of control to grant replacement options to the EMI option-holders.

Where they meet the requirements of para. 41 to 43, the replacement options will be treated as qualifying EMI options – and, for the purposes of the EMI Code and ER, treated as if they were the original option – with the same date of grant and same values used to calculate the scheme limits as the original options.

In order to be treated as a qualifying replacement option, all of the following conditions must be met:

- The options must be granted within the six month time-limit set out above.
- The employee must enter into an agreement to release the original EMI options in consideration for the grant of the replacement options.
- The replacement options must be granted over shares in the acquirer company and must be equivalent to the old options (meaning that the aggregate exercise price must be the same and the total value of shares under option before and after the replacement option is granted must be the same too).
- The employee must take up employment with either the acquiring company or a subsidiary of the acquiring company (including the old issuing company).
- The replacement option must be granted for purposes that meet the requirements of para. 4.
- The grant of the replacement option must not take the employee over the £250,000 limit on qualifying EMI options.

Part 5: Statutory share schemes

- The replacement options must meet the requirements for options set out in **section 13.4.3** above.
- The acquiring company must have "headroom" (i.e. it must have less than £3m of shares, valued at the date of grant, that are subject to EMI options).
- The acquiring company must meet the independence test and the qualifying trade test, but does not need to meet the other requirements of the EMI Code.
- HMRC must be notified of the grant of the replacement options using their online system, within 90 days of the date of grant.

Example: replacement options

Rachel holds options over 10,000 shares in Puppy Ltd, which had an AMV of £8.00 and a UMV of £9.60 when they were granted to her 18 months ago. The options' exercise price is £1.00 per share.

The shareholders decide to insert a new holding company and incorporate a new company, Puppy Holdings Ltd. At the time that it is incorporated, Puppy Holdings Ltd has no assets, other than its initial share capital, which is made up of subscriber shares.

Puppy Holdings Ltd acquires the whole issued share capital of Puppy Ltd and, in consideration, issues new shares to the shareholders on the basis of one new share for each old share that they held. There is no cash alternative. The next day, Rachel signs an agreement with Puppy Holdings Ltd to release her old option in exchange for new options over an equal number of shares, with the same strike price.

The transaction between Puppy Ltd and Puppy Holdings Ltd will constitute a qualifying exchange of shares for the purposes of the EMI Code. The new options granted to Rachel by Puppy Holdings Ltd will be treated as if they were the original options granted to Rachel by Puppy Ltd. No tax charges will arise on the exchange of the options.

Three months later, Hound Inc. acquires all of the issued share capital of Puppy Holdings Ltd for consideration of £20.00 per share. Rachel is allowed to exercise half of her option and sells the shares that she acquires. Her tax position is as follows:

Sale proceeds (£20 x 5,000)		£100,000
Aggregate exercise price (£1 x 5,000)	£5,000	
Taxable employment income ((£8-£1) x 5,000)	£35,000	
Total base cost		£40,000
Chargeable gain		£60,000

As Rachel is treated as having held the options since the date that the old options in Puppy Ltd were granted, she has held the options for more than 12 months and is entitled to claim entrepreneurs' relief on the gain (assuming that she has not already used up her lifetime allowance).

One of the effects of the legislation is that it is possible for companies that would not normally be qualifying companies to grant qualifying options as replacement options to the employees of companies that they acquire.

Example: replacement options (2)

At the time of the transaction between Hound Inc. and Puppy Holdings Limited, Hound Inc. and its subsidiaries employ 150,000 people worldwide, it has gross assets of $50bn and a significant number of joint ventures with companies in Asia. Hound Inc.'s trade is to license software that it has developed.

Hound Inc. is listed on the New York Stock Exchange and its stock is priced at $127.35 per share, which equated to £94.72 on the date of the transaction. Its largest single stockholder is an investment fund manager, which holds 11% of its stock.

Although Hound Inc. does not meet most of the tests for granting qualifying EMI options, it meets the qualifying trade test and the independence tests. This means that Hound Inc. can grant replacement options over its own shares to the Puppy Holdings Limited employees.

Rachel is offered a replacement option over 1,056 shares of stock in Hound Inc. in exchange for her option over 5,000 shares in Puppy Holdings Limited. The new option has an exercise price of £4.74 per share.

As the value of shares subject to the new option is equivalent to the value of the Puppy Holdings Ltd shares that were subject to the old option (i.e. 1,056 x £94.72 = £100,024) and the exercise price is similar to the aggregate exercise price of the old option (i.e. 1,056 x £4.74 = £5,005), the new option is treated as a qualifying replacement EMI option.

13.7.2 Variation of share capital

Companies may undertake a number of changes to the structure of their share capital; common examples include subdivisions, bonus issues, consolidations and rights issues.

Unlike the legislation governing the other statutory share schemes, the EMI Code does not have any specific provisions expressly regulating the treatment of variations of share capital. Instead, companies are free to approach variations of share capital as they see fit, with the proviso that some changes to options can be treated as giving rise to a disqualifying event if they have the effect of increasing the value of the shares under option or reducing the option price.

Typically, option plan rules will allow options to be adjusted to take into account any changes in share capital so that the employees hold options over the same percentage of the company's share capital, with the same aggregate exercise price:

- on a bonus issue, rights issue or subdivision of share capital, the number of shares under option will be increased and the exercise price per share will be reduced;
- on a consolidation, the number of shares under option will be reduced and the exercise price per share increased.

For bonus issues, subdivisions and consolidations, the calculation of the adjustment factors is straightforward.

Example: bonus issue and consolidation

Anna holds options over 2,000 Puppy Ltd ordinary shares of £0.01 each with an exercise price of £1.00 per share. The shares under option constitute 1% of the company's fully diluted share capital.

Enterprise management incentives

The company resolves to capitalise its reserves and undertake a bonus issue, issuing shares on a 1:1 basis to its shareholders. The company's fully diluted share capital is now 400,000 shares.

In order to ensure that Anna doesn't lose out, her option is adjusted, so that it is now an option to acquire 4,000 ordinary shares of £0.01 each, with an exercise price of £0.50 per share.

The following year, Puppy Ltd consolidates its share capital so that for every 100 ordinary shares of £0.01 held by shareholders, they now hold 10 shares of £0.10 each.

To reflect this transaction, Anna's option is adjusted again, so that she now holds an option over 400 ordinary shares of £0.10 each and the exercise price of her option is now £5.00 per share.

Following each transaction, Anna's options represent the same percentage of the company's fully diluted share capital and have the same aggregate exercise price, meaning that neither the variations of share capital nor the variations of Anna's options constitute disqualifying events and the options continue to be qualifying EMI options.

The position with rights issues is more complex and at ETASSUM 44250 HMRC have published a formula for adjusting options that is generally acceptable to HMRC Shares and Assets Valuation (SAV). The formula works by calculating the value effect of the rights issue and it is advisable to seek HMRC's confirmation that they agree with any adjustments proposed following a rights issue.

Rights issues are most often encountered in a quoted company context and will typically be set out as an opportunity to acquire *x* number of new shares for every *y* number of old shares held for a fixed price, usually a discount to the company's current share price.

The steps to making the calculation are as follows:

- Step 1: calculate the average value of a share after the rights issue ("A") using the following formula (definitions given below):

    $(N \times M + R \times P) \div (R + N)$

- Step 2: establish the mid-market value of a share on the last day the shares were listed cum rights ("M" i.e. the price

219

of a share on the last day that a shareholder had to be registered as a shareholder to join in the rights issue);

- Step 3: multiply the number of shares under option by A/M;
- Step 4: multiply the exercise price by M/A.

Where:

N is the number of existing shares that need to be held to create an entitlement to receive rights shares;

M is given above;

R is the number of rights issue shares that can be acquired per N; and

P is the price at which each rights share is issued.

An example of the operation of this formula is given at ETASSUM 44250. The purpose of this process is to increase the number of shares under option and to reduce the exercise price per share, so that both the aggregate market value of the option shares and the aggregate exercise price remain unchanged.

Law: ITEPA 2003, s. 536

13.7.3 Demergers

HMRC have taken a consistent position that a demerger transaction does not constitute a variation of share capital for the purposes of the statutory share schemes. This means that it is not generally possible to adjust existing share options to compensate employees for the loss of value in their shares resulting from a demerger.

The most straightforward approach to dealing with a demerger would be to grant a second option to employees over shares in the demerger entity. Such an option would not constitute a qualifying option, as the employees are unlikely to meet the working time requirement in both the original and demerged entities.

An alternative approach would be to allow the options to be exercised (assuming that the terms of the grant of options permit this), which would mean that the employees would take part in the demerger transaction alongside the other shareholders.

13.8 Amending options

13.8.1 Making changes

Qualifying EMI options are individual to each option-holder, meaning that there is no legal reason why any two grants of options made by the same employer should be made on the same terms; an employer can adapt new grants of options to meet the commercial needs at the time that the options are granted.

The only limitations on the variation of the terms on which new options are granted are:

- the formal requirements for an option to be a qualifying option set out in the EMI Code;
- corporate governance considerations (for example, the need to seek shareholder approval); and
- any restrictions imposed by financial markets and regulators that might affect the company.

Changing the terms of existing options is more involved, as the options will take the form of contractual agreements between the individual employees and the grantor. Any change to the terms of an existing option will generally need to be set out in a formal agreement between the option-holder and the grantor; it is not generally possible for an employer to change the terms of an existing option unilaterally.

13.8.2 Taxation

There are two main tax risks attaching to variations of option rights:

- that the variation constitutes a disqualifying event (see **13.5.2** above); or
- the variation effectively constitutes the release of the old option and the grant of a new option.

If the variation of an option right constitutes the grant of a new option, the option is not likely to constitute a qualifying option, as the effective grant of the option will not have been notified to HMRC within the time limits set out in the legislation and the form of the grant of the new option is unlikely to meet the requirements of Part 5 of Sch. 5.

HMRC's practice is based on two key cases: *Eurocopy* and *Reed International*.

In *Eurocopy*, the company sought to amend the terms of its share scheme so that options could be exercised on the sixth anniversary of grant and not on the ninth anniversary of grant. The court held that the effect of the alteration was to give the option-holders new rights and, for that reason, the proposed change would constitute a new option right.

The *Reed* case concerned a proposal to remove a time limit for employees to exercise their share options. In that case it was held that the proposal constituted the variation of a pre-existing right and not the creation of new rights for the option-holders. For that reason, it was held that the proposal did not constitute the grant of a new option.

In summary, the principles that can be derived from these cases are as follows:

- a change to an option right that confers a right that an option-holder did not have before the amendment will constitute the grant of a new option right;
- variation of a pre-existing right does not constitute the grant of a new option; and
- a *de minimis* change to an option will generally be disregarded.

Cases: CIR v Eurocopy plc (1991) 64 TC 370; CIR v Reed International plc (1995) 67 TC 552

13.9 Leavers

Because the EMI Code does not impose a minimum period for an option to be held before it benefits from tax advantages, it does not confer specific tax reliefs on options exercised by defined classes of "good leavers". Instead, the legislation's approach is to treat the cessation of employment as a disqualifying event (see **13.5.2** above):

- If the terms of the option permit leavers to exercise it, and the option is exercised within 90 days of the date of cessation of employment, the option will be treated as a qualifying option, with all of the tax advantages attaching to such options.

- If the option is exercised more than 90 days after the date of cessation of employment, the special treatment applicable to options exercised after a disqualifying event will apply.

The key point is that any options exercised by leavers will only benefit from any relief under the EMI Code if the option is exercised in accordance with the terms on which it was granted.

This can create problems where the terms on which options are granted are too restrictively framed; a typical example is the employer who has framed the terms of an EMI option so that they invariably and automatically lapse if an employee is a leaver, discovering that a long-standing promise to a valued retiree cannot be met through the EMI option.

Law: ITEPA 2003, s. 532, 535

13.10 Reporting

13.10.1 Option registration

The reporting regime for EMI options is based on the same platform as that used for reporting other transactions in employment-related securities (see **8.1** above).

When an employer establishes an EMI plan, a new "scheme" should be set up on the *Employment-Related Securities for Employers* portal on the HMRC website.

The grant of qualifying options must be undertaken using the online system within 92 days of the date of grant. If the options are not notified to HMRC within this time limit, they will not have qualifying status.

It is possible to apply to make a late notification of the grant of options, on the grounds of reasonable excuse for having failed to file the notification. The application must be made by email to shareschemes@hmrc.gsi.gov.uk setting out details of the options, the grantor and the reasons for late notification.

13.10.2 Annual reporting

An annual return must be filed with HMRC in each year that the EMI plan is active, even if the return is a nil return.

The report must include details of any transactions in the options (options exercised, lapses, released options).

13.10.3 Enquiries

HMRC may enquire into the grant of an EMI option by giving notice to the grantor company within 12 months of the end of the 92-day period from the date of grant in which the option should be notified to HMRC.

14. Company share option plans (CSOP)

14.1 Eligibility for a Schedule 4 CSOP

14.1.1 Eligibility – shares

A Schedule 4 CSOP scheme (that is, a share option scheme that qualifies for tax relief under the CSOP Code of ITEPA 2003) can only be granted over fully paid-up, irredeemable shares that form part of the ordinary share capital of the issuing company (see **15.1.1** for the definition of "ordinary share capital").

The issuing company must be the "scheme organiser" (i.e. the company that has established and is running the scheme for its employees and for the employees of its subsidiaries), the parent company of the scheme organiser or one of a consortium of companies that controls the scheme organiser. A consortium is defined as five or fewer companies which each hold at least 5% of the issued share capital of the scheme organiser and which between them hold at least 75% of the shares (Sch. 4, para. 36(2)).

The shares must be either:

i. shares in a company that is not under the control of another company;
ii. shares of a class listed on a recognised stock exchange; or
iii. shares in a company which is subject to an employee-ownership trust that meets the conditions set out in TCGA 1992, s. 236I-236U.

Unlike SIP or EMI, the CSOP Code prevents a company from using a special "employee share class". It does so by imposing a condition on the ownership of shares of the same class (if the issuing company has only one class of shares and the options will be granted over shares of that class, this condition can be disregarded). The shares must either be:

- "employee-control shares"; or
- "open market shares".

These terms are defined in Sch. 4, para. 20:

- shares will constitute employee-control shares if:
  - that class confers control of the issuing company on its holders, and
  - the persons with control of the company are either current or former employees or directors of the company or any of its subsidiaries;
- open market shares are defined as a class of shares the majority of which are beneficially owned by people who did not acquire them by reason of office or employment, unless they were acquired as part of an offer to the public.

An important point to note is that HMRC may regard shares as belonging to a separate class if their terms are such that their holders have differing rights depending on their status.

Example: share classes

Toffee Ventures Ltd has two classes of shares: ordinary shares and deferred shares. The terms of the articles state that shares acquired through any of the company's share schemes do not confer voting rights on their holders.

Although the ordinary shares formally constitute only one class, the fact that they confer different rights on different holders means that they are treated as two classes for the purposes of the CSOP Code.

Law: ITEPA 2003, Sch. 4, para. 15-20, 36(2)

14.1.2 Eligibility – employees

Qualifying CSOP options can only be granted to someone who is an employee of the scheme organiser or one of its subsidiaries. There is no working time requirement for most employees, but only full time directors are eligible to be granted Schedule 4 CSOP options.

As with EMI, CSOP options cannot be granted to someone with a "material interest" in the company (i.e. an interest in 30% or more of the company's share capital, or the right to receive more than 30% of its assets on a winding up).

The rules are largely the same as those applying to EMI options, which are set out in more detail at **13.3.2**; the main point of difference is the treatment of share options held by an employee. Unlike the rules in the EMI Code, ITEPA 2003, Sch. 4, para. 11 does not disregard EMI options and CSOP options held by the employee for the purposes of the material interest test.

Law: ITEPA 2003, Sch. 4, para. 7-14

14.2 Establishing the scheme

14.2.1 Scheme requirements

Qualifying CSOPs differ from EMIs in one fundamental respect: essentially EMI is a framework within which option grants can qualify for relief if they individually meet the requirements of the EMI Code; CSOP, on the other hand, is a regime under which an over-arching scheme must meet the legislative requirements of the CSOP Code – if the scheme as a whole qualifies, the options granted under the scheme will also qualify.

A CSOP scheme must meet two criteria:

- the scheme's purpose must be to provide benefits in the form of share options and must not provide other forms of benefit; and
- the scheme must provide that no person may hold CSOP options over shares with an unrestricted value of more than £30,000 (measured at the date of grant of the options).

The limitation on option grants takes into account all of the unexercised qualifying CSOP options granted to a person by the scheme organiser or any associated company.

Examples of unacceptable features in CSOP scheme rules that are highlighted by HMRC in their guidance at ETASSUM 41140 are rules that enable:

- paying the exercise price in instalments or in advance;
- paying the exercise price in shares;
- settling the options in cash instead of in shares;
- stock-appreciation rights (see **9.1** above);

- making the grant of options conditional on the employee entering into a "put option", under which the employee could be forced to buy shares at a disadvantageous price;
- forcing the participants to relinquish rights to participate in other statutory share schemes; and
- loan arrangements connected with the options.

The scheme must provide that the exercise price of options should not be manifestly less than the market value of shares of the same class at the time that the option is granted (HMRC may allow the value to be determined at an earlier date to make the plan administration more straightforward in the case of a quoted company).

The scheme must also provide that the options cannot be transferred.

The legislation also provides for a number of optional features that can be included in scheme rules. Serious consideration should be given to including all of these features, as they increase the flexibility of the scheme to deal with changes to the employees' and company's circumstances.

The scheme can also provide the following features:

- for the price and number of shares to be varied where there is a variation of share capital. This is a recommended inclusion in the scheme rules – see **14.5.2** below;
- for the participant's personal representatives to exercise options after his or her death – see **14.6**;
- allowing the employee to exercise the options on cessation of employment – see **14.6**; and
- allowing options to be exercised on a sale of the company – see **14.5**.

Law: ITEPA 2003, Sch. 4, para. 5-6, 21-25A

14.2.2 Implementation process

The implementation of a Schedule 4 CSOP broadly follows the same process as the implementation of an EMI scheme, as set out at **13.4.2**:

- the company's articles of association should be reviewed to ensure that they cater for employee share ownership and that the rights of the shares under option reflect the commercial intention of the shareholders – any changes to the articles should ideally be made before the options are granted;
- the terms of the options should be determined:
  - will there be performance conditions?
  - how will leavers' options be treated?
  - what happens if the company is taken over?
  - when will the options be exercisable?
- any shareholders' agreements will need to be reviewed to ensure that the rights of other shareholders have been taken into account and that any approvals process can be fully factored into the implementation timeline;
- plan rules and ancillary documents will need to be drafted;
- the plan will need to be adopted by the company; and
- the scheme will need to be set up on HMRC's online reporting system.

14.2.3 Granting CSOP options

Once a plan has been established, the following steps are needed to grant options:

- the company needs to finalise to whom options will be granted and the terms on which the selected employees will benefit from the options;
- a valuation exercise should be undertaken, to determine whether the options fit within the scheme limits and also to ensure that the exercise price is equal to the shares' market value, so that the options can be qualifying CSOP options;
- it is strongly recommended that the valuation is agreed with HMRC Shares and Assets Valuation ("SAV") before options are granted;
- option grants should be timed to fall within the period of validity of the agreement with SAV;

- options are typically granted by deed, meaning that the option grants will be treated as having been made once the grantor company has executed the deed;
- option certificates should be distributed to the employees.

When options are granted, a number of items must be notified to the option holders as soon as possible after the date of grant:

- the exercise price of the option;
- the number and class of shares under option (or the mechanism for calculating the number of shares);
- any restrictions on the shares;
- when an option may be exercised; and
- when an option will lapse or be cancelled, including any performance conditions.

It is advisable to include all of this information in any option certificates given to the participants, so that it can be clearly shown that the grantor has fulfilled its obligations under the legislation. Section **13.4.3** above sets out the practicalities of notifying option-holders about the complexities of the rights attaching to shares.

If the options are to be granted over shares held by an EBT, a parallel process of consultation with the trustees should take place and, ideally, they will be made party to the grant of options.

The grant of options must be notified to HMRC as part of an annual return process (unlike EMI, no in-year notification is required), see **14.8**.

Law: ITEPA 2003, Sch. 4, para. 21A

14.2.4 *Performance conditions and the exercise of discretion*

The considerations about setting performance conditions and exercising discretion apply equally to EMI and CSOP options and are discussed in more detail at **13.4.4** above.

14.3 Employee tax treatment

14.3.1 Income tax and NIC – grant of options

The CSOP Code contains an anomaly in the post-FA 2003 legislative scheme, in that it is possible for tax charges to arise when CSOP options are granted.

Although the CSOP Code very clearly stipulates that a CSOP option must not be granted with an exercise price that is less than the market value of a share on the date of grant, the legislation allows a margin of error: if, by an oversight, a CSOP option is granted with an exercise price that is up to 15% less than the market value of a share, then the option will still be a qualifying option, but the difference between the market value of the shares and the exercise price will be treated as taxable employment income on the date of grant.

If the options are granted with an exercise price that is more than 15% less than the market value of a share, the option will not be a qualifying CSOP option and, if it is valid at all, will only take effect as a non-statutory option.

Law: ITEPA 2003, s. 526

14.3.2 Income tax and NIC – exercise of options

Provided that the CSOP scheme remains a qualifying Schedule 4 CSOP throughout the life of the options, then the exercise of the options will not give rise to tax charges where the conditions set out in ITEPA 2003, s. 524 are met.

In order to qualify for tax-free treatment, the following conditions must be met:

- the option must be exercised in accordance with the terms of the CSOP scheme;
- there is no avoidance motive underlying the grant or exercise of the options;
- the options are not exercised after the tenth anniversary of the date of grant; and

- either –
  - the options are exercised after the third anniversary of grant, or
  - the options are exercised before the third anniversary by a statutory "good leaver" (see **14.6**) or as a result of a transaction (see **14.5**).

Law: ITEPA 2003, s. 524

14.3.3 Capital gains tax

Unlike EMI options, options granted under CSOP do not confer any automatic right to entrepreneurs' relief ("ER"). Unless the employee's other shareholdings meet the requirements for ER, an employee will pay CGT at the standard rate on selling his or her shares.

In calculating the employee's CGT liability, the base cost of the shares acquired under CSOP will be the exercise price paid to acquire them.

Example: CGT treatment

Toffee Ventures Limited grants Reshma a qualifying CSOP option over 15,000 shares, with an exercise price of £2.00 per share, which is their market value as agreed with HMRC.

Five years later, Fudge Capital PLC acquires Toffee Ventures Limited for consideration of £18.00 per share. Reshma exercises her option and sells her shares as part of the transaction. Her tax position is as follows:

Proceeds of sale (15,000 x £18.00)	£270,000
Exercise price (15,000 x £2.00)	(£30,000)
Chargeable gain	£240,000
CGT at 20%	(£48,000)
Reshma's net position	£192,000

14.4 Company tax treatment

14.4.1 Corporation tax relief

As with EMI, the employer company will be entitled to claim corporation tax relief under the ordinary provisions in CTA 2009,

Part 12 provided that the other conditions for relief are met (see **Chapter 6** above for more information).

14.4.2 PAYE and NIC

Whether any tax liabilities arising under a Schedule 4 CSOP are subject to PAYE and NIC will depend on the status of the option shares at the time of the chargeable event: if the option shares are readily convertible assets (RCAs) at the time of the chargeable event, PAYE will need to be operated and NIC will also arise. If the shares are not RCAs, any tax charges will be self-assessment matters for the employee.

The rules on RCAs and PAYE are set out in more detail at **7.4** above.

14.5 Transactions

14.5.1 Takeovers

Where a grantor company is taken over by another company, it may be possible for the employees holding CSOP options to exercise them before the third anniversary of grant without incurring income tax charges. Alternatively, the CSOP options may be swapped for new options with the same tax benefits.

Under ITEPA 2003, Sch. 4, para. 25A, a CSOP scheme is allowed to provide that share options may be exercised in the period of six months following the date on which:

- control of the company has passed to a person who made a general offer to shareholders;
- the court sanctions a compromise or arrangement under CA 2006, s. 899;
- there is a non-UK reorganisation that meets the requirements of sub-para (6A); or
- a person becomes bound or entitled to acquire shares in the company under CA 2006, s. 979-982 or s. 983-985 (the statutory "drag-along" and "tag-along" provisions (see **10.4.2**)).

If the transaction would result in the shares failing to meet the requirements of the CSOP Code, then the legislation allows 20 days for the options to be exercised.

Part 5: Statutory share schemes

The CSOP rules are also permitted to allow an employee to exercise options in the 20 days leading up to the events mentioned above, with the exercise of the option being conditional on the transaction actually taking place.

Where an option is exercised in accordance with para. 25A, the exercise of the option will be exempt from income tax and NIC, even if the option was exercised less than three years from the date of grant (ITEPA 2003, s. 524).

The rules of the scheme must provide for options to be exercised in these circumstances in order for the relief to apply.

Provisions are made for options to be replaced with new options where there is a company transaction that involves the grantor company being taken over by another company (Sch. 4, para. 26 and 27). The replacement options must be granted in the six month period following the date of the transaction (this is determined in the same way for the purposes of para. 26-27 as it is for para. 25A).

The new options will stand in the place of the old options for tax purposes provided that:

- the new options are to acquire shares in a different company;
- the shares are in a company that is obtaining control of the scheme organiser responsible for the old options;
- the shares and the options meet the requirements of the CSOP Code;
- the new options are exercisable in the same way as the old options;
- the total market value (UMV, see 2.6 above) of the shares under option is the same; and
- the aggregate exercise price payable is the same.

Example: Company transactions

Toffee Ventures Limited has granted a qualifying CSOP option to Zahra to acquire 10,000 shares at an exercise price of £2.00 per share.

Two years after the date of grant, Toffee Ventures Limited is acquired by Fudge Capital PLC for £18.00 per share and Zahra agrees to release her option in consideration for the grant of a replace option over shares in Fudge Capital PLC.

Zahra's replacement option entitles her to acquire 60,000 shares in Fudge Capital PLC at an exercise price of £0.33 per share. Fudge Capital PLC's share price is £3.00 per share on the date of the exchange of options.

Because the aggregate value of shares under option has remained unchanged and the aggregate exercise price of the options is also the same, the replacement option can be a qualifying CSOP option and Zahra will be able to exercise it in a year's time (i.e. three years after the date of grant of the old options) without incurring income tax charges.

Law: ITEPA 2003, s. 524; Sch. 4, para. 25A-27; CA 2006, s. 899, 979-985

14.5.2 Variation of share capital

Specific provision is made for the option exercise price and number of shares under option to be varied following a variation of share capital.

See **13.7** above for a detailed outline of HMRC's approach to variations of share capital and to demergers.

Law: ITEPA 2003, Sch. 5, para. 22(3)

14.6 Leavers

14.6.1 The basic rules

The legislation permits a number of courses of action for dealing with leavers. In each case the relieving provisions must be explicitly included in the scheme rules:

- the scheme may provide for options to be exercised after someone has left employment with the company;
- the personal representatives of a deceased participant may be permitted to exercise the option in the 12 months following his or her death;
- the scheme may also provide that certain fixed categories of statutory good leavers can exercise their options up to six months after their leaving date.

Where a leaver exercises a qualifying CSOP option before the third anniversary of the date of grant, and does so within six months of the end of his or her employment, ITEPA 2003, s. 524(2B) exempts the option gain from income tax if that person is leaving:

- by reason of injury, disability, redundancy or retirement;
- because the employee's employment has been transferred to another employer in a transaction covered by the *Transfer of Undertakings (Protection of Employment) Regulations* 2006 ("TUPE"); or
- by reason of the employee's employer company ceasing to be a member of the same group as the scheme organiser.

If an option-holder leaves for any other reason, and is allowed to exercise his or her option before the third anniversary of grant, the option gain will be taxed as if the option is a non-statutory option, meaning that the difference between the market value of the option shares at the date of exercise and the exercise price will be treated as taxable employment income.

If, however, the plan rules allow leavers to continue to hold their options and to exercise them after the third anniversary of grant, they will benefit from tax relief, as their options will be treated as qualifying CSOP options.

Example: leavers

Megan, Hannah, Reshma and Zahra are granted qualifying CSOP options by Fudge Capital PLC.

On the first anniversary of the date of grant, Reshma leaves the company to take up a directorship elsewhere. The company agrees to allow Reshma to retain her options, which she exercises on the third anniversary of grant. The exercise of the option is taking place on or after the third anniversary of the date of grant and is therefore exempt from income tax.

Six months later, the company disposes of Toffee Ventures Limited, which is Zahra's employer. Zahra is allowed to exercise her options under a provision in the scheme rules. As Zahra is a statutory good leaver within ITEPA 2003, s. 524(2B)(a)(iii), the option exercise is not treated as giving rise to taxable employment income.

On the second anniversary of the date of grant, Megan leaves to travel the world. She is allowed to exercise her options. Because Megan is not in one of the classes of statutory good leavers, and is exercising her option before the third anniversary of grant, the option gain will be treated as taxable employment income and, as Fudge Capital PLC is a quoted company, whose shares will be RCAs, PAYE withholding will need to be operated and NIC levied.

On the fourth anniversary of the date of grant, Hannah leaves to set up her own business. She exercises her option and, as it is more than three years from the date of grant, she will benefit from relief from income tax on her option gain.

14.6.2 Restriction on use of discretion

It is not uncommon for EMI options to be framed so that the owners of the company have a broad discretion as to how to deal with leavers.

For qualifying CSOP schemes, HMRC's long-standing practice, set out at ETASSUM 44470, is to restrict the use of discretion, especially where a leaver falls within one of the categories of statutory good leavers. In short, a CSOP scheme must either allow statutory good leavers to exercise their options or must give them no right to exercise their options.

This means that if a scheme gives the directors the ability to allow leavers to exercise their options, the statutory good leavers must be carved out from that discretion.

Law: ITEPA 2003, s. 524; Sch. 4, para. 24-25A

14.7 Amending options

As a qualifying CSOP is a scheme, it is quite difficult to change the terms of options between grants without amending the scheme as a whole (other than varying performance conditions between participants). Because the scheme as a whole is adopted by the company, the company's own internal governance may mean that shareholders may need to be consulted on any changes (not necessarily an onerous proposition in a private company, but far more difficult in the context of a quoted company).

Varying the terms of options once they have granted is possible, but may require the consent of the option holders (in a public company setting this is often quite straightforward, as the bulk of options granted under a scheme are likely to be held by a small number of senior managers, who will exercise their majority to push through any changes).

The same caveats apply to CSOP as apply to EMI about the risks associated with amending options (see **13.8.2**).

14.8 Reporting

As with SIP, the employing company must register the CSOP with HMRC after the first options have been granted, not later than 6 July following the end of the tax year in which they are granted.

The company will also have an annual reporting obligation to HMRC in respect of CSOP transactions. If no transactions have been undertaken, then a nil return will need to be filed.

15. Share incentive plans (SIP)

15.1 Eligibility for a Schedule 2 SIP

15.1.1 Eligibility – shares

Shares used in a Schedule 2 SIP (i.e. a SIP that qualifies for relief under the SIP Code – see **12.1** above) must be fully paid up, irredeemable shares that form part of the ordinary share capital of the issuing company.

The term "ordinary share capital" is defined in ITA 2007, s. 989 as being all of a company's issued share capital except for shares that have a fixed rate of dividend and have no other right to participate in the company's profits. In practice, unless the shares are fixed rate preference shares, the likelihood is that they will count as "ordinary share capital".

The shares must be one of the following:

   i.   shares in a company that is not under the control of another company;
   ii. shares of a class listed on a recognised stock exchange;
   iii. shares in a company which is subject to an employee-ownership trust that meets the conditions set out in TCGA 1992, s. 236I – 236U; or
   iv. shares in a company which is under the control of a listed company.

For conditions (ii) or (iv) to apply, the company must not be under the control of five or fewer persons.

Shares in a service company will also not qualify for use in a SIP. A service company is a company whose only significant activity is providing the services of its employees to:

- the person who controls the service company (for example, the parent company of a larger trading group);
- the persons who jointly control the service company; or

- a company associated with the service company (for example, another company in the same group of companies, or a company under common control).

The purpose of this rule is to prevent groups of companies from establishing a SIP to save tax without giving the employees a stake in the group's actual trade.

Law: ITEPA 2003, Sch. 2, para. 25-29

15.1.2 *Eligibility – employees*

Individuals will be eligible to participate in the plan if they are employed by the company whose shares are being used in the plan (the "issuer company") or one of its subsidiaries.

It is possible to stipulate a minimum period of service before employees can participate in awards under a SIP. This qualification period cannot exceed two years and must apply to all of the employees able to take part in the SIP. Where a company specifies a minimum service period, an individual must have remained in employment with a group company throughout the qualifying period.

The individual must not be currently participating in another Schedule 2 SIP established by a connected company or have previously participated in another Schedule 2 SIP in the same tax year.

Eligibility is tested at the following times:

- in the case of free shares, when the award is made;
- for partnership and matching shares, when the first deduction to acquire partnership shares is made from salary.

The legislation does not stipulate a minimum number of hours that an employee must work and does not prevent employees with other shareholdings from participating.

Law: ITEPA 2003, Sch. 2, para. 13-18A

15.2 Establishing the scheme

15.2.1 *Scheme requirements*

The scheme must be for the benefit of employees and should be structured to give the employees a continuing stake in the issuer company.

The same offer to participate must be made to every employee and, if they choose to participate, they must do so on the same terms. The scheme should not wholly or mainly be for the benefit of directors or employees receiving the highest levels of remuneration.

There should be no other conditions set for employees to participate or to benefit from their share awards other than what is contained within the scheme.

The scheme must not be a part of any loan arrangement or provision associated with a loan to any employees.

A SIP will require an instrument to define who the settlor, trustees and beneficiaries will be. The employee trust would be structured as a discretionary trust for the benefit of the employees.

The trustees will be the legal owners and have control of any assets held within the trust. The trustee could be a company within the group, or a professional trustee could be appointed, but the trust must be an onshore trust.

Law: ITEPA 2003, Sch. 2, para. 6-12

15.2.2 *Implementation process*

The following steps are needed to implement a SIP:

- Preparing SIP documentation, including the SIP rules, a declaration or deed of trust for the SIP trust and the ancillary documents for the employees. HMRC have published a number of "model" documents for SIP that would be acceptable for most companies' purposes.
- Deciding who will act as trustee of the SIP trust.
- Ensuring that the company's articles of association are in a form suitable for use in a SIP and that they meet the company's commercial objectives with regard to issues like

Part 5: Statutory share schemes

the treatment of leavers, drag-along and tag-along (see **10.4.2** for an explanation of these terms).
- Determining the source of the shares to be used in the SIP, whether they are to be newly issued shares or shares acquired from other shareholders.
- Notifying HMRC of the establishment of the SIP when the first awards are made.

15.2.3 Making SIP awards

In outline, the following steps will need to be taken to make SIP awards:

- If the shares are not listed on a recognised stock exchange, a valuation will need to be agreed with HMRC before shares can be awarded.
- Invitation letters are sent to employees, setting out the terms of the SIP offer.
- Applications are collected from employees.
- Applications are reviewed and assessed against the maximum dilution that the shareholders have allowed, scaling back awards as necessary.
- Free shares awards are made.
- The accumulation period for partnership shares begins and deductions from salary are made.
- At the end of the accumulation period, the deductions are applied to acquire partnership shares, and matching shares are awarded.

15.3 SIP awards

15.3.1 Terms of the offer

Participation in a SIP must be offered to all of the eligible employees of a participating company. The offer must be made on the same terms to all of the employees and they must be permitted to participate on the same terms.

Where a SIP is established by a group of companies, it would be a breach of this rule if lower paid employees were predominantly employed by companies that did not participate in the SIP, while companies employing higher paid employees did participate.

Where an employer has a hard limit to the number of shares that can be used in the scheme (for example, a private company may only have a fixed pool of shares that it is willing to give away to employees or a public company may be bound by dilution limits agreed with its investors), then any steps taken to scale back awards of shares to employees under SIP must be taken on the basis that they apply proportionately across the employee population and do not disproportionately advantage higher paid employees.

15.3.2 Partnership shares and matching shares

Employees can be given the opportunity to contribute up to £1,800 from their gross salary to purchase partnership shares (or 10% of their annual earnings if lower). The partnership share money can be taken as a regular deduction from salary or as a single lump sum (for example, an employee could use a bonus payment to make a one-off contribution to the SIP).

The organising company may specify in the SIP scheme rules that there is a minimum amount that can be contributed to the SIP, but this cannot be more than £10 and must apply across the board to all employees, irrespective of their individual pay scale.

The partnership share money must be handed over to the SIP trustees as soon as possible after it has been deducted and the SIP trustees must hold the money in an account with a properly regulated bank. Any interest that arises on the money held in the SIP trustees' bank account will belong to the employee absolutely, may not be applied to purchase partnership shares and will be taxable interest income in his or her hands.

The SIP trustee may either immediately purchase partnership shares as soon as it receives the contributions from the employees or it may collect the partnership share money over a period (known as an accumulation period) and then use all of the money collected during the period to purchase shares.

Where a company elects to operate its SIP with an accumulation period:

Part 5: Statutory share schemes

- the accumulation period must be of a fixed duration;
- the period can last no longer than 12 months;
- the accumulation period must be the same for all employees; and
- SIP trustees must apply the money that they have collected not later than 30 days after the end of the accumulation period.

The SIP trustee can apply the collected money to purchase shares in the market, if the shares are traded, to subscribe for new shares or exchange it for shares that they already hold.

The number of shares that an employee will acquire will depend on whether there is an accumulation period or not. If there is no accumulation period, the number of shares will be calculated by dividing the money held by the trustee by the value of a share on the date that the shares are acquired.

If there is "change" from a share purchase (i.e. where the employee's contributions divided by the relevant share price does not result in a whole number of shares), it should be carried forward to the next partnership share offering.

Any partnership share money held by the SIP trustees should be repaid to the employee where:

- he or she leaves employment before the last deduction has been taken in an accumulation period;
- a repayment is requested by the employee;
- the plan ceases to qualify as a Schedule 2 SIP; or
- the employer company gives a scheme termination notice.

Partnership share money repaid to an employee will be treated as taxable employment income in his or her hands and subject to PAYE and NIC withholding – any repayment should be made via the employer company's payroll.

The employer may also choose to award a maximum of two matching shares for each partnership share acquired by an employee.

Law: ITEPA 2003, Sch. 2, para. 43-61

15.3.3 Free shares

In any tax year, free shares worth up to £3,600, valued on the date of award, can be awarded to each employee.

The number of shares awarded can be varied by reference to one of three factors:

- length of service;
- hours worked; and
- remuneration.

Where an employer wishes to use a combination of these measures, they will have to do one of the following:

- effectively split their award of free shares into two or more separate awards, each governed by its own eligibility criteria; or
- adopt a "points" system to determine the total number of free shares that each employee is entitled to.

These award factors cannot be used to determine eligibility to receive an award – each employee who is eligible for free shares must receive free shares – but these measures can only be used to determine whether that is a greater or lesser number of shares.

Example: free shares

Bobs plc decides to begin making awards of free shares under its SIP.

In the first year, the company decides to vary the awards by reference to length of service, with employees who have more than 20 years' service receiving the maximum award.

- Aimee has 21 years' service with the company and receives the maximum award over shares worth £3,600.
- Elsa has 13 years' service and so qualifies for free shares worth £2,340 (i.e. £3,600 x 13 ÷ 20).

In the second year, Bobs plc decides to vary the awards by a combination of length of service and remuneration, allocating half of the award to each measure. The length of service criterion is measured in the same way as the previous year, while the remuneration criterion is based on the maximum award being given to employees earning in excess of £45,000:

- Aimee now has 22 years' service with the company and receives £25,000 per annum. Her award will be free shares worth £2,800 (i.e. (£1,800 x £25,000 ÷ £45,000) + £1,800);
- Elsa has 14 years' service and is paid £75,000 per annum. Her award of free shares will have a value of £3,060 (i.e. (£1,800 x 14 ÷ 20) + £1,800).

Law: ITEPA 2003, Sch. 2, para. 34-42

15.3.4 Dividend shares

If an employer decides to offer dividend shares, then any dividends an employee receives from the shares held within the plan can be used to purchase more shares. If dividend shares are acquired in this way, the dividends used to purchase shares are exempt from tax. This means that these dividends can be omitted from the income tax computation in the tax year in which they are received.

If the employee wishes to keep the dividends, and not use the cash to purchase more shares, the dividends not reinvested are taxable in the normal way.

The shares purchased using the dividend income cannot be subject to any forfeiture and must be of the same class and carry the same rights as the shares from which the dividend was received.

Law: ITEPA 2003, Sch. 2, para. 62-69

15.3.5 Performance conditions

It is possible to make awards of free shares subject to performance conditions (none of the other award types can have performance conditions). The employees must receive notice of any performance conditions, which must be:

- applicable to all employees who receive awards;
- based on the performance of a business unit comprising more than two employees (i.e. it is not permissible to use performance measures that are personal to each employee); and

- be based on objective criteria, like business results, and be fair measures of the performance of the business unit.

The performance conditions must be operated in one of two ways, either:

- Method one, where whole company performance conditions are imposed. At least 20% of the shares in the award must be awarded without reference to performance, with the remaining shares made subject to the performance condition. Or
- Method two, where the performance conditions are being tailored to separate business units. Some or all of the shares in the award must be awarded by reference to performance; the awards to the employees in that performance unit must be made on the same terms and must be consistent with the performance conditions set for other business units.

Law: ITEPA 2003, Sch. 2, para. 38-42

15.3.6 Leavers

On the termination of an employee's employment, any shares awarded must be removed from the plan.

Certain classes of leavers will benefit from tax exemptions even if the shares have not been held throughout the holding period. These are people leaving:

- by reason of injury or disability;
- by reason of redundancy;
- because their employment is transferred to another entity in a transfer to which the *Transfer of Undertakings (Protection of Employment) Regulations* 2006 apply;
- because the employing company is taken over and leaves the group;
- by reason of retirement; or
- by reason of death.

Free and matching shares can be subject to forfeiture, meaning that they can be taken back from leavers for little or no consideration.

Although shares held by leavers under partnership and dividend share awards cannot be subject to forfeiture, it would be possible to compel leavers holding dividend or partnership shares to sell them at market value when they leave.

Law: ITEPA 2003, s. 498; SI 2006/246

15.4 Employee tax treatment

15.4.1 Operation of PAYE and NIC

Tax charges arising in connection with the SIP will be subject to PAYE withholding and NIC charges if the SIP shares are readily convertible assets ("RCAs") (see **7.4**).

Where the shares in the SIP constitute RCAs, tax at the employee's highest rate must be withheld and PAYE and NIC must be paid to HMRC by 22nd of each month by electronic payment. Details would be reported on the full payment submission to HMRC under RTI.

There are no specific forms that would need to be submitted with the withholding, but the taxable amounts would have to be included on the annual statement of employment income for each employee (forms P14 and P35) for the relevant tax year and filed by the May 19th following the end of the tax year. Any taxable employment income arising from a SIP that is subject to PAYE withholding would also need to be included in the employer's year-end reporting, including form P60.

If the SIP shares are not RCAs, then any taxable employment income arising when an employee withdraws shares from the SIP will need to be included in that person's self-assessment return and any tax paid by 31 January following the end of the tax year.

As set out at **7.4**, an RCA is (in essence) any asset that can be easily converted into cash. This includes assets that can be used to realise a cash sum (e.g. the asset can be used as collateral to secure a loan or advance).

The legislation treats shares as being convertible into cash if they are listed on a recognised stock exchange or if "trading arrangements" exist or are likely to come into existence. Examples of trading arrangements include listing on a non-recognised exchange, such as AIM, or if the company is in the process of being acquired by a third party.

The SIP legislation at ITEPA 2003, s. 509 adjusts the usual rules on RCAs by ignoring any market for the shares which is created because the SIP trustees are acquiring shares to be used in the plan.

15.4.2 Employee tax treatment of awards – income taxes and NIC

Once shares have been awarded under SIP they are held in a dedicated employee share trust. No tax will arise while the shares are held in the SIP trust provided that the company, the employee and the SIP scheme itself continue to qualify.

The tax treatment of the shares on their withdrawal from the trust will depend on the type of share award and the length of time that they have been held by the trustees.

Partnership shares:

- These are bought out of gross salary. No tax charges or NIC arise on the salary used to buy partnership shares.
- If the shares are kept in the trust for five years, they can be withdrawn from the trust tax free (i.e. no amounts will be treated as taxable employment income).
- If the shares are withdrawn after the third anniversary, but before the fifth anniversary, the employee will be treated as having received taxable employment income equal to the lesser of:
  o the market value of the shares on the date of withdrawal; and
  o the amount of salary originally sacrificed to buy the partnership shares.
- If the shares are withdrawn before the third anniversary, the value of the shares on the date of withdrawal will be treated as taxable employment income.

Free and matching shares:

- No tax charges arise when free and matching shares are awarded;

- If the shares are kept in the trust for five years, they can be withdrawn tax free.
- If the shares are withdrawn after the third anniversary, but before the fifth anniversary, the employee will be treated as having received taxable employment income equal to the lesser of:
  - the market value of the shares on the date of withdrawal; and
  - the market value of the shares on the date that they were awarded to the employee.
- If the shares are withdrawn before the third anniversary, the value of the shares on the date of withdrawal will be treated as taxable employment income.
- The transfer or assignment of the beneficial ownership of the shares by an employee (for example, if the employee executes a trust deed over the shares) will be treated as a withdrawal.

Dividend shares:
- There is no tax charge on dividends reinvested in dividend shares.
- If they are retained within the SIP trust for more than three years they are free from tax.
- If the dividend shares are distributed within three years of the date of acquisition, the employee will be treated as if he or she received taxable dividend income equal to the amount used to acquire the dividend shares under ITTOIA 2005, s. 394.

Where an employee withdraws shares from a SIP, the shares that are withdrawn from the trust are matched on a first in, first out basis, so that employees are given the benefit of the longest holding periods available.

Example: SIP matching

Bobs plc offers partnership and matching shares to its employees. It does not offer dividend shares and has yet to make an award of free shares.

Share incentive plans

Aimee participates in the plan, contributing £750 per year from her gross salary. As Aimee is a higher rate taxpayer, the impact on her net salary is a reduction of £435 per year. Bobs plc matches each of Aimee's partnership shares with one matching share.

At the end of each accumulation period under the plan, the following awards are made to Aimee:

Plan Year	Relevant share price	Number of partnership shares	Number of matching shares	Running total
1	£2.50	300	300	600
2	£3.00	250	250	1,100
3	£4.00	187	187	1,474
4	£4.50	167	167	1,808
5	£5.50	136	136	2,080

Mid-way through year 6, Aimee decides that she wants to take flying lessons and elects to withdraw and sell 1,000 of her SIP shares, which are then priced at £5.75 per share. Aimee realises proceeds of £5,750.

Aimee's tax position is as follows:

- 600 of the shares will be matched with the shares that she was awarded in year 1. Because Aimee has held them for more than five years, she will not have any employment taxes to pay on these shares.
- 400 of the shares are matched with the shares that she was awarded in year 2. As more than three years have elapsed, but than five, Aimee is treated as having realised taxable employment income equal to the initial price/value of the shares – in this case, £1,200 in total (i.e. £3.00 x 400), and Bobs PLC will have to operate PAYE and NIC withholding on this amount.

15.4.3 Employee tax treatment of awards – CGT

Part 1 of Sch. 7D to TCGA 1992 sets out a number of different reliefs for employees and trustees of SIP trusts. The key relief for employees is that they are treated as acquiring their SIP shares at

251

market value for CGT purposes when they withdraw them from the trust; this is because the withdrawal of the shares is treated as a market value disposal by the trustee (which is exempt from tax in the trustee's hands).

It is possible for an employee to retain shares in the SIP trust indefinitely, provided that he or she remains an employee. This means that it is possible for employees to keep shares in the tax-free SIP "wrapper" until they are ready to sell them and to do so without realising a chargeable gain.

Example: CGT treatment

In the example above, Aimee's withdrawal of shares from the SIP is treated as a disposal by the trustees and an acquisition by Aimee at market value – this means that Aimee will not have any tax to pay on her gains.

SIP shares may also be transferred directly to an ISA or to a stakeholder or personal pension, allowing them to retain their CGT free status, even after the employee leaves employment and has to withdraw from the SIP.

15.5 Company tax position

15.5.1 CTA 2009, Part 11

SIP plans fall outside the usual rules on corporation tax deductions set out in CTA 2009, Part 12 and instead have their own regime of rules in CTA 2009, Part 11, Chapter 1, which forms part of the SIP Code.

Where relief is allowed under Part 11, it is given as a deduction in the company's corporation tax calculations, while deemed receipts arising from the SIP are treated as taxable income in the company's hands.

Part 11 allows reliefs for the following expenses:

- the costs associated with establishing a Schedule 2 SIP;
- the running costs of the SIP (for example, trustee fees, fees associated with filings) including the incidental costs of acquiring shares for the plan, including:

- interest paid on borrowing by the trustees to fund share acquisitions,
- incidental costs, including fees, commission, stamp duty and stamp duty reserve tax; and
• contributions to the SIP trust if certain conditions are met.

An additional deduction can be claimed when shares held by the SIP trustees are awarded to employees. The deductions can be revoked or withdrawn if the SIP loses its status as a Schedule 2 SIP.

15.5.2 Deductions for contributions

Provided that there is no tax avoidance motive, CTA 2009, s. 989 provides that a deduction may be claimed by a company that makes contributions to a SIP if:

- the SIP trustees acquire shares from individuals; and
- at the end of 12 months from the acquisition (called the "interim period" in the legislation), the SIP trustee holds shares constituting 10% of the ordinary share capital of the company (or its parent company, in a group setting), which confer rights to 10% of:
  - any distribution of profits by the company; and
  - the assets available for distribution to shareholders on a winding up.

It does not matter if the trustee has awarded shares to employees at the point that the interim period ends; so long as they are held by the trustee under the terms of the SIP, they will count. The relief is given in the accounting period in which the interim period ends.

Under CTA 2009, s. 990, the relief can be clawed back by HMRC if the trustees have not awarded at least 30% of the shares before the fifth anniversary of the date that they were acquired by the SIP trustees, or if the trustees have not awarded all of them before the tenth anniversary. The clawback would be reversed when and if qualifying awards are made over all of the shares.

15.5.3 Deductions for share awards

An employer company can claim relief under Part 11 when free, matching or partnership shares are awarded to its employees in the period that the awards are made. No deductions are given for the provision of dividend shares

For free and matching shares, a deduction is given equal to the market value of the shares on the date that they were acquired by the SIP trustee (and where the trustee acquires shares in a number of tranches, they are matched on a FIFO basis). For partnership shares, the relief is given on the amount, if any, by which the market value of the partnership shares at the date that they were originally acquired by the SIP trustee exceeds the price paid by the employee to acquire them.

These deductions may only be claimed if:

- the employee is UK resident and taxable under ITEPA 2003, s. 15 on his or her earnings, or is taxable on the remittance basis under s. 20;
- the shares do not have any feature that could cause them to depreciate in value, which other classes of shares in the company do not have (for example, a mechanism to convert shares held by leavers into deferred shares);
- no other deduction has been claimed for the shares;
- no deduction has been claimed under s. 989 of CTA 2009 (see **15.5.2** above) in respect of the shares; and
- the shares have not previously been forfeited by a participant.

15.5.4 Deductions for partnership share money deducted from salary

Although the salary deducted from an employee's pay to acquire partnership shares does not count as taxable employment income in the employee's hands, it remains part of the employer's remuneration expense and deductible for corporation tax purposes.

15.5.5 Stamp taxes

Under FA 2001, s. 95 the transfer of dividend and partnership shares to an employee is exempt from both stamp duty and stamp duty reserve tax.

Acquisitions of shares by the SIP trustees from other shareholders will be subject to stamp taxes in the usual way.

15.6 Employee share trust taxation

As set out above, a SIP trust would be structured as an onshore discretionary trust for the benefit of the employees.

The SIP trust will need to be registered with HMRC using the online trust registration service for self-assessment. New trusts will need to register online by 5 October following the end of tax year in which the trust has been set up or, if later, when it starts to make income or chargeable gains. For ease of compliance it may be easier to register the trust at the point when it is set up.

A UK resident trust will be subject to UK taxes on any worldwide income or gains generated within the trust (subject to double tax relief) and should be reported on a self-assessment trust tax return. The SIP Code at ITA 2007, Part 9, Chapter 5 provides exemptions for dividends arising on un-awarded shares held by the SIP trustees – provided that the shares have not been held for more than a certain period, no tax charges will arise on the dividends. If the shares were acquired using a contribution that qualified for relief under CTA 2009, s. 989 the time period is ten years; otherwise it will be:

- for shares that are readily convertible assets (RCAs), two years;
- for shares that are not RCAs, five years.

15.7 Disqualifying events

A disqualifying event will occur when the value of the shares subject to the plan is affected because of either:

- an alteration made to the share capital of the company (any of whose shares are subject to the plan trust); or
- the rights attached to any shares within the company.

A disqualifying event can also include where shares of a class in a plan receive a different treatment – for example on the dividend payable, repayment or offer of substituted or additional shares, securities or rights of any description in respect of the shares.

The effect of a disqualifying event is that the plan loses its status as a Schedule 2 SIP and no further awards may be made under it. Awards made before the date of the disqualifying event are

Part 5: Statutory share schemes

"grandfathered", meaning that they continue to be treated as qualifying awards of SIP shares and will benefit from the reliefs in the SIP Code.

15.8 Company transactions

Where a company that operates a SIP is taken over, the employees can benefit from the full value of the SIP tax relief – even if they have not held their shares for the full holding period – if the takeover transaction meets certain criteria. In order to qualify, the transaction must take one of three forms:

- a compromise, arrangement or scheme that affects all of the ordinary share capital of the company or shares of the same class as the SIP shares;
- a general offer that is made to all of the holders of shares of the same class as the SIP shares, that is made conditional on the person making the offer obtaining control of the company; or
- the acquirer is exercising rights under CA 2006, s. 979-982, to drag-along minority shareholders to join a transaction, or the SIP shareholders are entitled to exercise their rights under CA 2006, s. 983-985 to tag-along with majority shareholders as part of the transaction.

The employees must be given no choice as to whether they receive cash – if there is a share alternative, that can be taken up or refused, the employee will not benefit from relief if he or she takes cash instead.

If the employee receives shares or loan notes, these can potentially be retained in the SIP trust until the holding period has been met and then withdrawn.

Where the offer is a combination of cash and shares, without any option being given to the SIP participants about the mix between cash and shares, then the cash element may qualify to be taken without being treated as giving rise to taxable employment income, while the shares are retained by the trust.

15.9 Reporting

The employing company must register the SIP with HMRC after the first awards have been made, not later than 6 July following the end of the tax year in which they are made.

The company will also have an annual reporting obligation to HMRC in respect of SIP transactions. If no transactions have been undertaken, then a nil return will need to be filed.

Table of legislation

Companies Act 2006
...... 3.3.4, 10.4.3
288 ...... 10.4.2
566 ...... 10.4.3
682 ...... 10.4.4
899 ...... 13.7.1, 14.5.1
979-985 ...... 13.7.1, 14.5.1, 15.8
1166 ...... 10.4.3

Contracts (Rights of Third Parties) Act 1999
...... 5.5.4

Corporation Tax Act 2009
Pt. 11 ...... 15.5.1
Pt. 11, Ch. 1 ...... 6.1, 15.5.1
Pt. 11, Ch. 2 ...... 6.9
Pt. 12 ...... 1.1, Ch. 6, 7.4, 8.2.4, 11.7, 11.8, Ch. 12, 13.6.1, 14.4.1
Pt. 12, Ch. 2 ...... 6.3
Pt. 12, Ch. 3 ...... 6.4
Pt. 12, Ch. 4 ...... 6.5
Pt. 12, Ch. 5 ...... 6.6
Pt. 20 ...... 1.1, 6.8, 9.4.3, 11.3.2, 11.7, 11.8
989 ...... 15.5.2, 15.5.3, 15.6
990 ...... 15.5.2
1007A 6.7
1015A 6.7
1016 ...... 6.4
1023 ...... 6.4
1024 ...... 6.4
1025A 6.7
1027 ...... 6.5
1290 ...... 6.8
1030A 6.7
1034 ...... 6.6
1038A 6.1

Corporation Tax Act 2010
449 ...... 6.2
450 ...... 13.1.3
451 ...... 13.1.3
455 ...... 11.3.1

259

1033-1043	5.6.2
1033	9.4.2

Finance Act 1966
25	3.5.1

Finance Act 2000
	12.5.1

Finance Act 2001
95	15.5.5

Finance Act 2003
	2.1, 3.3, 8.1
Sch. 22	1.1
Sch. 23	1.1, 6.1
Sch. 24	1.1

Finance Act 2005
	4.5.1

Finance Act 2013
	5.7.2
Sch. 24	13.5.5

Finance Act 2014
	5.2.3, 8.1, 12.1

Finance Act 2017
	11.7

Higher Education Act 2004
41(2)	4.5.4

Income Tax Act 2007
Pt. 9, Ch. 5	15.6
Pt. 10A	1.3.2
Pt. 13, Ch. 1	11.4
188	13.1.3
191A	13.1.7
383	3.4.4
392	3.4.4
496A	11.1
496B	11.1
497	11.1
698	9.4.3
701	11.4
989	15.1.1

993	13.1.2
995	13.1.2

Income Tax (Earnings and Pensions) Act 2003

	1.1, 12.1
Pt. 2, Ch. 1	3.3.6, 3.3.7
Pt. 3, Ch. 1	3.1, 3.4.1
Pt. 3, Ch. 7	3.4.2
Pt. 7	Ch. 1, 2.1, 2.6, 3.1, 4.1, 4.5.1, 4.5.5, 5.3.2
Pt. 7, Ch. 2	2.5, 3.3, 5.2.2, 5.6.1
Pt. 7, Ch. 3	3.2, 3.3.6, 4.3.1, 4.5.2
Pt. 7, Ch. 3A	Ch. 4, 6.5
Pt. 7, Ch. 3B	Ch. 4, 6.5
Pt. 7, Ch. 3C	3.3.6, 3.4, 5.4, 5.5.1
Pt. 7, Ch. 3D	2.5, 5.5, 5.6.1
Pt. 7, Ch. 4	4.4.1, 4.4.3, 4.5.3, 10.3.2
Pt. 7, Ch. 4A	4.5
Pt. 7, Ch. 5	3.2, 3.3.6, 3.5.1, 3.5.2
Pt. 7A	3.5.4, 9.4.3, 11.6.1, 11.6.3, 11.8
Pt. 9	1.3.2
4	1.3.1
5	1.3.1
15	15.5.3
20	15.5.3
62	1.3.2, 2.1, 2.6
62(3)	2.2, 3.1
175	3.4.2
178	3.4.4
180	3.4.4
222	7.1, 7.5
225	7.6
226	7.6
420	1.3.2
420(1)(b)	11.6.3
421	2.1, 5.5.2
421B	1.3.4, 1.4, 1.5, 3.5.2
421C	5.2.1
421L	8.1.2
423	3.3.3
424	3.3.3
425	3.3.5, 3.3.8, 4.2.3
426	3.3.5, 6.5, 7.6
427	3.3.7, 5.2.3
428	3.3.7, 5.2.2
430	3.3.8, 5.2.3

430A	5.2.3
431	5.2, 5.6.1, 6.5, 9.3
431(1)	3.3.8, 4.5.2, 5.2.3, 5.6.1, 8.1.3, 10.3.2, 13.5.4
431(2)	3.3.8
431A	3.3.8, 13.5.4
431B	3.3.8
437	5.3.2, 5.3.3
438	6.6, 7.6
439	4.3.4
440	4.3.7, 4.3.8
441	5.3.3
442	5.3.1
442A	5.3.4
443	5.3.2
446A	4.2.2
446C	4.2.3
446D	4.2.3
446E-446I	4.2.4
446K	4.2.2, 4.2.5
446Q	3.4.3
446R	3.4.4
446S	3.4.2
446U	5.4.1, 5.4.2
447	4.4.3
449	4.4.2
452	4.5.2
453	4.5.3
454	4.5.2
455	4.5.3
459	4.5.4
471	3.5.2
475	3.5.3
476	6.4, 7.6
480	3.5.4
481	3.5.4
483	3.5.5
498	15.3.6
509	15.4.1
524	14.3.2, 14.5.1, 14.6
526	14.3.1
530	13.5.1
531	13.5.1
532	13.5.3, 13.9
535	13.9

536	13.7.2
554A	11.6.1
554E	11.6.2
554J	11.6.3
554K	11.6.3
554L	11.6.3
554M	11.6.3
696	7.2
698	7.3
700	7.2
702	7.4
Sch. 2	12.1, 12.5, Ch. 15
Sch. 2, para. 6-12	15.2.1
Sch. 2, para. 13-18A	15.1.2
Sch. 2, para. 25-29	15.1.1
Sch. 2, para. 27	13.1.2
Sch. 2, para. 34-42	15.3.3
Sch. 2, para. 38-42	15.3.5
Sch. 2, para. 43-61	15.3.2
Sch. 2, para. 62-69	15.3.4
Sch. 3	12.1, 12.4
Sch. 4	3.5.3, 12.1, 12.3, Ch. 14
Sch. 4, para. 5-6	14.2.1
Sch. 4, para. 7-14	14.1.2
Sch. 4, para. 11	14.1.2
Sch. 4, para. 15-20	14.1.1
Sch. 4, para. 20	14.1.1
Sch. 4, para. 21-25A	14.2.1
Sch. 4, para. 21A	14.2.3
Sch. 4, para. 24-25A	14.6.2
Sch. 4, para. 25A-27	14.5.1
Sch. 4, para. 25A	14.5.1
Sch. 4, para. 26	14.5.1
Sch. 4, para. 27	14.5.1
Sch. 4, para. 36(2)	14.1.1
Sch. 5	Ch. 13
Sch. 5, Pt. 2	13.1.1
Sch. 5, Pt. 5	13.8.2
Sch. 5, Pt. 6	13.7.1
Sch. 5, para. 3-7	13.4.1
Sch. 5, para. 4	13.4.1, 13.7.1
Sch. 5, para. 5	13.3.3
Sch. 5, para. 6	13.3.3
Sch. 5, para. 9	13.1.2

Sch. 5, para. 10	13.1.3
Sch. 5, para. 12	13.1.4
Sch. 5, para. 12A	13.1.5
Sch. 5, para. 13	13.1.6
Sch. 5, para. 14A	13.1.7
Sch. 5, para. 16-23	13.1.6
Sch. 5, para. 22(3)	14.5.2
Sch. 5, para. 24-27	13.3.1
Sch. 5, para. 28-33	13.3.2
Sch. 5, para. 35	13.2
Sch. 5, para. 39	13.7.1
Sch. 5, para. 40	13.7.1
Sch. 5, para. 41-43	13.7.1

Income Tax (Trading and Other Income) Act 2005
394	15.4.2

Inheritance Tax Act 1984
13	11.2.3, 11.3.2, 11.3.3
13(4)	11.2.3
86	11.2.3, 11.3.2, 11.5.1
218	11.2.2
270	11.2.3

Joint Stock Companies Act 1856
	10.1

Social Security Contributions and Benefits Act 1992
Sch. 1, para. 3A	7.6
Sch. 1, para. 3B	5.3.4, 7.6, 9.6

Statutory instruments
SI 2006/246	15.3.6
SI 2008/3229	10.1

Taxation of Chargeable Gains Act 1992
	Ch. 2
Pt. VIII	2.1, 3.1, 3.3.2, 4.2.3, 5.5.2, 5.5.3
17	5.6.1, 9.6, 11.5.1
28	5.2.3
86	11.5.2
87	11.5.2
119A	9.4.2
119A-120	5.6.1
127	13.5.5
135(3)	13.5.5
144ZA	9.6, 11.5.1

144(3)	11.5.1
169I	13.5.5
169S	13.5.5
239	11.3.3
239ZA	9.6, 11.5.1
236I-236U	14.1.1, 15.1.1
272(1)	2.1
273	2.1, 2.5
Sch. 7D	11.5.1, 15.4.3

Index of cases

Abbott v Philbin (1960) UKHL 1 .... 3.5.1
CIR v Burton (1990) 63 TC 191 .... 13.4.4
CIR v Eurocopy plc (1991) 64 TC 370 .... 13.8.2
CIR v Reed International plc (1995) 67 TC 552 .... 13.8.2
Grays Timber Products Ltd v HMRC (Scotland) [2010] UKSC 4 .... 2.5, 5.5.4
HMRC v P A Holdings Ltd [2012] STC 582 .... 4.4.3
Hunters Property plc v HMRC [2018] UKFTT 96 .... 13.1.3
James H Donald (Darvel) Ltd v HMRC [2015] UKUT 514 .... 4.4.3
Mansworth (HMIT) v Jelley [2003] BTC 3, STC 53 .... 9.6, 11.5.1
Sjumarken v HMRC [2015] UKFTT 375 (TC) 3.3.3
Weight v Salmon (1935) 19 TC 174 .... 2.1, 3.1

General index

Accounting for share awards
    accounting entries 8.2.3
    generally 8.2
    interaction with tax rules 8.2.4
    valuation and amortisation 8.2.2

Acquisition of securities
    at below market value
      . exemptions 3.4.4
      . partly paid shares 3.4.3
      . seven-year window 4.2.3
      . subsequent tax charges 3.4.5
      . tax principles 3.4.1, 4.2.3
      . unpaid consideration treated as loan 3.4.2
    changes following .... Ch. 4
    conditional shares regime 3.3.1
    corporation tax relief on 6.3
    elections (effect of) 3.3.8
    employee benefit trusts, by 11.4
    forfeitable securities 3.3.5
    generally .... Ch. 3
    money's worth 3.1
    private companies – Companies Act model articles 3.3.4
    reporting obligations 8.1.3
    restricted securities 3.3
    share options
      . common law position 3.5.1
      . corporation tax relief 6.4
      . exercise of options 3.5.4
      . grant of options 3.5.3
      . release for consideration 3.5.5
      . scope of statutory scheme 3.5.2
    status of securities 3.2
    tax charge
      . on acquisition 3.3.6
      . on future events 3.3.7
    tax principles 3.1
    terms of offer 3.2

Anti-avoidance
    acquisition of convertible securities 4.3.3
    beneficial loan treatment 3.4.4

    dividends (not usually caught) 4.4.3
    non-commercial changes in value 4.2
    post-acquisition changes to shares .... Ch. 4

Articles of company
    choice of shares for scheme 10.1
    treatment of leavers 9.4.5

Beneficial loan
    employee pays less than market value 3.4.1
    exemptions 3.4.4
    unpaid consideration 3.4.2

Capital gains tax
    acquisition by trustees of employee trust 11.4
    company reorganisations (EMI) 13.7.1
    company share option plans 12.3.2, 14.3.3
    computation 5.6.1
    designing a share scheme 9.6
    dilution 9.6
    disposals of securities 5.6
    employee benefit trusts 11.5, 11.8
    enterprise management incentives 13.5.5
    growth shares 10.3.2
    joint share ownership plans 10.3.3
    market value 5.5.2
    nil consideration transfer to employee trust 11.3.3
    offshore trusts 11.5.2
    SAYE 12.4.2
    share incentive plans 12.5.2, 15.4.3

Cash cancellation
    securities options 3.5.5

Classes of shares
    employee shares 10.2

Close companies
    beneficial loan treatment (exemptions) 3.4.4

Communication
    with participants 9.7

Company law considerations
    authority to issue shares 10.4.3
    changing company constitution 10.4.2
    financial assistance 10.4.4
    generally 10.4
    nominal value 10.4.5

Company reorganisations
    EMI considerations.. 13.7.1

Company share option plans
- alternative to EMI 12.6
- amending options 14.7
- annual return 14.2.3
- approved scheme 12.1, 12.3.1
- capital gains tax
  - . entrepreneurs' relief 14.3.3
  - . generally 14.3.3
  - . use of EBT 11.5.1
- corporation tax relief 14.4.1
- counted towards limit re EMI options 13.3.3, 13.5.2
- discretionary nature of 12.1
- disqualifying event re EMI 13.5.2
- eligibility
  - . employees 14.1.2
  - . scheme requirements 14.2.1
  - . shares 14.1.1
  - . value cap 14.2.1
- employee-control shares 14.1.1
- entrepreneurs' relief 14.3.3
- establishing the scheme 14.2
- exercise of options 12.3, 14.3.2
- generally ....Ch. 14
- grant of option...3.5.3, 12.3.2, 14.2.3, 14.3.1
- immediate ownership (contrasted) 9.2.1
- implementation process 14.2.2
- income tax and NIC 14.3
- leavers, treatment of
  - . generally 9.4.1, 9.4.4, 14.2.2, 14.6
  - . restriction on use of discretion 14.6.2
- material interest restriction 14.1.2
- open market shares 14.1.1
- PAYE and NIC..14.4.2
- performance conditions 12.3.1
- relaxation of rules over successive years 12.3.1
- reporting 8.1.4, 14.8
- scheme organiser 14.1.1
- scheme requirements 14.2.1
- share right restrictions 12.3.1
- takeovers 14.5.1
- tax relief for costs of establishing scheme 6.9
- tax treatment of 12.3.2
- taxation of employees
  - . exercise of options 14.3.2

271

 . generally 14.3
 . grant of options 14.3.1
 unacceptable features 14.2.1
 value per employee (limit on) 12.3.1
 variation of share capital 14.5.2
Conversion rights
 disposals 5.3
 generally .... Ch. 4
 tax principles 3.2
Convertible securities
 chargeable events after acquisition 4.3.4
 corporation tax relief 6.6
 disposals taxed as employment income 5.3
 flowering shares 4.3.2
 gain when benefit received 4.3.8
 gain when conversion right surrendered 4.3.7
 gain when converted 4.3.5
 gain when sold before conversion 4.3.6
 general principle 4.3.1
 tax on acquisition 4.3.3
Corporation tax
 company share option plans 12.3.2, 14.4.1
 employee trusts (funding of) 11.3.1
 employee trusts (satisfying share awards) 11.7
 enterprise management incentives 12.2.2, 13.6
 generally .... Ch. 6
 readily convertible assets 7.4
 relief
  . acquisition of shares 6.3
  . conditions for 6.2
  . convertible securities 6.6
  . costs of establishing share scheme 6.9
  . employee trusts 6.8, 11.3.1, 11.7
  . mobile employees 6.7
  . other reliefs 6.8
  . qualification conditions 6.2
  . restricted securities 6.5
  . share incentive plans 15.5
  . share options 6.4
 SAYE 12.4.2
 share incentive plans 12.5.1, 15.5
 statutory schemes 12.1
Definitions
 all employee share ownership plans 12.5.1

AMV (actual market value)	2.6.2, 3.3.6
approved schemes	12.1
associate	13.3.2
associated persons	1.3.3, 5.2.1
authorised share capital	10.4.3
avoidance options	3.5.2
benefit (of loan)	3.4.2
by reason of employment	1.3.4
cash cancellation	3.5.5
commercial association of companies	6.2
company reorganisation	13.7.1
connected	11.2.3, 13.1.2
consideration	9.6
consortium	6.2, 14.1.1
control	13.1.2, 13.1.3
corporation tax deductible	7.4
DC (disposal consideration)	5.3.1
deductible amounts	3.5.4
discretionary scheme	12.1
disguised remuneration	11.6.1
disqualifying events (SIPs)	15.7
employee	1.3.1
employee benefit contributions	11.3.2
employee benefit trusts	11.1
employee-control shares	14.1.1
employee share class	14.1.1
employee share ownership plans	12.5.1
employees' share scheme	10.4.3
excluded trades	13.1.6
exercise price	3.5.4
financial assistance	10.4.4
flowering shares	4.3.2
freezer shares	10.3.4
grandfathering	15.7
growth shares	10.3.1
interest in securities	10.3.3
interim period	15.5.2
making good	7.5
market value	5.5.2, 6.3
material interest	14.1.2
money's worth	3.1
non-commercial increase	4.2.5
open market shares	14.1.1
ordinary share capital	5.7.1, 15.1.1

over-funded 11.6.2
partly paid 3.4.3
permanent establishment 13.1.7
property managing subsidiary 13.1.3
qualifying exchange of shares 13.7.1
qualifying subsidiary 13.1.3
qualifying trade 13.1.6
readily convertible asset 7.4
relevant benefits 11.6.3
relevant EMI shares 13.5.5
relevant linked persons 1.3.3
relevant steps 11.6.1, 11.8
research institution 4.5.4
restricted securities 3.3.3
restricted stock units 9.1
restricted value 2.6.1
reverse ratchet 5.3.2
Schedule 2 SIPs 12.1
Schedule 3 SAYEs 12.1
Schedule 4 CSOPs 12.1
scheme 10.4.3
scheme organiser 14.1.1
securities 1.3.2
securities option 1.3.2
spin-out company 4.5.4
spread 3.5.1
strike price 3.5.4
subsidiary (EMI Code) 13.1.3
substantial 13.1.6
swamping rights 13.1.2
trading arrangements 7.4, 15.4.1
transaction in securities (EBT) 9.4.3
unrestricted market value (UMV) 2.6.3, 3.3.6
underwater 10.3.3
vesting 9.3
working time 13.3.1

Designing a scheme
  buy back by employee benefit trust 9.4.3
  choice of shares
    . customisation 10.2
    . employee classes 10.2
    . freezer shares 10.3.4
    . generally .... Ch. 10
    . growth shares 10.3

    communication with potential participants 9.7
    company law considerations 10.4
    dilution of existing shareholdings 9.6
    essentials 9.1
    exit strategy 9.5
    generally .... Ch. 9
    immediate ownership v options 9.2
    leavers, treatment of 9.4
    performance conditions 9.3
    private companies 9.2.2
    public companies 9.2.3
    purchase of own shares 9.4.2
    vesting 9.3

Dilution of existing shareholdings
    strategic considerations 9.6

Disguised remuneration
    use of employee benefit trusts 11.6

Disposals of securities
    acquired at below market value 5.4.1
    capital gains tax 5.6, 11.4
    company reorganisations 5.2.3, 5.3.3
    convertible securities 5.3
    dilution 9.6
    employee tax charge 3.3.7, 5.2.2
    employee trusts 11.5.1
    for more than market value 5.5
    generally .... Ch. 5
    leavers 9.4.1
    PAYE and NIC 5.3.4, 7.3
    purchase of own shares 5.6.2
    reorganisations 5.2.3, 5.4.2
    reportable events 8.1.3
    restricted securities 5.2

Dividend reinvestment plans
    reporting obligation 8.1.3

Dividend shares (SIP schemes)
    income tax and NIC 15.4
    reinvestment by employees 12.5
    terms of offer 15.3.4

Dividend yield
    share valuation 2.3.3

Dividends
    received by employee benefit trusts 11.1
    taxation of 4.4.3

Due diligence
    non-commercial changes in value 4.2.1
Elections
    gifts to employee trust 11.3.3
    limited effect of 1.6
    NIC (transferring liabilities) 7.6
    opting out of restricted securities regime 3.3.8, 5.2.1
    overview of different types 3.3.8
    paper for paper transactions 5.2.3
    restricted securities 8.1.3, 13.5.4
    SIP (accumulation period) 15.3.2
    time limits 3.3.8
Employee benefit trusts
    acquiring shares from employees 11.4
    capital gains tax 11.5
    corporation tax relief 11.7
    dividends received by 11.1
    enterprise management incentives 13.1.2
    establishing 11.2
    funding 11.3
    generally .... Ch. 11
    inheritance tax reliefs 11.2.3
    offshore trusts 11.5.2
    purchase of leaver shares 9.4.3
    satisfying share awards 11.6
    SIP shares 12.5.2, 15.6
    situs of 11.2.2
    transactions 11.8
Employment-related securities
    acquired before FA 2003 .... 1.4
    acquisition of .... Ch. 3
    application of regime 1.3.3
    awarded by unconnected company 1.3.3
    corporation tax .... Ch. 6
    directors 1.3.1
    disposals of .... Ch. 5
    founders' shares 1.5
    general tax principle 3.4.1
    growth shares 10.3.2
    options 3.5.2, 3.5.3
    PAYE and NIC .... Ch. 7
    reporting regime .... Ch. 8, 13.10.1
    scope of regime 3.5.2

spin-out companies 4.5.1
spouses 1.3.3
Enterprise management incentives
    advance assurance 13.1.8
    alternatives to 12.6
    amending options 13.8
    annual reporting 13.10
    capital gains tax 13.5.5
    cash cancellation (example) 3.5.5
    cessation of employment 13.9
    company transactions
      . company reorganisations 13.7.1
      . demergers 13.7.2
      . generally 13.7
      . variation of share capital 13.7.2
    corporation tax 13.6.1
    demergers 13.7.2
    design (lighter regime) 10.2
    discretionary nature of...12.1
    disqualifying events 13.5.2, 13.5.3
    elections (restricted securities) 13.5.4
    eligibility
      . company 13.1
      . employees 13.1.5, 13.3
      . gross assets 13.1.4
      . scheme requirements 13.4.1
      . shares 13.2
      . trade 13.2, 13.5.2
    employee benefit trusts 11.5.1, 13.1.2
    employee numbers 13.1.5
    entrepreneurs' relief 13.5.5
    establishing the scheme 13.4
    exercise of option and sale of shares on same day 5.7.2
    flexibility 12.2.1
    generally ....Ch. 13
    granting options 13.4.3
    gross assets test 13.1.4
    HMRC enquiries 13.10.3
    implementation costs 13.6.3
    implementation process 13.4.2
    income tax and NIC 13.5.1
    independence requirement 13.1.2
    leavers 9.4.4, 13.9
    limit on options held 13.3.3

material interest 13.3.2
options
  . amending 13.8
  . granting of 13.4.3
  . registration of 13.10.1
performance conditions 13.4.4
permanent establishment in UK 13.1.7
private companies 9.2.2
qualifying trade 13.1.6
reporting 8.1.4, 13.10
restricted securities 13.5.4
scheme requirements 13.4.1
share-for-share exchanges 13.5.5
state aid 13.1.1
subsidiary (meaning) 13.1.3
tax treatment
  . amending options 13.8.2
  . corporation tax relief.. 13.6.1
  . disqualifying events 13.5.3
  . employees 13.5
  . exercise of option 12.2.2
  . grant of option 12.2.2
  . implementation costs 13.6.3
  . income tax and NIC 13.5.3, 13.6.2
  . overview 12.2.2
variation of share capital 13.7.2

Entrepreneurs' relief
company share option plans 14.3.3
EMI options 5.7.2
qualifying for relief 5.7.1

Exit strategy
designing a share scheme 9.5

Extra statutory concessions
B18 .... 11.1

Financial assistance
company law considerations 10.4.4

Forfeitable securities
acquisition 3.3.5
company structures 9.2.3
election to disapply regime 3.3.8
future events 3.3.7
non-commercial transactions pre-acquisition 4.2.3

Founders' shares
as employment-related securities 1.5

Free shares (SIP schemes)
    awarded by employers 12.5
    income tax and NIC 15.4
    performance conditions 15.3.5
    terms of offer 15.3.3
Freezer shares
    inheritance tax planning 10.3.4
Funding
    contributions 11.3.2
    employee benefit trusts 11.3
    gifts of assets 11.3.3
    loan funding 11.3.1
Growth shares
    joint share ownership plans 10.3.3
    tax analysis 10.3.2
    use for employee schemes 10.3
Industry-specific valuations
    share valuation 2.3.5
Information standards
    market value (determining) 5.5.3
    share valuation 2.2
Inheritance tax planning
    employee benefit trusts 11.2.3
    freezer shares 10.3.4
Intellectual property
    relief for spin-out companies 4.5
Joint share ownership plans
    tax planning with growth shares 10.3.3
Joint ventures
    enterprise management incentives 13.1.3
Leavers
    articles (interaction with) 9.4.5
    company share option plans 9.4.1, 9.4.4, 14.2.2, 14.6
    enterprise management incentives 13.9
    purchase of own shares 9.4.2
    retention of options 9.4.4
    statutory schemes 9.4.1
    treatment of (when designing scheme) 9.4
    SIPs 15.3.6
Legislation
    elections (limited effect of) 1.6
    employees (defined) 1.3.1
    employment-related securities (defined) 1.3.3
    founders' shares 1.5

generally	Ch. 1
principles	1.2
retrospective effect of	1.4
scope	1.3
securities (defined)	1.3.2

Market value
manipulation of	4.2.4
non-commercial increases in	4.2.5

Matching shares (SIP schemes)
given by employers	12.5
income tax and NIC	15.4
terms of offer	15.3.2

Minority shareholdings
share valuation	2.4

Money's worth
interaction with share schemes	3.1
residual charge	3.3.6

Multiple of earnings
share valuation	2.3.4

National Insurance
borne by employees	3.5.4, 5.3.4, 6.5, 7.6
company share option plans	14.4.2
convertible securities	5.3.4
dividends	4.4.3
employee benefit trusts	9.4.3, 11.6, 11.7
enterprise management incentives	13.6.2
generally	Ch. 7
non-commercial transactions	4.2.2
readily convertible assets	7.4, 7.5
relevant steps (EBTs)	11.6.1
restricted securities	6.5
sale of shares	Ch. 5
share incentive plans	15.4
transferring liabilities	7.6

Net asset value
share valuation	2.3.2

Nominal value
company law considerations	10.4.5

Non-commercial transactions
acquisition value depressed	4.2.3
anti-avoidance provisions	4.2
hypothetical value	4.2.3
increases in market value	4.2.5
statutory examples	4.2.2

280

Offshore trusts
    capital gains tax 11.5.2
Options – *see* **Share options**
Partly paid shares
    sale of shares 3.4.5
    tax effect for employee 3.4.3
Partnership shares (SIP schemes)
    funds held by trustees 15.3.2
    income tax and NIC 15.4
    salary sacrifice 12.5
    terms of offer 15.3.2
Pay As You Earn (PAYE)
    acquisition of securities 7.2
    company share option plans 14.4.2
    employee benefit trusts 9.4.3, 11.6, 11.7
    enterprise management incentives 13.6.2
    failure to operate 7.5
    generally .... Ch. 7
    making good by employee 7.1
    persons not registered for 8.1.2
    post-acquisition charges 7.3
    readily convertible assets 7.4, 7.5
    share disposals 5.1
    share incentive plans 15.4.1
Personal representatives
    company share option plans 14.2.1
Post-acquisition benefits
    exemptions from charge 4.4.2
    tax charge 4.4
Private companies
    classes of shares 10.2
    Companies Act model articles 3.3.4
    company law considerations 10.4.1
    company reorganisations 13.7.1
    dilution of other shareholdings 9.6
    EMI as natural choice 12.6
    exit strategy 9.5
    financial assistance 10.4.4
    immediate ownership v share options 9.2
    information standards 5.5.3
    joint share ownership plans 10.3.3
    leavers 9.4
    nominal value, paying up 10.4.5
    PAYE on post-acquisition charges 7.3

    readily convertible assets 7.4
    restricted securities 3.3.3
    SAYE (generally not suitable for) 12.6
    share valuation 2.3, 5.5.3, 8.2.2
    share incentive plans 12.6, 15.3.1
    statutory schemes used for 12.6
    tailoring share rights 9.1
    trust assets, treatment of on company transactions 11.8
    valuation approaches 2.3
    vesting and performance conditions 9.3

Public companies
    company law considerations 10.4
    dilution limits 15.3.1
    financial assistance 10.4.4
    immediate ownership v share options 9.2.3
    valuation approaches 2.3

Purchase of own shares
    double taxation 5.6.2, 9.4.2
    leavers 9.4.2

Qualifying trade
    enterprise management incentive 13.1.6, 13.5.2

Readily convertible assets
    PAYE and NIC 7.4, 7.5

Reporting to HMRC
    enterprise management incentives 13.10
    form 42 .... 8.1.1
    obligation to report 8.1
    practicalities 8.1.4
    reportable events 8.1.3

Research institutions
    relief for spin-out companies 4.5

Restricted securities
    acquisition 3.3, 6.3
    capital gains tax 5.6
    corporation tax 6.5
    definition 3.3.3
    disposals 5.2, 5.6
    election to disapply regime 3.3.8
    enterprise management incentives 13.5.4
    forfeitable securities 3.3.5
    future events 3.3.7
    growth shares 10.3.2
    listed companies 3.3.3
    market value manipulation 4.2.4

    NIC liabilities (transfer of) 7.6
    non-commercial transactions pre-acquisition 4.2.3
    private companies 3.3.3
    reorganisations 5.2.3
    reportable events 8.1.3
Restrictions
    lifting or variation of 3.3.7
Rights issues
    reporting obligation 8.1.3
Save As You Earn
    all-employee requirement 12.4.1
    capital gains tax re use of EBT 11.5.1
    corporation tax deduction 6.9
    generally 12.4
    leavers, treatment of 9.4.1
    non-discretionary nature of 12.1
    private companies (rarely suitable for) 12.6
    reporting 8.1.4
    tax treatment 12.4.2
Scrip dividends
    reporting obligation 8.1.3
Securities options – *see* **Share options**
Service companies
    shares not eligible for SIP 15.1.1
Share-for-share exchanges
    reporting obligation 8.1.3
Share incentive plans
    all-employee requirement 12.5.1
    approved scheme 12.1
    capital gains tax
      . generally 15.4.3
      . re use of EBT 11.5.1
    company takeovers 15.8
    corporation tax deduction 6.1, 15.5
    non-discretionary nature of 12.1
    disqualifying events 15.7
    dividend shares 12.5
    eligibility of shares for 15.1.1
    EMI (disregarded re) 13.3.2
    employee benefit trust 12.5.2, 15.6
    employees (eligibility of) 15.1.2
    employees (taxation of) 15.4
    establishing the scheme 15.2
    free shares 12.5

implementation of 15.2.2
ineligible shares 15.1.1
leavers, treatment of 9.4.1, 15.3.6
making awards 15.2.3, 15.3
matching shares 12.5
partnership shares 12.5, 15.3.2
PAYE and NIC 15.4.1
performance conditions 15.3.5
private companies 12.6
public companies 9.2.3
reporting 8.1.4, 15.9
scheme requirements 15.2.1
service companies 15.1.1
stamp taxes (exemption from) 15.5.5
tax relief for costs of establishing scheme 15.5.1
tax treatment of 12.5
terms of offer.. 15.3.1
Share options
   accounting 8.2.3
   acquisition 3.5
   amending 13.8.2, 14.7
   bad leavers 9.4.1
   cash cancellation 3.5.5
   chargeable events re 3.5.5
   company share option plans 12.3
   corporation tax relief 6.4
   deductible amounts 3.5.4
   dilution 9.6
   disguised remuneration 11.6
   employee trusts 11.1
   enterprise management incentives .... 5.7.2, 12.2, Ch. 13
   entrepreneurs' relief 5.7.2
   exchange for other options 3.5.5
   exercise of 3.5.4, 12.3.2
   good leavers 9.4.1
   grant of 3.5.3, 12.3.2, 13.4.3
   growth shares 10.3
   immediate ownership contrasted 9.2
   leavers 9.4
   mobile employees 6.7
   nominal value 10.4.5
   not treated as security 1.3.2, 3.5.1
   partnerships (options granted to) 3.5.1
   PAYE 7.2

    private companies (pros and cons of options) 9.2.2
    public companies 9.2.3
    reportable events 8.1.3
    SAYE 12.4
    securities (definition) 1.3.2
    self-employed (options granted to) 3.5.1
    United States companies 9.1
    trusts 11.1, 11.5.1
    valuation and amortisation 8.2.2
Share valuation – *see* **Valuation of shares**
Spin-out companies
    post-acquisition changes in value 4.5.3
    reason for special rules 4.5.1
    relief from tax 4.5
Stamp taxes
    exemption for SIP shares 15.5.5
State aid
    EMI scheme 13.1.1
Targeted anti-avoidance rule
    convertible securities 4.3.3, 4.3.4, 5.3.2
    employee benefit trusts 11.6.2
    restricted securities 5.2.2
    spin-out companies 4.5.4
    statutory share schemes 11.6.2
Taxation (overview)
    accounting entries (interaction with) 8.2.4
    acquisition of securities ....Ch. 3
    corporation tax ....Ch. 6
    disposals of shares ....Ch. 5
    enterprise management incentives ....Ch. 13
    entrepreneurs' relief... 5.7
    growth shares..10.3.2, 10.3.3
    PAYE and NIC ....Ch. 7
    post-acquisition changes ....Ch. 4
    purchase of own shares 5.6.2
    share incentive plans ....Ch. 15
    statutory schemes ....Ch. 12
    trusts ....Ch. 11
Trusts – *see* **Employee benefit trusts**
Valuation of shares
    accounting for share awards 8.2
    dividend yield 2.3.3
    generally ....Ch. 2
    HMRC approach 2.3

industry-specific methodologies 2.3.5
information standards 2.2
market value 5.5.2
minority status 2.4, 5.5.5
multiple of earnings 2.3.4
net asset value 2.3.2
share rights 2.5, 5.5.4
terminology 2.6
use of CGT principles 2.1

Printed and bound in Great Britain by
Marston Book Services Limited, Oxfordshire